THE GREAT CENTRAL
THEN AND NOW

MAC HAWKINS

David & Charles

Frontispiece: **New Basford** (129 SK 562428) A truly classic study of a typical Woodford–Annesley 'runner' at work. Having just emerged from Sherwood Rise Tunnel in the background, Class 9F 2-10-0 No 92068 storms past New Basford on its way towards Annesley exchange sidings, just a few miles to the north. *Photo: Tom Boustead. Date: 31 August 1963.*

Title page: The skyline is familiar, but little else bears any resemblance. The former stationmaster's house, previously obscured by the locomotive, can be seen in the middle distance. A mixture of new housing and industrial development has encroached on the entire area the station and goods yard once occupied. *Date: 5 November 1989.*

The author and publishers have made every effort to ensure that the 'then and now' photographs are exact facsimiles. Due to normal production and printing practices, certain details may have been 'bled off' by the binding or trimming of this book.

The differences will be minor, and therefore it is hoped that they do not detract from the accuracy that this publication endeavours to achieve.

British Library Cataloguing in Publication Data
Hawkins, Mac
The Great Central: then and now.
I. Title
385.0942022

ISBN 0-7153-9326-X

First published 1991
Reprinted 1994

© Mac Hawkins 1991

Designed by Michael Head
Typeset by ICON Exeter
and printed in Great Britain by Butler & Tanner Ltd
for David & Charles
Brunel House Newton Abbot Devon

CONTENTS

FOREWORD

When invited to write this foreword to THE GREAT CENTRAL THEN AND NOW, I was both delighted and honoured, but to find such an excellent and readable chronicle of the line in which I have been so keenly interested for as long as I can remember, makes my task doubly enjoyable.

Not only has Mac Hawkins provided a book that, for me, fills a gap in the many books written on railways, but his photography will be a joy to any enthusiast, showing as he has the tremendous and so often heartbreaking changes that have taken place over the years.

My own family have been involved with the Great Central Railway from the outset. My grandfather fought tirelessly, and I am happy to say unsuccessfully, to stop the line from being built across our estate at Swithland, and I am sure must have turned in his grave to find his grandson fighting with even greater determination to keep at least part of the line for the benefit and enjoyment of future generations. It was certainly not easy, with British Rail being so far from encouraging, and clearly convinced that we would never raise enough money to buy the stretch of line we were after.

We are, however, a persistent band, and having now got the line running to Leicester North – previously known as Belgrave and Birstall – our next target is to run north of Loughborough as far as Ruddington.

Many, I am sure, who read this book, will set out to retrace the Great Central line as it is today – following every step of the way with the help of this book with its marvellous photography.

One thing comes through very clearly – Mac Hawkins enjoyed the intense care he has taken in writing with such detail and accuracy.

On another personal note, one of my happiest memories is of when I rode on the footplate of the 'Master Cutler', from Leicester to Marylebone, returning on the 'South Yorkshireman'. Our two best known express trains. Happy days indeed!

I shall write no more, because this is a book you must get on and read!

THE RIGHT HONOURABLE
THE EARL OF LANESBOROUGH, T.D., D.L.

PREFACE

'The lifting of tracks does not obliterate a railway — it simply removes its life, leaving a corpse.' Colin Walker, author of *Main Line Lament*, 1973.

I became interested in this particular 'corpse' some twenty-three years ago, although at first I had little idea of its significance. Every summer since then, whilst staying with friends in Brackley, a town which was served by the Great Central's London Extension, I have managed to visit parts of the old line and have been constantly impressed by the magnificence of some remaining structures, and the grand scale of certain cuttings, like those at Helmdon and Rugby; all these things left me with the impression that no space nor, seemingly, expense was spared in its construction.

Being particularly awed by the enormous 22 arch blue-brick viaduct which lay at the bottom of our friends' garden, and bestrode like a Colossus the valley through which runs the Great Ouse — what a fabulous piece of architecture it was — imagine how dismayed I was when it was demolished in 1978 to supply hardcore for making up housing estate roads in Milton Keynes. What Philistines I thought . . . the structure would have stood for at least another thousand years!

In 1987 I decided to carry out a thorough survey of the formation from Aylesbury to Rugby, and in October 1988 made a trip as far as Annesley to see what remained of the old Great Central northwards to that point, in order to ascertain whether it presented a feasible subject for me to embark upon a comprehensive 'then and now' study, as I did with the former Somerset & Dorset line. I was surprised at what was to be found — although my forays usually seemed to be carried out in atrocious weather, soaking me to the skin each time I ventured along the former line. Nevertheless I enjoyed sampling the delights of the Great Central's ghostly magic, despite the inclemency!

Finally, after obtaining sufficient original photographs of good quality upon which my study could be based, I started in earnest the daunting task of recording what remained of the line. Several exhausting months of hard graft ensued and many sorties were made between the early spring of 1988 and autumn 1990 along the Great Central's former main line from Sheffield to Marylebone, often returning to individual locations several times before certain shots could be

satisfactorily obtained. This process resulted in over 5,000 photographs being taken, some of which then had to be matched with the originals and printed — a long and tedious job in itself. By the end of that period my task was all but complete, save the writing and compilation of the book itself, which was done over the next few months. As a consequence of unforeseen delays in publication of the title, not of my making, I was able somewhat to revise and update the book both photographically and textually, particularly with regard to the changes and modernisation carried out on the Chiltern Line, as well as the progress made by the preservationists of the Great Central Railway at Loughborough.

Time and logistical reasons made it impossible to include other Great Central lines, particularly the Woodhead route from Manchester to Sheffield, also the different routes to Immingham and Cleethorpes on the Humber estuary. One such, via Penistone, took in Barnsley, Mexborough, Doncaster and Scunthorpe; links from Sheffield to the East Coast were made via Rotherham which connected at Mexborough, whilst another passed through Worksop, Retford and Gainsborough, with a loop to Lincoln and Market Rasen; these all met at Barnetby between Scunthorpe and Grimsby.

A further deciding factor in limiting the book to the GC main line was, apart from the Woodhead route, most of the others survive in much the same form today, so provide as yet little by way of comparisons for a 'then and now' study,

During the time spent working on the project I have had the good fortune to meet many delightful people, especially during my photographic expeditions. The kindness, generosity, and in some cases tolerance, shown by individuals, especially when their privacy was being assailed by the need to photograph from their property, never failed to impress me. I also thoroughly enjoyed the company of fellow author Robert Robotham who joined me on some of the safaris, for his enthusiasm and extensive knowledge of the line proved invaluable; coupled with his sense of humour, we had some hilarious moments during our jaunts together.

I have endeavoured to select photographs both for their quality and content and have tried to include as

8

many as possible that have not been published before, but make no apology for a few others that have; for being the best or only ones available of a particular location, they have served my purpose well. My one regret is that many superb examples of the original photographs gathered have not been included, either because they duplicated areas already covered, or it simply was physically impossible to take an accurate facsimile and at best the end result would have been disappointing.

Most stations and important locations along the route have been included, but just a few were not able to be represented because no suitable photographs could be found in the time available to me to complete this book; a fact which I hope will not spoil readers' enjoyment. However, I trust the comparison photographs selected and accompanying text give some flavour of how the former Great Central main line from Sheffield to London has changed over the years.

Mac Hawkins COSSINGTON, SOMERSET, 1991

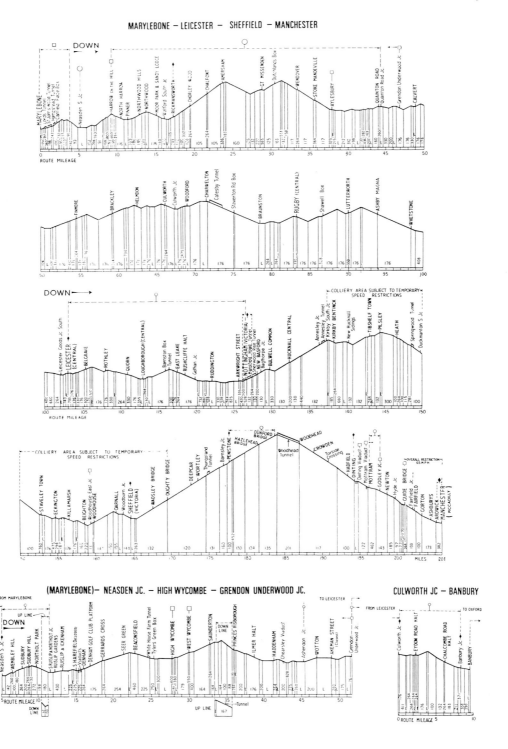

INTRODUCTION

In many people's eyes the day of 3 September 1966 was one of infamy, when the last main line built to reach London closed for ever. The Great Central's route to the capital was the first major casualty of the Beeching era, although closure had been mooted ten years before. On 15 March 1899 the Great Central had opened its extension constructed from Annesley in Nottinghamshire, joining with the Metropolitan Railway at Quainton Road in Buckinghamshire, thus providing a fast link from Manchester and Sheffield to a new terminus built at Marylebone, arriving in the capital some fifty years after its rivals.

Originally it had been the dream of Sir Edward Watkin, son of a Manchester cotton baron and chairman of various northern railway companies, who was blessed with big ideas and an ambition to match in becoming a railway magnate, to connect his series of regional railways with the Continent via a fast link constructed from Manchester to the South Coast and then through a channel tunnel; but, as with so many grandiose schemes, lack of funds precluded the goal. Although the Channel Tunnel Co Ltd, which had been formed in 1872, fought with vigour to have its *raison d'être* fulfilled, the various bills it promoted that were set before Parliament were defeated, including one in December 1906, mainly for nationalistic reasons. Renewed efforts were made in May 1912, but World War I effectively put paid to the scheme and therefore prevented Watkin's dream becoming a reality – at least, as it has turned out, for the next eighty years, despite a further attempt in June 1939 when that bill was rejected.

From its inception the Great Central was a thorn in the sides of the other railway companies, for it competed directly with the Midland main line and also provided a shorter route between Nottingham and Leicester than its neighbouring rival. From the outset the company met with stiff opposition, although it later proved no more than an irritant. Links with other systems were not actively encouraged, although it was to connect with the old Metropolitan Railway: Sir Edward Watkin was chairman of both companies at the time of conception. The railway also managed to link with the GWR at Banbury via a junction near Woodford Halse, together with other connections made at Princes Risborough and Northolt Junction.

Despite this, however, the 'Central' tended to operate as a self-contained and compact system, which had the benefiting effect of fostering great loyalty to the company by its employees who soon developed a 'family'-type atmosphere on the railway, like that experienced on the Somerset & Dorset Joint Railway.

The company perhaps could be best described as having 'grit', moulding its railwaymen accordingly, developing them into individuals who exuded this. The homely atmosphere of the Great Central proved infectious in that it benefited the customers, who were always made to think that they were of paramount importance and great value. The frequent appearance of the same engines on particular trains also helped give the Great Central a certain intimacy, which continued well into BR days.

Although the London Extension from Annesley to Marylebone had a ruling grade of 1:176 and undulated like a switchback for most of its length with relatively few level stretches, it was the only main line built to the Berne loading gauge standards and had no level crossings. Together with the Great Western, with whom it jointly built and operated the section between the junctions at Ashendon and Northolt, the Great Central was also the last company to employ navvies engaged in building a railway in the country. The construction itself was based on simplicity and quality, so that the careful pathing of the double track enabled fast running times to be achieved. The engineering at Leicester was substantial: from the southern outskirts the station was reached through a cutting, then passed the goods yards on a level stretch before climbing briefly to stride over the city across a long blue-brick viaduct upon which the station was built, and on a slight plateau. After dipping briefly half a mile from the station, the line climbed steadily towards Belgrave & Birstall, which ensured that the pyrotechnics of engines leaving Leicester for the North was a spectacle worth watching. Similarly, in other parts, the construction of the line took on major proportions: Catesby Tunnel in the heart of the Northamptonshire countryside, was some 3,000yd long; bridges that spanned the very wide cuttings and rivers were extremely impressive and usually constructed in blue brick, like the 22 arch viaduct over the Great Ouse at Brackley. Although not the longest by 70yd, it certainly was the most prodigious.

The Great Central had managed to attract respectable custom due to some high quality advertising and fast running times that its services offered, which had been marketed by Dean & Dawson of Manchester, the first railway travel agents. The management, enlightened and imaginative, was led by chairman Sir Alexander Henderson. The work of men such as J. G. Robinson, the Chief Mechanical Engineer; Sam Fay, the General Manager; Joseph Rostern, the Line Superintendent and A. F. Bound, the head of the signalling department at the age of twenty-eight, ensured that the Great Central won a high reputation amongst its customers.

The railway's patrons from the shire counties soon christened the Great Central the 'Countryman's Line', as it connected not only the industrial north with the capital, but also the rich rural counties of Oxfordshire, Northamptonshire and Leicestershire, which with their large estates, country houses and field-sporting facilities, provided revenue from an otherwise sparse population it served. Friday night trains from Marylebone would often be well patronised by invited house guests for weekends in the country.

The tight timing of trains led to the crews earning a reputation for outstanding performances achieved with their locomotives, whose rapid acceleration and scorching stops were to become legendary: it was nothing for a train still to be doing 60mph under a mile out from the next stop! The fastest service was the 'Sheffield Special' afternoon flyer from Marylebone — 2hr 50min to Sheffield, an average speed of 58·15mph. The track alignment also meant that goods trains were sharply timed and travelling at almost express speeds by comparison with other lines. Some of the expresses were allowed only 23 minutes for the 23·5 miles between Leicester and Nottingham.

The major re-grouping of 1923 saw the Great Central amalgamated into the LNER. Therefore it was able to enjoy the benefits of being part of a much larger system, including the revenue earned from the East Coast route; also it attracted much freight traffic from the South Midlands and South-West via Woodford Halse up to the Nottingham and Sheffield areas, thence connected with the rest of the LNER system.

In the years after World War II, the Great Central line had two officially named express trains, the premier of which was the 'Master Cutler'. Known to all simply as the 'Cutler', this service was introduced in 1947 and was an attempt to revitalise the élite business market. The train had a loyal following of regular patrons, especially from Nottingham and Leicester. It left Sheffield at 07.40 and returned from Marylebone at 18.15. The other named train was the 'South Yorkshireman', which was the 10.00 service from Bradford to Marylebone, returning at 16.50. Other unofficially named trains were the 'Newspaper', which left Marylebone at 01.45 and the 'Breakfast', which departed from Manchester at 08.30. These trains, except during the peak periods, were usually made up of nine-coach sets and included a restaurant car. There was a weekday service of seven trains in the down direction to Sheffield, Manchester or Bradford, with six in the up direction.

Until the autumn of 1957 express trains were mostly hauled by Gresley A3 Pacifics, which were supplemented by V2 2-6-2s, B1 4-6-0s and later Stanier Class 5s. The Great Central's own designed locomotives, including the handsome Director class 4-4-0s had been relegated to the North-West and Lincolnshire, but occasionally could be found on locals between Nottingham and Sheffield — a service known as the 'Spitfire'. BR Standard Class 9Fs were introduced in the summer of 1958 to supplement the motive power available. Their performance soon became legendary, especially when working the fast freight services, known as 'windcutters' or 'runners'. The line had the added attraction of having a variety of locomotive power use its metals: GWR, LNER, LMS, Southern and Standard classes were all to be seen in latter years.

Following nationalisation and the subsequent transfer of the system in 1958 to the London Midland Region, the writing was on the wall for the Great Central route to London. Although better in many respects than its direct competitor and brilliantly engineered — the minimum radius of curves was one mile — it was competing with the longer-established route to the Midlands, together with its cross-country connecting services. It served less populated areas between Rugby and the capital, as the extension was built primarily to provide a fast run to link the Great Central's homeland in the North to London.

Almost inevitably services were run down: through expresses ceased on 2 January 1960 and for the next few years only three semi-fast trains a day, mainly hauled by 'Black Fives', Royal Scots or Standard Class 5s, were operated between Marylebone and Sheffield — indeed an act of enervation for a once proud line. With diesels being introduced on other routes, the GC became a dumping ground for surplus and mechanically-exhausted steam engines. Decay had set in everywhere and revenues were lost because of the lack of services. The London Midland Region had dealt a mortal blow to its latter-day rival, which was therefore doomed and destined not to survive the Beeching era.

GREAT CENTRAL RENAISSANCE?

Since the start of the preparation of this book, one of the most imaginative and exciting schemes for decades has emerged, involving a proposal to build Britain's first privately run main line this century, designed to link the Channel Tunnel with the Midlands.

During the summer of 1989, the *Sunday Times* reported that a consortium made up of engineers, banks and property interests called the Central Railway Group was in the process of formation and headed by Andrew Gritten, which intends to build a 175 mile rail freight link from a point north of Rugby to Kent. The aim of this £1·3 billion project is to bring the benefits of the Channel Tunnel directly to the Midlands and is designed to ease road congestion in the South East, by creating inland 'ports'. Following a two-year build programme, the line is intended to be operational by 1996, but detailed plans have yet to be finalised regarding the logistics involved with the actual construction. By the time these words are read, a bill which was planned to be set before Parliament in November 1991 could be approved and the necessary finance on the way to being raised.

With particular relevance to this book, and almost strikingly obvious by its choice, part of the plan is the intention to use almost sixty miles of the abandoned former Great Central route from the Midlands. This will commence from a point near Whetstone, possibly with a connection to the Midland line between Leicester and Nuneaton, then south via Grendon Underwood Junction to Ashendon Junction, where it will join the Chiltern Line between Banbury and Marylebone. The route will then use existing BR metals through London and on to the Channel Tunnel via Redhill, Tonbridge and Ashford.

Major engineering work will be necessary on the existing network in the southern portion, to bring it up to modern European standards. Many stations, tunnels and bridges will have to be widened, particularly through London, to enable the line to be capable of taking continental freight traffic; this will be carried out at the consortium's expense and is an integral part of the funding. Little will have to be done in this regard from Ashendon northwards, save alteration to some occupation overbridges, as the GC line was initially constructed to the Berne loading gauge.

The railway will be geared towards the most profitable market: the primary purpose of the line's creation being its potential to move large volumes of road freight at reasonable cost, working on the principle of carrying not only conventional ISO containerised traffic, but complete lorry loads on trains, including tractors, the freight wagons being specifically designed for the purpose. The time saving will be of enormous benefit to businesses in the North and Midlands; similarly the advantages will also be apparent to companies on the Continent wishing to avoid the inevitable delays that road traffic causes in London and the Home Counties, which are costly both in time and money. The line is intended to cope with freight trains capable of doing 110-20mph.

Roll-on roll-off terminals will be built along the route to handle the freight traffic. Although details have yet to be finalised, it is likely that the main terminal will be sited north of Rugby near the junctions of the M1, M6 and M69: this appears to the Group as the most logical and ideal location from which to capture much of the freight traffic generated from the North and Midlands that is funnelled to the bottleneck of motorways near to this point. A major terminal will also be built in west London, with a possible link to Heathrow.

The projected costs include about thirty train sets, which will be similar in design to those already ordered for the Channel Tunnel. From its inception, the line will be fully electrified along its entire length. Although not a priority in terms of profitability, the Central Railway is likely to offer a passenger service, but no specific plans have been made for the precise location or number of stations needed: these will be sited according to local demand, and as passenger forecasts dictate. Double-decker coaches may be considered desirable for passenger trains, but detailed design work has not yet been embarked upon for such rolling stock, or for the freight wagons.

With the inevitable increase in road traffic, both commercial and domestic, by as much as 40 per cent over the next ten to fifteen years, as some forecasts predict, this scheme appears to make economic sense. An annual turnover of at least £100 million is forecast initially, but is more likely to exceed that figure. To be profitable, the line will be highly utilised and it will offer a freight service about every fifteen minutes in either direction.

This corridor, or one like it, will be needed, as by all accounts British Rail is unlikely to be able to cope with the projected increase in rail traffic generated by the link with the Continent and is already running into some difficulty in finding corridors for much of the existing freight in the region. This is aside from the problems already being experienced in the building of a new high-speed link from the tunnel to the capital, which has already caused much controversy, both environmentally and in terms of cost — and which the Government has refused to fund directly.

Conversely, although it is inevitable that objections will be raised, the revitalisation of the former Great Central line is unlikely to make much of a detrimental environmental impact, for most of the formation from Ashendon to Whetstone is still extant: very little development that obstructs the route, either domestic, agricultural or industrial, has taken place over the past twenty-five years, save certain portions which have been landfilled.

In terms of engineering there are relatively few problems involved in restoring the line. The two major hurdles to overcome would be to rebuild a viaduct at Brackley across the River Ouse flood plain, and that of the River Avon to span a section north of the West Coast main line bridge at Rugby, where a large viaduct and embankment between the Midland line and the Grand Union Canal have been demolished. In both locations new industrial estates have been built, but at Brackley this happens to be nearer to the site of the former station. These two sections will require substantial funding if the line is to follow the same

course. A slight route deviation may be deemed to be more practical in both cases.

It is ironic that if the Parliamentary Bill is successful and this giant project gets the green light, Sir Edward Watkin's dream of a railway linking a channel tunnel to the Midlands and the North nearly a century before, will have finally been realised — at least in part!

Postscript: *In the summer of 1990, the Labour party put forward its plans for a fast rail link connecting Scotland, the North and the Midlands to the Channel Tunnel and published a fifty-page document entitled* Moving Britain into Europe, *which outlined its ideas. Part of the proposals included the use of the former Great Central route north of London to Rugby, where it would connect with the West Coast Main Line, so this affirms the Central Railway Group's thinking that this section is ripe for use.*

With the Conservative party's recent pledge to privatise British Rail eventually, the Secretary of State for Transport, Malcolm Rifkind, quite unexpectedly announced in May 1991 a major Government initiative (in what would appear to be a complete reversal of previous policy) to encourage, particularly through the involvement of the private sector, the greater use of railways for the movement of both freight and passengers, in an attempt to ease the burden on the roads. This is certain to give encouragement to the Central Railway Group's plan and other similarly inspired schemes. The outcome of this initiative will be awaited with great interest by many.

MAPS AND TRACK PLANS

Map references
In the pages following map references are given for the 1:50,000 OS Landranger Series of Great Britain, and represent the point from which the photographs were taken. A grid reference, as in the example below quotes: sheet no(s) (110/111), 100,000m square identification letters (SK), eastings (360), northings (881). The references are accurate to within 50 metres.

Sheffield Victoria station (1)
110/111 SK 360881

Notes:
1: Location maps are mainly derivatives of the second and provisional editions of Ordnance Survey 6" to 1 mile series, whereas the majority of track plans are on the second editions of the 25" to 1 mile series.

2: Whilst every endeavour has been made to reproduce location maps and track plans to a high standard, it has not been helped by the age, condition and poor printing quality of some of the original maps, which are not of the high cartographic standards achieved today, but nevertheless are of great historical importance.

3: Windows on certain location maps represent areas covered by track plans, which have been annotated accordingly and not duplicated.

Location map and track plan key

55 ↗ Photograph number and location (arrow indicates directional view)

5 ↗ Colour photograph number and location

●—**255** Bridge/viaduct/tunnel location and designated number

＊**1** Supplementary/inset photograph location (numbered as appropriate)

Location map scale

10 Chains 5	0	10	20	30	40	50	60	70	80 Chains

1000 Feet 500	0	1000	2000	3000	4000	5000	5280 Feet

1 Furlong 0	¼	½	¾	1 Mile

Track plan scale

Links 100	0	5	10	15	20 Chains or ¼ Mile

Feet 100	0	500	1000	

SHEFFIELD VICTORIA–STAVELEY TOWN

I
Sheffield Victoria station (I)
110/111 SK 360881

An unusual view facing east taken from the cab of a DMU as it approaches Sheffield Victoria, showing the general layout well. The lines on the left are the passing loops which obviated the need for goods trains having to pass the platforms. The track alongside platform 2 (west) has already been removed and the station by this date is only a shadow of its former self, with little or no activity — and certainly no passengers are seen on the platforms. A portent of things to come.

The bridge in the foreground is the one spanning the Wicker, whilst the building seen behind the DMU's cab divider is the Royal Victoria Hotel. *Photo: Gordon Buck. Date: 30 September 1971.*

Just one track of the former route from Manchester remains and snakes past the last vestiges of the station. Only a platform edge abuts the line, which is no more than a siding to service the Stocksbridge steelworks, where it now terminates. Class 20 and Class 31 locomotives often perform this duty; however, the occasional football special pass through here serving the Hillsborough ground from the now much vandalised Wadsley Bridge station.

The railings of the bridge over the Wicker signify that the vantage point is the same. The Royal Victoria Hotel is undergoing a face-lift and has had a new extension built, which now covers part of the former station site. One remaining mast shorn of its electric wires stands as a useless artefact, or perhaps as a memorial of Britain's first overhead electrified main line. *Date: 24 September 1989.*

With the impending closure of the Woodhead route this fine but sad view of Sheffield Victoria, then partly demolished, shows the layout of the station to good effect. Seen leaving is the 11.38 train for Huddersfield. The carbuncular blocks of flats of monstrous proportions still dominate the skyline today, dwarfing the church which seems entirely threatened by them; but most are empty and will eventually be demolished. However, there were plans to renovate some to house students competing in the World Student Games, to be held at Sheffield in 1991. *Photo: Les Nixon. Date: 29 July 1980.*

Sheffield Victoria station (2)
110/111 SK 360880

Class EM1 1,868hp Bo-Bo electric No 26056 *Triton* enters Sheffield Victoria with an up haul of coal empties as it passes over the celebrated Wicker Arch. The Morning Star Flour buildings are visible behind the locomotive.

The fifties-style electrification gantries and wires make this aspect looking north-west from the station appear rather a tangled mess, unlike modern systems which are better, but still not ideal aesthetically.
Photo: Brian Stephenson. Date: 22 July 1963.

The old flour mill buildings have gone and only a sixties-vintage office extension remains, but itself appears to be partly demolished. The last few remaining gantries of the once electrified Woodhead route still stand as a reminder of the recent past, but it must be a matter of time before they too are removed for scrapping. However, the much older Wicker Arch is due to play a prominent part in the Sheffield Development Corporation's plan for the renaissance of the Lower Don Valley which is designed to revitalise its business potential and environmentally improve the area. The bridge is to be enhanced by pseudo pavilions mounted on its parapets: Sheffield's answer to the Arc de Triomphe perhaps?
Date: 24 September 1989.

The Woodhead route

Initially it was intended that this book should also include the Woodhead route from Manchester London Road to Sheffield Victoria, but the former Great Central line from Sheffield to London, being some 165 miles in length, was considered to be the more important part to cover in as much detail as possible, due to the radical changes that have taken place in the last quarter of a century, particularly north of Nottingham.

Although the Great Central's through route to Manchester was finally closed in 1981 and lifting the major portion of the track over the Pennines started in earnest in 1986, taking almost two years to complete, the changes are not as yet so apparent; for if 'then and now' photography is to succeed in its objective, it is surely the dramatic contrast that makes it work so effectively. The comparatively recent demise of the Woodhead route did not therefore meet this criterion.

3
Sheffield Victoria station (3)
110/111 SK 361880

Brush Type 4 (Class 47) No D1868 has come to a stop in the station adjacent to platform 2 (west). It was not usual for freight trains to run past the platforms; they were normally kept to the through roads on the north side of the station behind a screening wall, well away from view, probably to the chagrin of many a rail spotter. Of interest is the LNER tail lamp sported by the diesel-electric locomotive.

The proximity of the Royal Victoria Hotel is evident from this photograph, which portrays the rather gloomy atmosphere of Sheffield Victoria. It begs the question as to how many guests opened their bedroom windows at night only to be enveloped by choking black smoke that might have been arising from engines 'brewing up' in the station below! *Photo: William P. Power. Date: 27 August 1966.*

The large annexe to the hotel is almost complete and now encroaches on the platform area shown in the original photograph, but the building has been tastefully designed, blending in well with the main structure and is a worthy extension to a fine Victorian building. The occasional platform edging slabs can be picked out under the debris created during the refurbishment and extension of the hotel, enabling the spot to be identified. *Date: 24 September 1989.*

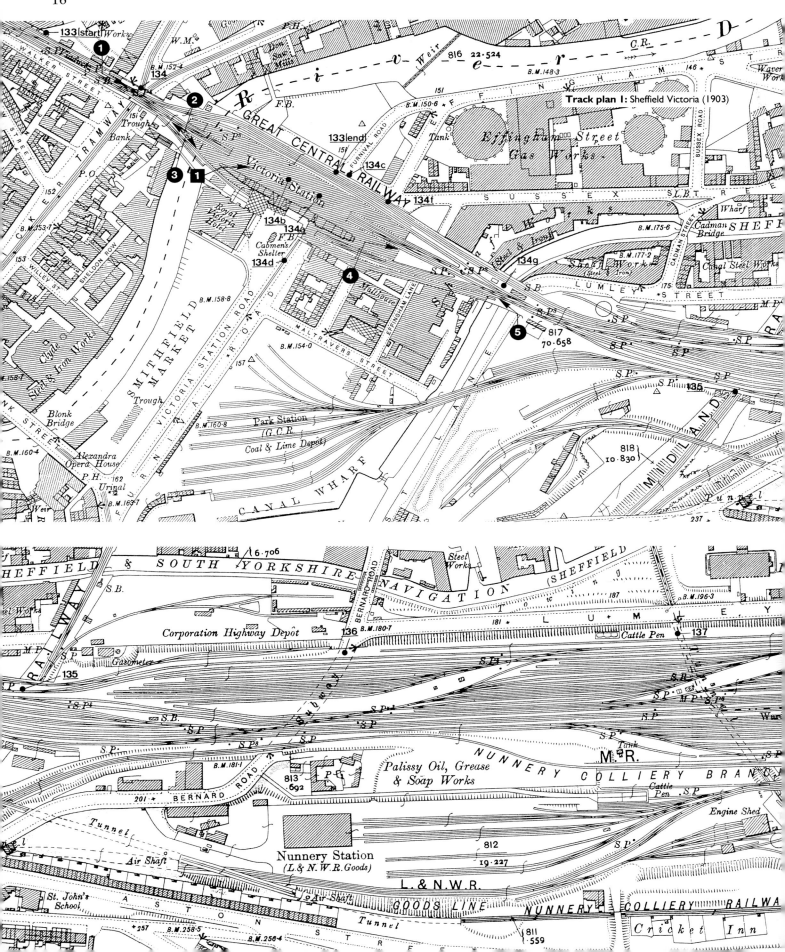

Track plan 1: Sheffield Victoria (1903)

4

Sheffield Victoria station (4)
110/111 SK 363879

This view off the east end of the station shows Director 4-4-0 No 62662 *Prince of Wales*, having worked a down train to Sheffield, running light engine back to Darnall shed, whilst Ivatt Class 4 2-6-0 No 43058 stands behind in the bay platform. Seen in the distance approaching the station from behind the No 4 signal box and its attendant buildings housing the electrical switchgear, is an unidentified 2-8-0 with a goods train from Nunnery sidings. *Photo: J. H. Turner. Date: 25 July 1959.*

The shell of the signal box and other associated buildings were finally demolished during 1989. On the extreme right the last vestiges of platform 3 remain together with one illuminated station signpost, a few yards beyond which the platform ramp is still exposed, but is not visible from this vantage point. Just out of view to the right, there is a small compound which is occupied by BR, which uses it as an engineers' depot and store. *Date: 24 September 1989.*

Supertrams for Sheffield

A 30km Light Rapid Transit (LRT) railway is planned for the area; rumours had suggested that part of the system would use the station site, but subsequent investigation proved this detail to be incorrect. However, two Supertram systems, similar to those in many European cities, sponsored by the South Yorkshire Passenger Transport Executive in conjunction with the city council, received Government approval on 27 November 1990. The first line of 22km will extend from Middlewood in northern Sheffield, via the city centre to Halway in the south, the second line running from the city centre along the Lower Don Valley to the Meadowhall shopping centre in the east. The system will be constructed in eight phases and will not use existing or disused tracks. An area on the southern portion of Nunnery sidings, approximately one mile east of this site, is where a proposed Supertram depot would be built, with access from Woodburn Road.

The major part of the £230 million scheme is to be financed by resources allocated by the Department of Transport; the Sheffield Development Corporation, Sheffield City Council and private backers will also contribute to the costs. It is hoped to get the scheme under way in August 1991 and to commence operation in 1993. The system will eventually be transferred to the private sector under the auspices of South Yorkshire Supertrams Ltd.

Reservations on track, signalling (ordered from Balfour Beatty) and twenty-five articulated tramcars (Siemens), were placed with manufacturers in 1990.

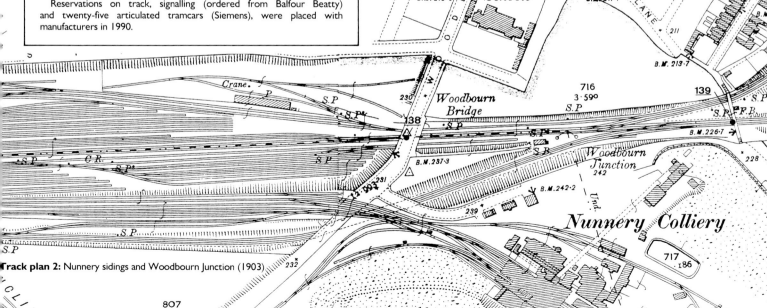

Track plan 2: Nunnery sidings and Woodbourn Junction (1903)

Sheffield Victoria station (5)
110/111 SK 365878

This classic study of Class A3 Pacific No 60103 *Flying Scotsman* departing from platform 4 with an up express also provides a pre-electrification view of the station, albeit minus its central overall roof, which had recently been dismantled.

The 38C shed plate signifies that *Flying Scotsman* was then shedded at Leicester Central, where having come that far south it would be uncoupled and another engine would then take over to work the train on to Marylebone. *Photo: J. F. Henton. Date: 11 February 1952.*

Apart from the retaining wall buttress on the right of the photograph, the platform ramps are the only remaining evidence of the same spot today, save the two concrete posts which once supported illuminated signs that told travellers they had reached Sheffield Victoria, on this eastern approach to the station. At least the weather was glorious on this day for photography, which helped an otherwise depressing scene.

The single line runs eastwards from here and gains double track just east of the overbridge carrying Bernard Road, where the link from the now local-authority-supported line from Sheffield (Midland) to Retford, Gainsborough and Lincoln is made. It is not uncommon on winter Sundays for HSTs to use part of the GC, when the Midland line to London is closed for engineering work. Trains are then diverted to Chesterfield on to the 'old road' via Darnall, Woodhouse Junction and Beighton Junction. *Date: 24 September 1989.*

6
Darnall MPD
110/111 SK 384878

The store lines at Darnall hold a variety of types, including two Class D11 Directors, No 62664 *Princess Mary*, and No 62668 *Jutland*. Introduced in 1920, both have had their day. Also seen in this view is K2 No 61761, which had recently undergone a works overhaul only to be ignominiously consigned for scrap without ever entering service again. The steam shed closed in 1965, but DMUs and coaches were serviced here well into the seventies. *Photo: B. N. Collins. Date: 1959.*

In recent years the shed has been used to store redundant DMU stock. Today it is empty and remains in a partly demolished state, as this view from Kettlebridge Road shows. On the left are the roofs of the famous Cravens works.

A little further down the track both Darnall and Woodhouse stations survive, but the buildings on the former have been demolished and only a bus-type shelter is provided for passengers on this subsidised route. *Date: 23 September 1989.*

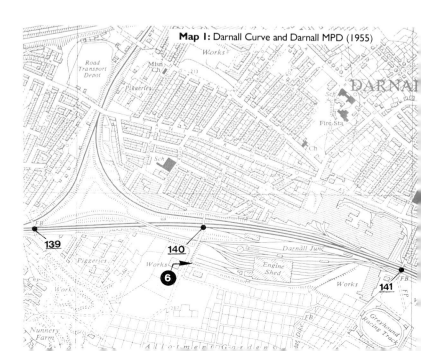

Map I: Darnall Curve and Darnall MPD (1955)

Woodhouse Junction
120 SK 435850

On a cold and dismal Sunday, track maintenance gangs are busy working on the old GC line to Worksop and Retford. The GC's London line branched right at this point, as seen in this shot, where the last vestiges of track remain as far as Beighton Junction. *Date: 23 April 1989.*

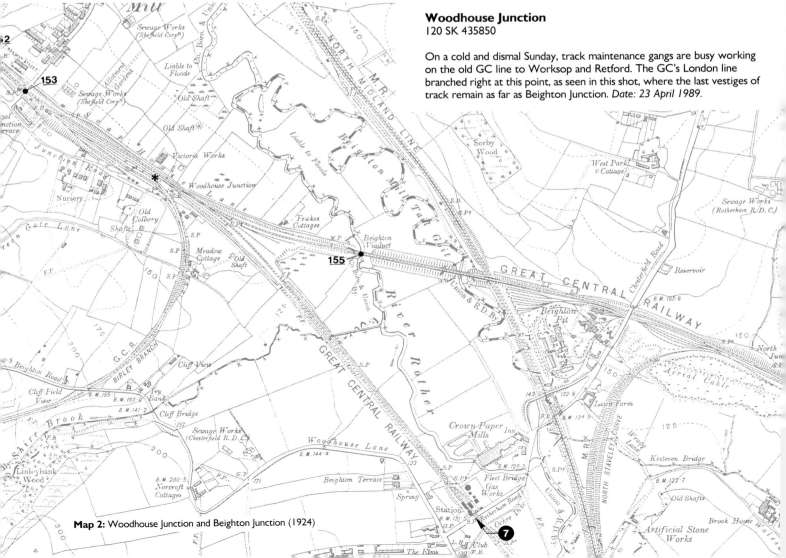

Map 2: Woodhouse Junction and Beighton Junction (1924)

7
Beighton station and level crossing
120 SK 443840

A view of Beighton station taken at the turn of the century with the staff posing for the camera: standing on the up line the shunters adopt a suitable stance with their poles. *Photo: Lens of Sutton. Date: c1900.*

The station is no longer, but the only level crossing on the entire GC route between Sheffield and Marylebone survives together with its attendant signal box on the now secondary route to Chesterfield, which is mainly used by mineral trains.

   Beighton Junction, a few hundred yards south of this point, is where the MR's North Midland line from Chesterfield to Rotherham, the GC's Beighton branch, (the ex-Lancashire, Derbyshire & East Coast Railway's line to Spinkhill, Clowne and Langwith Junction) and the GC's route to London once met. Until recently a few miles of the latter survived as a single track to service the now closed Arkwright Colliery, just south of Staveley. *Date: 23 April 1989.*

COMMENT: A true facsimile could not be obtained, as the original photograph was not available at the time of my visit here, but I hope that these contrasts will enable the changes to become apparent.

Beighton Junction today. *Date: 23 September 1989.*

8

Killamarsh North and South Junctions
120 SK 448823

An O1 class 2-8-0 struggles up the 1:176 gradient with a goods train towards Killamarsh Junction and is about to cross the girder bridge under which the Midland line passes. The disused branch on the right once served Holbrook Colliery. *Photo: G. Newall. Date: 1963.*

Map 3: Killamarsh (1924)

The girder bridge survives in reasonable condition and was used until recently to carry the line on to Arkwright Colliery. Nature takes no time at all in staking her claim and the trackbed is rapidly becoming overgrown.

The footbridge carrying Meadow Gate Lane, from which these photos were taken, now leads from large new housing estates built in the area to the Rother Valley Country Park, seen in the background on the left, which was created from industrial wasteland and slag heaps. This provides all kinds of excellent amenities for the local community, including water sports, fishing, camping facilities and a nature trail; also a golf course and driving range are planned. *Date: 23 September 1989.*

9
Killamarsh station
120 SK 448809

A view looking north of Killamarsh Central in the early years of this century. The down platform's rather elegant buildings were demolished in latter years and replaced with a miserable looking shelter with no other facilities available. The station was closed in 1963 along with all others between Woodhouse and Nottingham, when local passenger services were withdrawn. *Photo: A. R. Kaye collection. Date: c1900/1.*

The station roof and canopy are unmistakable but trees and shrubs have taken over the down platform during the relatively short time since the track was lifted through here. The trackbed, however, remains fairly clear and is used regularly by walkers and off-road motorcyclists.

The main booking office is now owned by Havenplan Ltd, which runs its world famous architectural emporium from here. It sells an amazing collection of memorabilia from bygone days. One can buy almost anything from, to quote the brochure: 'beautiful cast-iron pieces to rugged stonework steeped in history.' The firm also has many interesting railway artefacts that are too varied to list between these pages; it is well worth a visit for the rail enthusiast. *Date: 11 September 1989.*

COMMENT: *Proprietors John and Margaret Buckle were most welcoming and gave me a conducted tour of their premises crammed with the most fascinating and unusual items. Television and film companies regularly use their emporium to provide many artefacts for period productions. They really do a good line in kitchen sinks (complete with ornate taps) and most probably could supply anything from a pin to an elephant (china of course), if requested!*

A view of the station as it is today looking north from the footbridge. Note that a new housing development has started to encroach on to the track formation at the far end of the goods yard. *Date: 23 April 1989.*

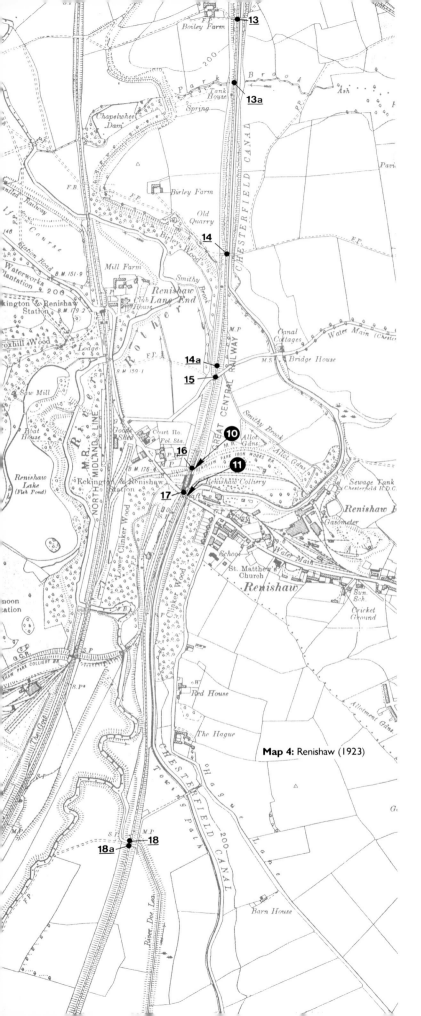

Map 4: Renishaw (1923)

10

Renishaw Central station
120 SK 445783

This view of Renishaw station, situated in a valley to the north-west side of the village on the A616 towards Eckington, was taken sometime around its closure. The booking hall was adjacent to the roadside and abutted the bridge. Although the buildings, graced by canopies supported on elaborate cast-iron trusses, looked substantial, they were in fact only built on a timber frame and faced with cladding boards. However, the effect achieved was one of permanence at a moderate cost and was typical of much of the railway architecture of the period.

About half way along the platforms the Midland Railway's Renishaw Park Iron Works branch passed underneath the station, having turned off in a north-easterly direction from the MR's line 200yd west and running parallel to here. It met the GC's own spur from the goods yard serving Renishaw Colliery 350yd due east of the station. *Photo: Lens of Sutton. Date: c1963.*

Since mineral trains last used this section of line, there has been much salvaging of materials from the station site itself; many of the platform edging stones have been removed, possibly for use in local gardens.

The old iron works branch bridge has recently been demolished and only the abutments remain, effectively cutting the station in half. Apart from the bridge carrying the A616 over the formation, the goods shed seen through it still stands more or less intact. *Date: 11 September 1989.*

11
Renishaw station goods yard
120 SK 445781

A trio of engines, headed by clean-looking Austerity 2-8-0 No 90358, with a grubby sister locomotive and a Class O2 goods run light past Renishaw goods yard.

The spacious goods yard, complete with crane, appears by this date to be little more than a scrapyard. *Photo: J. H. Turner. Date: 15 May 1960.*

Whilst much of the ballast has been removed, the whole area is remarkably clear of undergrowth and weeds. The goods shed used by a small engineering firm in recent years now stands abandoned, as does the crane's plinth and iron column in the middle of the yard.
Date: 11 September 1989.

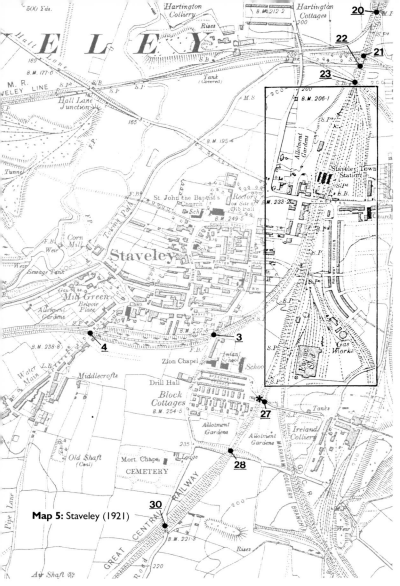

Map 5: Staveley (1921)

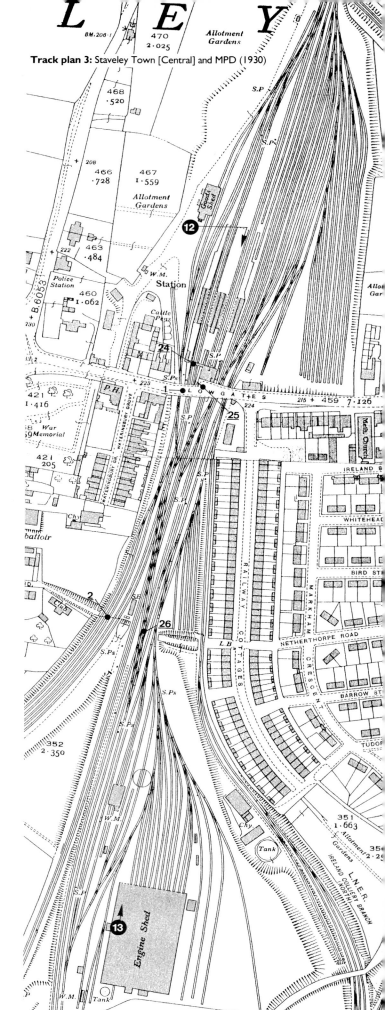

12
Staveley Town station
120 SK 437751

Staveley Town (latterly Central), its associated goods yard and locomotive depot were once a hive of activity, but this view, taken looking south towards the A619 road bridge during its last days, belies the fact. The station was extensive and could boast no fewer than four platforms and as many tracks running through it. The GC's Chesterfield loop came in from the west at Staveley Town South via Brimington & Sheepbridge station (closed 6 March 1963) at Wheeldon Mill, joining the main line just south of the station and road bridge; this ensured that Staveley had many and varied diagrams working through this section of line. *Photo: Lens of Sutton. Date: c1963.*

The same view of the station today provides little comfort for rail enthusiasts, as the last remaining track to serve the now-defunct Arkwright Colliery was lifted during 1988. Although still quite well ballasted south of this location, all that remains is a small portion of pointwork which has been cast aside and rests at the far end of the platform near the bridge.
    A new spur from the MR's Barrow Hill–Seymour line was constructed to serve Arkwright Colliery as recently as 1981, joining the GC's formation just north of the road bridge in the background and to the left of this shot. The spur was only used for a very short period before being placed 'under engineers' possession'; the last train having run in about 1985. *Date: 11 September 1989.*

13
Staveley MPD
120 SK 436744

The depot, situated a little to the south of the station, provided motive power for freight and local services. It was usually a centre for protracted activity, but spare capacity in its latter years meant it was home to a variety of types and often served as a final resting place for the Sheffield area's stored locomotives. Darnall's B1s were temporarily kept here from February 1962, in addition to which Millhouse's Jubilees and Royal Scots were transferred to Staveley upon the former's closure.

This view looking north from inside the structure shows Austerity 2-8-0 No 90227, a sister WD engine, Class O4 No 63701 and Class O1 No 63863, basking in the sun outside. *Photo: Les Nixon. Date: April 1965.*

The area is now just waste ground covered with rough grass and bushes. A couple of inspection pits, seen in the original photograph, are the only evidence that this was once a locomotive depot, or that a shed ever existed here at all. A true facsimile was impossible to effect, so a close-up of one of the inspection pits had to suffice as a tangible reminder of bygone days. *Date: 24 September 1989.*

A view looking north from the footbridge just south of the old Staveley depot, which was once situated in the area now covered by bushes beyond the lorry park on the right. *Date: 24 September 1989.*

2

THE CHESTERFIELD LOOP
AND STAVELEY–TIBSHELF

Chesterfield loop

The GC line to Chesterfield from Staveley, which left the main 'direct' route at Staveley Town South, but still following the Rother Valley and Chesterfield canal, had two intermediate stations. The first, Staveley Works station was near Hollingwood and literally spanned the canal 1½ miles west of the town; the second at Wheeldon Mill was Sheepbridge & Brimington station. Just south-west of this point the GC line passed under the Midland Railway, turning south towards Chesterfield, leaving the MR on its east side.

Chesterfield, noted for the crooked spire of St Mary's church, was once blessed with no fewer than three stations: the GC's Central and Midland stations were a matter of 250yd apart on the north-east side and not far from the centre, whilst Market Place station (closed in 1951), on the GC's Chesterfield to Lincoln branch (the ex-LD&EC line) was on the south-west side, it too being fairly central for the town.

Trains heading south from the station immediately entered a tunnel under the town to emerge at Hollis Lane, then turning south-east to duck under the Midland's line at Horns Bridge, and with the old LD&EC route, which closed completely in 1957, passing over them both at this point. Still heading in a general south-easterly direction, and on a rising gradient, the loop joined the main line between Temple Normanton and Heath at Heath Junction, with only one intermediate station on this section at Grassmoor.

In 1963 the town was left with only the Midland station, when Chesterfield Central shut following the closure of the GC loop on 5 March that year; it had opened on 9 March 1899. The last passenger train to run over the loop was on 15 June, being a commemorative special hauled by A3 Pacific No 4472 *Flying Scotsman*.

Little remains of the GC's Chesterfield loop today: the line from Staveley has been mostly obliterated. The Staveley Works station site is overgrown, but the platform edges are still visible. Five miles of navigation to the nearby canal in this area is being restored by a group of volunteers with help from British Coal. There is a possibility that part of the GC formation here may be used in a future scheme for a Staveley bypass road. At Wheeldon Mill, Sheepbridge & Brimington station's site is an untidy contractor's yard. The goods shed and station building on the up side survive, but are in a poor state.

The most notable obliteration of the GC loop came to a conclusion on 25 July 1985, when Mrs Linda Chalker, then Minister of Transport, declared the new A61 Chesterfield inner relief road officially open; it was constructed on much of the GC's route from Chesterfield's northern outskirts near Sheepbridge sidings, to a point where the old tunnel passed under the town. The relief road then swings briefly in a walled cutting towards the Midland station before taking up the old GC's route again at Horns Bridge. The tunnel was sealed and now hides behind the road's retaining walls.

A massive roundabout at Horns Bridge has been constructed near the point where the three railways once crossed. The GC's bridge under the Midland line has been demolished and only a small portion of a blue brick abutment wall near a footbridge survives. The recently constructed A617 dual carriageway link road between Chesterfield and the M1 at Junction 29, follows the major portion of the GC's formation to Heath and beyond the site of the former junction; virtually no trace of the railway is left, save a small section of embankment at Corbiggs.

Map 6: Chesterfield (1938)

14
Chesterfield Central
119 SK 386715

The crooked spire of St Mary's church acts as a backdrop to this deserted south-looking view of Chesterfield Central, taken during its final years of operation. Note the tunnel beyond the station buildings. Most local services called here until the loop's closure in 1963.
Photo: Lens of Sutton. Date: c1963.

Track plan 4: Chesterfield Central (1938)

The new A61 inner relief road seems to be deserted in this view, looking from precisely the same spot today. This is an illusion, for it now carries hundreds of vehicles an hour — a sure sign of the times — but Chesterfield's town centre has been partly relieved of its traffic burden.
Date: 24 September 1989.

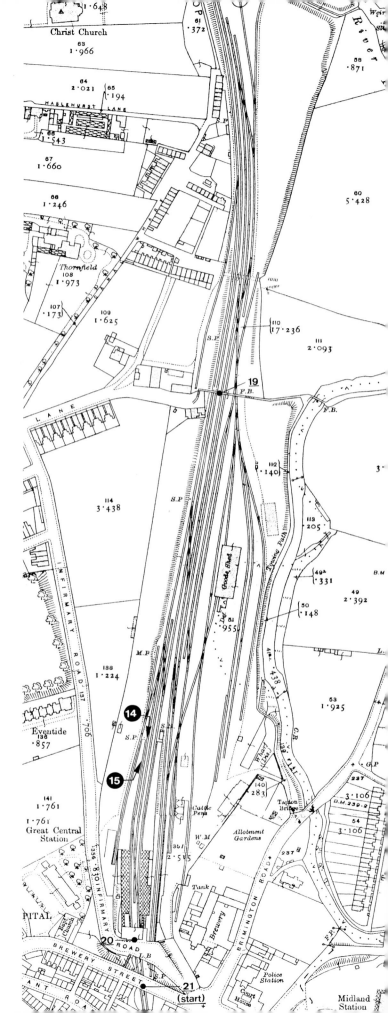

15
Chesterfield Central
119 SK 386715

Darnall B1 4-6-0 No 61312 enters Chesterfield Central with the 16.05 Manchester–Marylebone express. Locomotives were changed at Leicester for the run south.

All Chesterfield Central's sidings and goods shed were on the northerly approach to the station. Although spacious, they were not nearly so extensive as the MR's. *Photo: Neville Stead. Date: May 1958.*

There is not much resemblance to the same scene today, save for a few trees on the right. The new A61 inner relief road has totally taken the place of the railway, obliterating completely any last vestiges that might have remained until a few years ago. *Date: 24 September 1989.*

COMMENT: *My efforts to secure these photographs were taken at some considerable personal risk, for it was necessary to make several dashes across the busy dual carriageway to line the shots up accurately before attempting to take a photograph. Wearing a high-visibility vest, I then waited for a gap in the traffic (which was not often) before sprinting to the chosen spot where the camera mounted on its tripod was hurriedly erected, and looking about me all the while, took the shot before rapidly seeking the relative safety of the verge. This exercise is not to be recommended and lest I seek an opinion on the success of the outcome, perhaps these words from the Good Book ought to be borne in mind: 'Answer a fool according to his folly, lest he be wise in his conceit.' Fitting words indeed!*

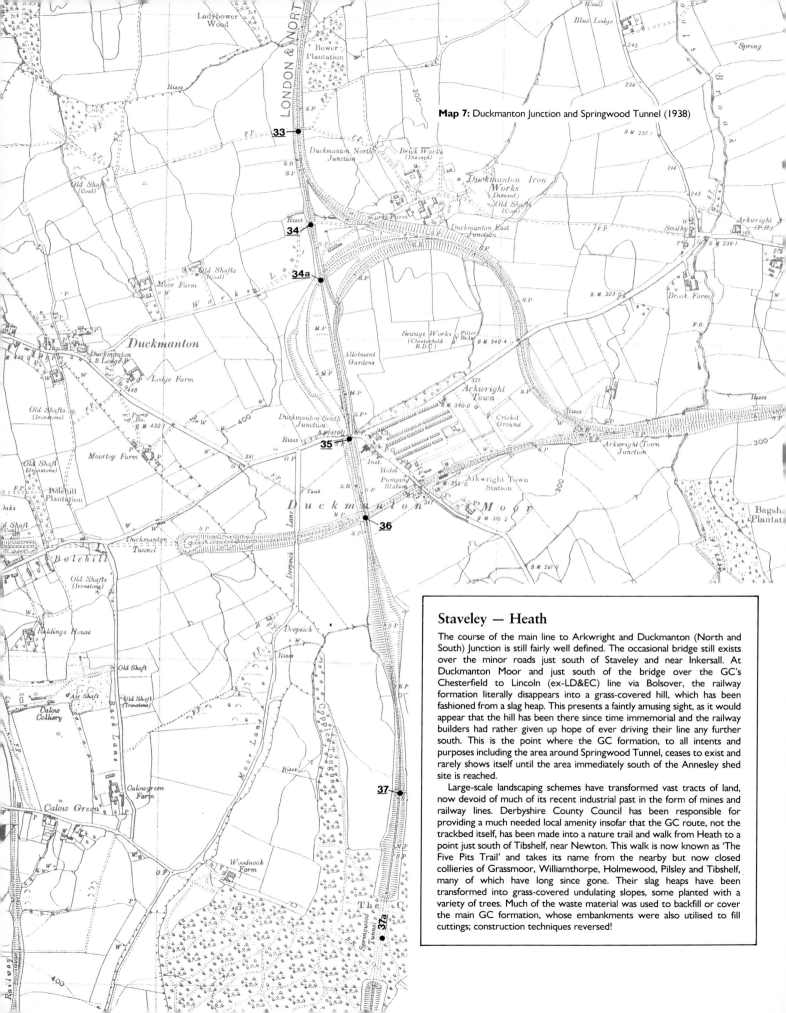

Map 7: Duckmanton Junction and Springwood Tunnel (1938)

Staveley — Heath

The course of the main line to Arkwright and Duckmanton (North and South) Junction is still fairly well defined. The occasional bridge still exists over the minor roads just south of Staveley and near Inkersall. At Duckmanton Moor and just south of the bridge over the GC's Chesterfield to Lincoln (ex-LD&EC) line via Bolsover, the railway formation literally disappears into a grass-covered hill, which has been fashioned from a slag heap. This presents a faintly amusing sight, as it would appear that the hill has been there since time immemorial and the railway builders had rather given up hope of ever driving their line any further south. This is the point where the GC formation, to all intents and purposes including the area around Springwood Tunnel, ceases to exist and rarely shows itself until the area immediately south of the Annesley shed site is reached.

Large-scale landscaping schemes have transformed vast tracts of land, now devoid of much of its recent industrial past in the form of mines and railway lines. Derbyshire County Council has been responsible for providing a much needed local amenity insofar that the GC route, not the trackbed itself, has been made into a nature trail and walk from Heath to a point just south of Tibshelf, near Newton. This walk is now known as 'The Five Pits Trail' and takes its name from the nearby but now closed collieries of Grassmoor, Williamthorpe, Holmewood, Pilsley and Tibshelf, many of which have long since gone. Their slag heaps have been transformed into grass-covered undulating slopes, some planted with a variety of trees. Much of the waste material was used to backfill or cover the main GC formation, whose embankments were also utilised to fill cuttings; construction techniques reversed!

16

Heath exchange sidings
120 SK 436663

This splendid and rare view taken from the overbridge at the north end of Heath station shows Austerity 2-8-0 No 90285 passing the exchange sidings with an up coal train. Having climbed almost continuously from Beighton, save for a few short stretches near Eckington, the summit will be reached a few miles up the line at Pilsley.

The line veering off to the right in a cutting served the Grassmoor and Williamthorpe collieries, swinging almost 180° to pass under the main line just beyond the signal box in the background, at which point the Chesterfield loop branched off westwards. The tracks on the extreme right served the Holmewood Colliery branch and passed just to the east of the station, before looping under the main line near the colliery, rejoining the GC just north of Broomridding Wood a mile or two south of the village.
Photo: J. S. Hancock/Ian Allan library. Date: 14 May 1965.

The lifting of the tracks commenced on 4 December 1967, the last trains having run the year before. The area has been totally landscaped and a link road passes under the old GC bridge, veers off and passes the now-closed Grassmoor Colliery. The horizon with its farm house essentially is the link, despite the depletion of mature trees; also the rows of terraced houses on the extreme right remain. *Date: 23 September 1989.*

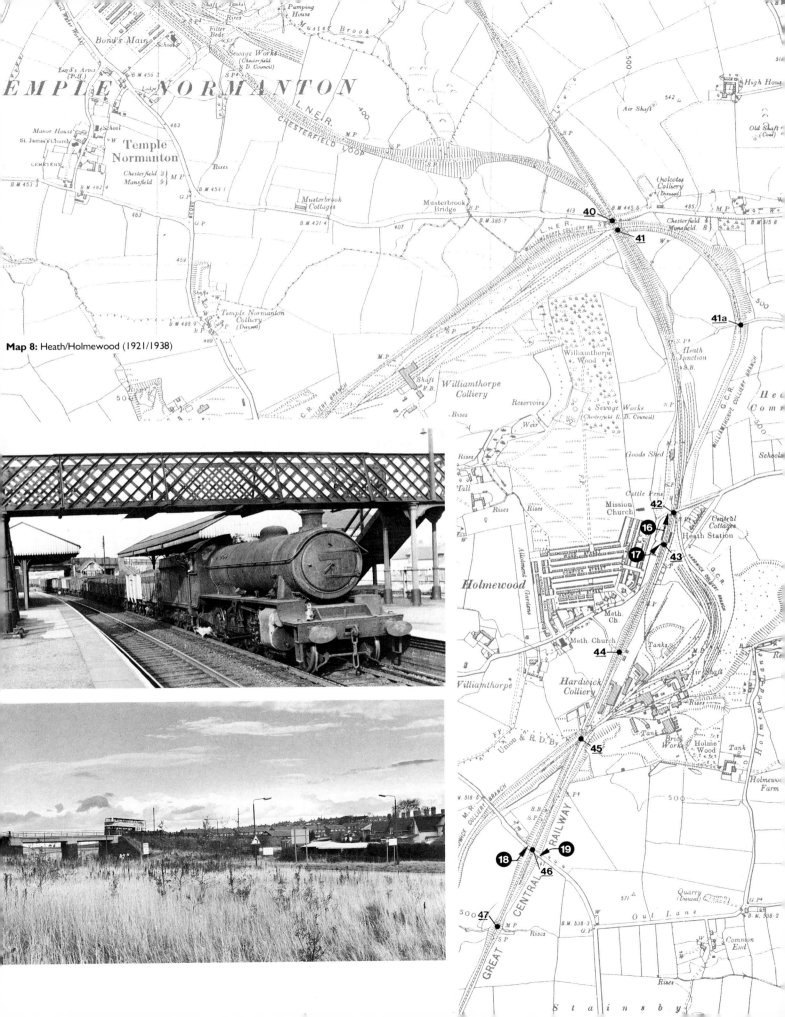

Map 8: Heath/Holmewood (1921/1938)

17 (Opposite)
Heath station
120 SK 435661

Having started out from the exchange sidings just beyond the bridge in the background, and with the rear wagons still snaking out from the yard, the rather grubby Class O1 2-8-0 No 63650 plods through Heath station (which was actually in the village of Holmewood) with a very long coal train, probably bound for Annesley.

Like the O4s, the O1s were powerful workhorses and did some splendid work for many years on the line, particularly on the northern section. From 1958 the class was gradually supplemented by the BR Standard Class 9F 2-10-0s, which performed supremely, especially when working the Annesley–Woodford 'runners'.

The station closed to passengers in 1963, along with others on this section. The neat signal box controlled the exchange sidings and the Holmewood Colliery branch. *Photo: K. Plant via Les Nixon. Date: c1955.*

The station area is now covered with rough grass and saplings. Apart from the adjacent stationmaster's house on the west side and a few remaining platform railings, the only survivor is the bridge, which has been rebuilt and carries the original road from Holmewood to the village of Heath. A new industrial estate has been built on the site of Holmewood Colliery and a large roundabout, into which the link road that passes under the bridge is connected, has been constructed on the south-east side of the station site. *Date: 4 November 1989.*

18 (Below)
Holmewood Colliery
120 SK 432652

Holmewood Colliery, with its associated coke ovens, and situated just to the south of the village, is seen in the background. Class O4 2-8-0 No 63701, with a heavy coal train from Staveley, slowly makes its way through the cutting and is about to pass under the iron bridge carrying the B6039. The structure (No 46) was known locally as the 'whistling bridge', due to the resonating sounds it made if pedestrians stamped their feet when walking across it. *Photo: Bob Tebb.*
Date: 12 September 1963.

Not only has the colliery been obliterated and the site turned into a modern industrial estate, which can be seen in the distance, but the cutting has been completely filled in and now is just sheep pasture. The path of the 'Five Pits Trail' is marked by the fence line on the left. 'Whistling bridge', sold in 1973, no longer survives and has been removed; the B6039 road being re-laid across the infilled land. It is easy to pass by without realising that a major railway ever existed here, the only marker being new post-and-rail fencing on the roadside.
Date: 23 September 1989.

19
Holmewood — Bridge 46
120 SK 432652

A view from the other side of the B6039 road shows K3 class 2-6-0 No 61974 heading south from under the 'whistling bridge' near Holmewood with the 10.09 Sheffield–Nottingham train. A large area of opencast mining is marked by spoil heaps in the distance, together with coal trucks on the MR's Pilsley extension which linked several mines in the area; this was connected to the GC south of this point and at Holmewood itself. *Photo: Michael Mensing. Date: 29 September 1959.*

Apart from the fence posts that mark the boundary on the down side, there is not much to link the former scene with that of today. The area once covered by spoil heaps from opencast mining has been amazingly turned back into pleasant pastures. The industrial lines have long since been removed, leaving virtually no trace of their existence.
Date: 4 November 1989.

Moorhouse Farm — Locko Road
120 SK 427638

B1 4-6-0 No 61078, with the 11.16 Bournemouth–Newcastle train, has just passed over Locko Road viaduct (No 51) north of Pilsley, which marks BR's Eastern and London Midland regional boundaries. Pilsley Colliery is seen on the extreme right, whilst the buildings on the left are those of Moorhouse Farm. This photo was taken from a footbridge (No 50) some 300yd north of Locko Road. *Photo: Michael Mensing. Date: 29 September 1959.*

Autumn sunshine casts long shadows across the field, which was once the GC line, and the area of Pilsley Colliery has now been planted with a variety of deciduous and evergreen trees. Some of the farm's older

outbuildings have been replaced. The only identifiable links are the two electricity poles and a solitary tree seen in the original photograph over the first and second carriages. *Date: 4 November 1989.*

COMMENT: *Not knowing the precise location from which the original shot was taken, the exact spot was very difficult to find and at first I headed off from Locko Road back towards Pilsley — completely in the wrong direction. I did, however, meet a charming financial consultant out for a walk with his young family and he kindly offered to organise my portfolio for me, but he could not help me with the topography! It bore no resemblance to the same scene the original portrayed and it was only after at least half an hour's search that I found the spot upon noticing the tree in the valley. It was then too dark for any photography, and due to indifferent lighting experienced here two further trips had to be made to the location before this photograph was obtained.*

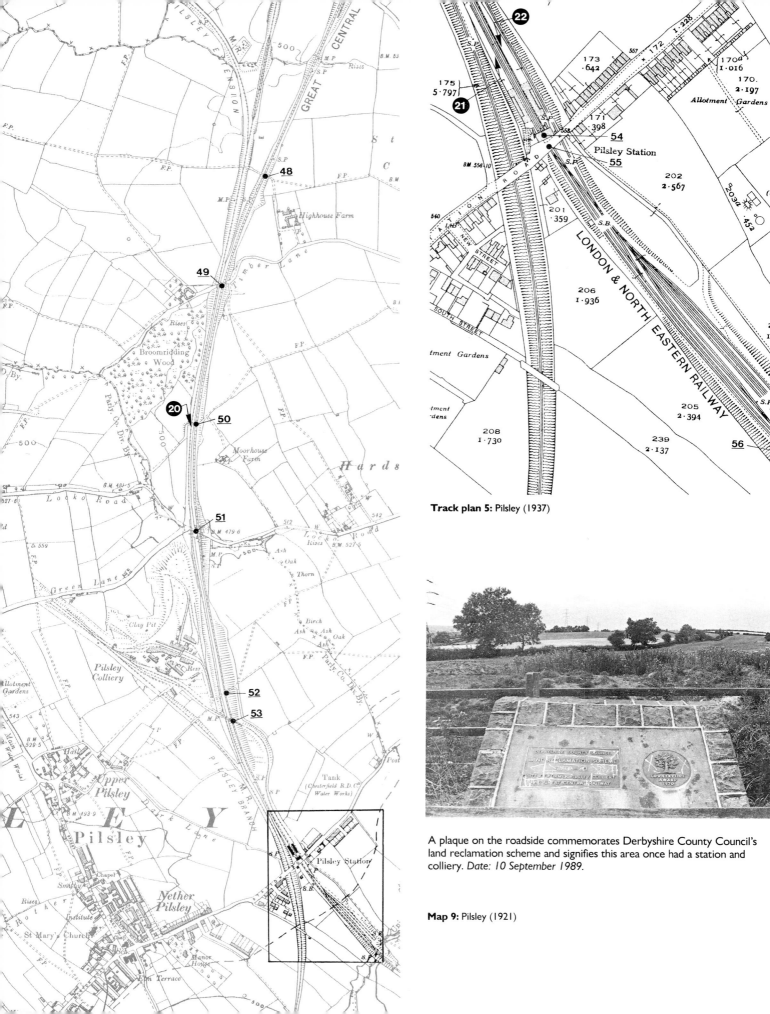

Track plan 5: Pilsley (1937)

A plaque on the roadside commemorates Derbyshire County Council's land reclamation scheme and signifies this area once had a station and colliery. *Date: 10 September 1989.*

Map 9: Pilsley (1921)

21
Pilsley station (1)
120 SK 429624

A Brush Type 2 (Class 31) diesel-electric roars past the weed-strewn platforms of Pilsley with a Sheffield–Nottingham train. This was the highest point of the line between Sheffield and Marylebone; the run would be mostly downhill to a point south of Nottingham just beyond milepost 120, save the short climbs to Kirkby and Bulwell Common. Pilsley Colliery is in the background. *Photo: Lens of Sutton. Date: c1963.*

A view looking north taken from approximately the same position today provides no evidence of a station once having been here, the colliery being another victim, but no sad loss visually. The fenced path of the 'Five Pits Trail' is seen on the right. *Date: 10 September 1989.*

22
Pilsley station (2)
120 SK 429624

Pilsley station looking south towards the rather elegant footbridge (No 55) and booking office on Station Road. The MR's Pilsley extension from its main line near Morton linked with the GC at this point and served the colliery here. The lines converged with the GC from behind the down platform on the right of this photograph and Pilsley's sidings were on the far side of the bridge in the background. The station closed in November 1959, after some sixty-seven years of use. *Photo: Lens of Sutton. Date c1963.*

The stationmaster's house which was obscured by the cottage (now demolished) in the original photograph, can now be seen. The removal of all railway artefacts has been achieved with ruthless efficiency, leaving no trace save the memorial stone on Station Road, which has even lost its bridge, having been sold to Derbyshire County Council in 1971. The only visible clue to the location is provided by a gable end of a cottage on the extreme right. *Date: 10 September 1989.*

COMMENT: Pilsley was renowned for one of its porters, a confirmed bachelor and World War I veteran, who rejoiced in the name of Fred 'Leaper' Wall. This man of eccentricity was something of an acrobat: he often used to ride his bicycle on the railway line itself and could balance it whilst static thus positioned for at least twenty minutes. His usual greeting of 'morning lady' to a female passenger was often accompanied by a flourishing 360° rotation of his cap on one finger. If asked by the lady for the time, he would first look up one arm, then the other — and up each leg in turn — only to produce a handsome timepiece from his waistcoat pocket!

23
Tibshelf (1)
120 SK 439610

B1 class 4-6-0 No 61157 has just passed Tibshelf Town with the 12.15 Marylebone–Manchester train and heads off in the direction of Pilsley, some two miles distant. The slag heap from Tibshelf Colliery dominates the skyline on the right.

Much of the line from Woodhouse to Bagthorpe Junction was dogged by mining subsidence and the line's general speed limit of 75mph was punctuated by several stretches where a limit of either 20mph or 30mph was imposed. The tight timings of expresses meant that an engine driver would have to brake hard where such restrictions were imposed; once clear, he would then accelerate away in spirited style, driving in true GC fashion in order to keep on schedule. *Photo: Michael Mensing. Date: 29 September 1959.*

A football pitch, complete with goalkeeper; a trail with walkers and somebody on horseback; but no railway — nor slag heap. The total transformation could not be more of a marked contrast than portrayed by this scene. The landscapers must be given due credit for turning the area into an excellent local amenity, if at the sad loss of the GC. The skyline with its trees and farm buildings, however, does provide some continuity. *Date: 5 November 1989.*

Map 10: Tibshelf (1921)

24 (Opposite)
Tibshelf (2)
120 SK 439610

A view in the opposite direction. Tibshelf church stands proudly on the hill overlooking the community it serves, whilst the 14.17 Sheffield–Nottingham train hauled by B1 4-6-0 No 61111 passes through the deep cutting which bisected the village. The station can just be made out in the distance under the High Street bridge (No 58). *Photo: Michael Mensing. Date: 29 September 1959.*

The location is unmistakable, as noted by the church. Some of the older houses have been demolished; new ones take their place, but the railway is lost for ever. Planted with a few trees and shrubs the infilled cutting provides this open space which is used for a variety of leisure activities. *Date: 4 November 1989.*

COMMENT: *Due to lighting and technical difficulties, three trips had to be made here; this was a pleasant task, as the local inhabitants were so friendly and readily told tales of the old railway and its folk. Despite the older generation appreciating the new walking amenities now provided by the 'Five Pits Trail', the GC is still greatly lamented.*

25 (Below)
Tibshelf Town station (1)
120 SK 440607

This vista of the line looking south from the B6025 road bridge dividing the town's High Street shows a Fowler Class 4MT 2-6-4T leaving Tibshelf with the 13.00 Leicester Central–Chesterfield Central service. The extent of the station layout with the goods yard, shed and signal box beyond can be seen to advantage.

Note the dominant colliery slag heaps that partly obscure the houses on the horizon, which are those in Newton.
Photo: Michael Mensing. Date: 29 September 1959.

An aspect with a difference; the extent of the landscaping that has taken place around Tibshelf is self evident. The final stretch of the 'Five Pits Trail' meanders off from a newly constructed underpass towards Newton, whose houses can now be seen well from here. The slag heaps have been flattened, no longer obstructing the view, and the area they once occupied is planted with trees: a dramatic and excellently executed transformation — even if it is at the cost of the Great Central's route. *Date: 10 September 1989.*

26
Tibshelf Town station (2)
120 SK 440606

Class O1 2-8-0 No 63784 with an up mineral train bound for Annesley trundles through the deep cutting and passes Tibshelf Town station. Coal traffic was the major revenue source of the line, particularly from the Nottinghamshire collieries, being fed into the network from Annesley yard.

Access to the station was gained on the west side by a steep path leading from the road. *Photo: J. F. Henton. Date: 9 May 1963.*

The site is now a rather attractive paddock bordered by post-and-rail fencing. The church still dominates the skyline, but there is little else that is so lasting in this view, taken in rather dull conditions. *Date: 10 September 1989.*

27
Crag Lane, Blackwell (1)
120 SK 444587

Having just skirted the village of Newton in the background, ex-NER B16/1 4-6-0 No 61458 coasts downhill around the sharp curve a mile south of Tibshelf with a fitted freight, and is about to pass under Bridge 64, the first of two carrying the B6026 over the line at Blackwell.
Photo: Michael Mensing. Date: 29 September 1959.

Apart from landscaping the station site at Tibshelf to the minor road south of the village, the line from there is marginally easier to define since much of the original railway fencing is still in situ, although most of the trackbed has been infilled, as here. A path now often trod by equine hooves replaces that pounded by the iron horses of yesteryear.
Date: 10 September 1989.

COMMENT: *The young lady on horseback stopped long enough to be shown the original photograph, despite the fact a howling gale was blowing which had made her horse skittish. She was amazed at the transformation and found it hard to believe that a railway ever existed here, especially since she was born after the demise of steam and could not remember the GC line at all.*

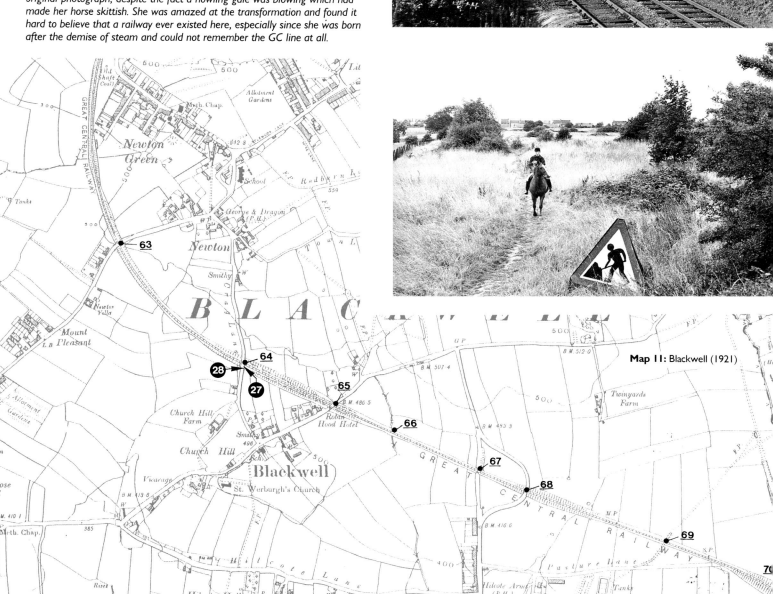

Map 11: Blackwell (1921)

Crag Lane, Blackwell (2)
120 SK 444587

BR Class 9F 2-10-0 No 92030 with a train of empties heads towards the second B6026 overbridge (No 65) at Huthwaite Lane, Blackwell, on its journey towards Annesley, passing through Kirkby Bentinck, some three miles south of this point. Before doing so, it will cross the viaduct over the MR's Blackwell branch and then pass New Hucknall sidings. *Photo: Michael Mensing. Date: 29 September 1959.*

An all too familiar sight of the GC north of Nottingham: sheep pasture, punctuated by a few jagged posts that remain from railway days.

However, the farm beyond seems to have changed little in the thirty years that separates the photographs. The gable of the Robin Hood public house is just perceptible on the extreme right.

The pastoral tranquillity of this view is but an illusion, for the roar of traffic on the M1, the embankment of which can just be discerned beyond the tree line and cuts across the GC's formation a matter of 200yd from this point, shatters the peace.

Track lifting commenced on this section from the MR's regional boundary north of Pilsley (Locko Road viaduct) only three days after the last train had run, the 22.45 Marylebone–Manchester 'Newspaper', which passed in the early hours of 4 September 1966. The reason for this haste was to salvage the rails before the construction of the M1 embankment severed the route here. *Date: 23 September 1989.*

29
Kirkby Bentinck station
120 SK 488556

Typical in design of the stations along the section to Annesley, the GC station of Kirkby Bentinck was situated at Castle Hill just under a mile south-west of Kirkby-in-Ashfield and once served a thriving mining community, but it had more than its fair share of competition, for as well as the GC's Kirkby-in-Ashfield Central station on the Mansfield line, the Midland Railway could offer a service from its station in the nearby town as well.

Maintenance problems and cost-cutting meant that like other stations, it suffered the indignity of losing some of its buildings over the years, which were replaced by utilitarian shelters as viewed here on the down side. *Photo: Lens of Sutton. Date: c1963.*

A couple of telegraph poles survive, otherwise roof lines with their chimneys signify that this was once Kirkby Bentinck station. The occasional view of a platform edge is to be had where the soil cover has thinned.

A much-loved horse now resides in the paddock, equipped with all the paraphernalia necessary for its well-being: a comfortable stable, food store and with personal transport provided. What more could an animal ask for? *Date: 27 October 1988.*

30
Kirkby-in-Ashfield — Mill House, Castle Hill
120 SK 492554

Having just passed Kirkby South Junction and crossed over the MR's branch off the Erewash Valley line at Pye Bridge to Mansfield, Class 9F No 92088 heads northwards with a long rake of coal wagons, on a dismal April day.

The line in the foreground is the GC's spur to Bentinck Colliery. This was rather awkward to operate in so far as it was necessary to construct a long headshunt with a spur rather than a direct loop to the colliery, because of the GC main line's much greater elevation to it. The difficult topography around Portland Park in the background also made it impractical to gain access from the south. Coal trucks can be seen on the line leading to the colliery spurred from the headshunt in the distance. The signals in the background are on the GC's Mansfield line via Kirkby-in-Ashfield and Sutton-in-Ashfield. *Photo: Tom Boustead. Date: 4 April 1959.*

Some thirty years later a sullen sky casts again its gloom, but over a very much changed landscape. Mill House has been extended and the footpath has had to be realigned to accommodate it. There is virtually no trace of the main line, for its embankments have been bulldozed into the surrounding fields. Remnants of the colliery spur form a track and footpath leading to the fields beyond the house. Portland Park in the background, through which the GC was cut, has been designated a Site of Special Scientific Interest, for it now is home to many species of wild plants and butterflies. The retaining walls of the railway cutting are still extant and visible in the undergrowth. *Date: 9 September 1989.*

COMMENT: *Farmer Edwin Sowter, of nearby Studfold Farm, acted as my guide. Leading with his van, we crossed several fields before he directed me to a remote spot to park my car, which can just be seen through a gap in the trees on the the GC's trackbed in the distance. Mr Sowter related that at least three D8 bulldozers were used to landscape the area, and that the contractors could not persuade a bridge they came across to budge, so had to abandon all attempts at demolishing it before covering it with soil.*

31
Kirkby South Junction
120 SK 502551

A Class 8F 2-8-0, with a brake van in tow, comes off the ex-GNR Leen Valley route from Langwith Junction to join the GC main line at Kirkby South Junction and heads south-east and is about to pass under Lindley lane footbridge (No 82) on the final few hundred yards to Annesley Tunnel. The GC's line from Mansfield, not constructed until the second decade of the century, merges with the main line behind the signal box. Note the speed restrictions in force here.

The GN line from here was often used as an alternative route in the off-peak hours by 'Starlight Specials' heading north to Scotland; the GC line being rejoined at Beighton via Langwith Junction. *Photo: Bob Tebb. Date: 1966.*

The boundary fences are all that remain of a once busy junction where trains once passed every few minutes, but which is now filled in with thousands of tons of colliery and industrial waste. However, trains will once again run past here, sadly not in the shape of Class 8Fs, but initially in the form of three-car Sprinter unit sets. *Date: 9 September 1989.*

The 'Robin Hood Line'

Because the area is now badly served by public transport, and with the worsening traffic problem around Nottingham, local councils in co-operation with BR have devised a £10 million scheme, first conceived more than eight years ago, to revitalise the Midland's route between Worksop and Nottingham via Mansfield. A newly constructed section built directly atop the old one at this point, will link the existing freight line at Kirkby with Annesley, where the now-disused MR route from Bestwood Park Junction, near Nottingham, terminates at Newstead Colliery. MR's Kirkby Tunnel under the Robin Hood Hills will be excavated and then resurrected to enable the systems to be joined; the 'Robin Hood Line', as it will be known, was projected to reopen in May 1992, but financial wranglings will mean a delay.

The limit of the Midland's disused line at Newstead, looking south-east. *Date: 18 June 1989.*

Map 12: Kirkby South Junction (1921)
Note GC line to Kirkby-in-Ashfield Central and Mansfield Central under construction

Annesley Tunnel (north-west cutting)
120 SK 506549

Class 9F 2-10-0 No 92069 in charge of the up 'South Yorkshireman' is about to enter the 1,000yd tunnel, having passed Kirkby South Junction, visible beyond Lindley Lane occupation bridge in the background. The structure spanning the cutting in the foreground is an aqueduct (Bridge 82).

Introduced to the route in 1958, Class 9Fs were occasionally employed on expresses to supplement available locomotive power, and speeds of between 80mph and 90mph were sometimes recorded. Not a bad achievement for a freight design, which proved it could undertake these duties with consummate ease like those similarly employed on the Somerset & Dorset line. However, the thought of the locomotives' 5ft 0in driving wheels being flailed so their spokes and rods were just a blur at such speeds caused much consternation with the powers-that-be, and a general restriction of 60mph was imposed on the type. Whether it was strictly adhered to was quite another matter!

The MR line from Mansfield crossed the GC's formation just above the tunnel's mouth, before entering its own of much shorter length (175yd) at a higher level, then running parallel, but at different levels, to each other some 45yd apart through the Robin Hood Hills.
Photo: J. Cupit/Ian Allan library. Date: 29 July 1959.

The steeple of Kirkby-in-Ashfield parish church on the horizon provides continuity when all else seems to change, apart that is from the northern parapet of the occupation bridge, which almost as if in an act of defiance, protrudes above the infill. All of the deep cutting between Kirkby South Junction and Annesley Tunnel has been made into two fields of considerable size, although a solitary horse is the only occupant of this particular one. *Date: 9 September 1989.*

33
Annesley North Junction
120 SK 519542

This rare view shows K2 class 2-6-0 No 61754 about to enter Hollin Well & Annesley station with the 10.10 Sheffield–Nottingham train. It has just passed the junction, having emerged from Annesley Tunnel, the southern portal of which can just be discerned in the cutting.

The Great Central's London Extension commenced at this junction situated some 15 chains south-east of the tunnel. Not only did the junction mark the entrance to Annesley's exchange sidings, shed and wagon works, but also the divergence of the GN's Leen Valley line, seen on the extreme left of the picture, from the GC's system, having 'shared' a passage through the Robin Hood Hills.

The building with the tall chimney in the background is Selston Pumping Station belonging to the Nottingham Corporation Water Works; the nearer water tower formed part of a pumping station built for the railway's requirements. *Photo: H. B. Priestley. Date: 16 July 1955.*

The Robin Hood Hills in the background remain unchanged, but the tunnel cutting has been completely filled with colliery waste, and the site of the junction now forms several fields. The one in the foreground is covered by tall grasses and is not grazed.

The water works pumping station survives as a shell, but minus its chimney, and now is used as a stable for horses. The houses on the skyline and the pylons make the area unmistakable. *Date: 9 September 1989.*

34
Hollin Well & Annesley station (GCR)
120 SK 519541

Ex-ROD Class O4/3 2-8-0 No 63835 trundles past Hollin Well & Annesley on the old GN Leen Valley line with a coal train, whilst Class O4/8 No 63683 enters Annesley yard from North Junction on GC metals with another mineral train, and is bound for the extensive exchange sidings, which had more than seventeen miles of track and could accommodate over 4,500 wagons, some one million of which were handled here during the course of a year.

In earlier times, golfers for the adjacent course also used this station. *Photo: H. B. Priestley. Date: 16 July 1955.*

Not one trace of the station or junction remains, but the embankment of the Midland's line can be observed in the middle distance; this is to be utilised once again following the rebuilding of the route between Worksop and Nottingham. The cutting to Kirkby Tunnel's south-east portal can just be spotted above the roof of the old pumping station.

Immediately to the rear of this view rises an enormous landscaped slag heap, under which lies the site of Annesley sidings, works and MPD. *Date: 9 September 1989.*

Selston Pumping Station building today. *Date: 18 June 1989.*

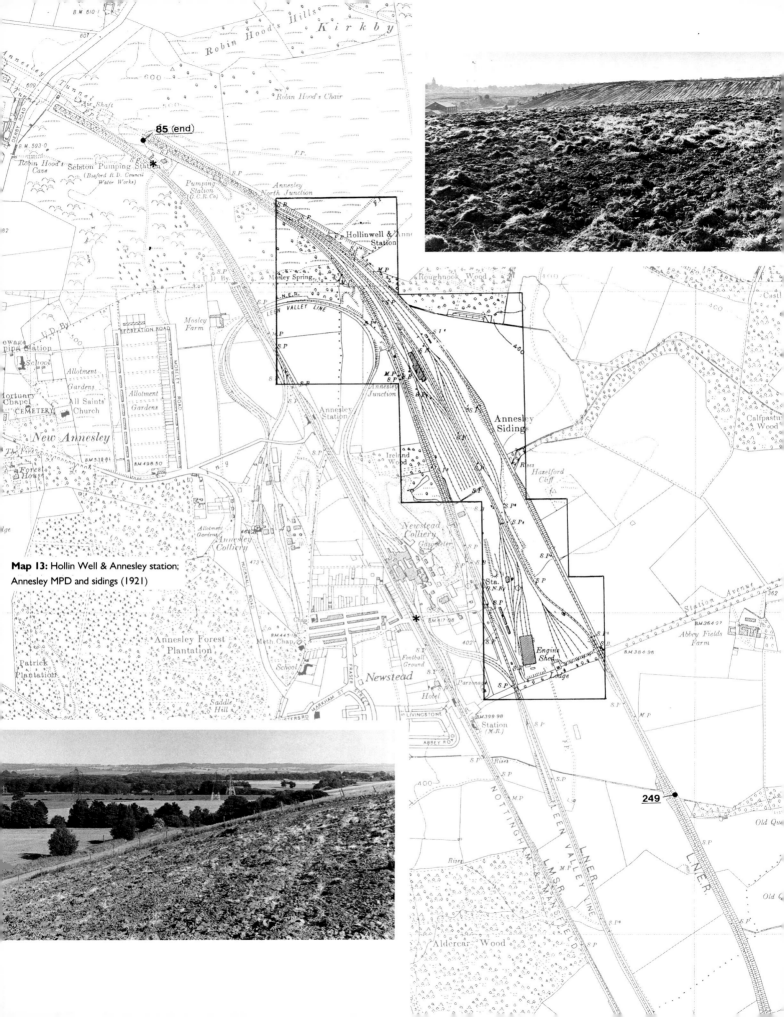

Map 13: Hollin Well & Annesley station;
Annesley MPD and sidings (1921)

85 (end)

249

The 'Windcutters' and 'Runners'

Due to three railway companies' routes running in close proximity at Annesley, it could boast no fewer than three stations: the GNR, GCR and MR each having built its own. In reality this was totally out of all proportion necessary to serve such a small centre of population, but was brought about by the fact that the three competing pre-Grouping systems met here, at the heart of the Nottinghamshire coalfield, thus holding the promise of much revenue from the mineral traffic it would generate.

Coal, and to some extent other freight traffic passing through here for the GC, played a vital role in the line's economy. The introduction of the Annesley to Woodford freight service in 1947 was significant in the system's survival until its withdrawal in June 1965: there were some 192 movements to and from the yard in a 24 hour period. Run to a high standard of efficiency, this provided an excellent fast service between the two yards, which also handled many cross-country freight workings.

These freights, although mostly loose coupled, soon became famed for their speed, particularly when Class 9Fs were rostered, and often achieved 50mph plus, so causing the minimum of disruption to passenger workings; thus the legendary 'windcutters' or 'runners' were born.

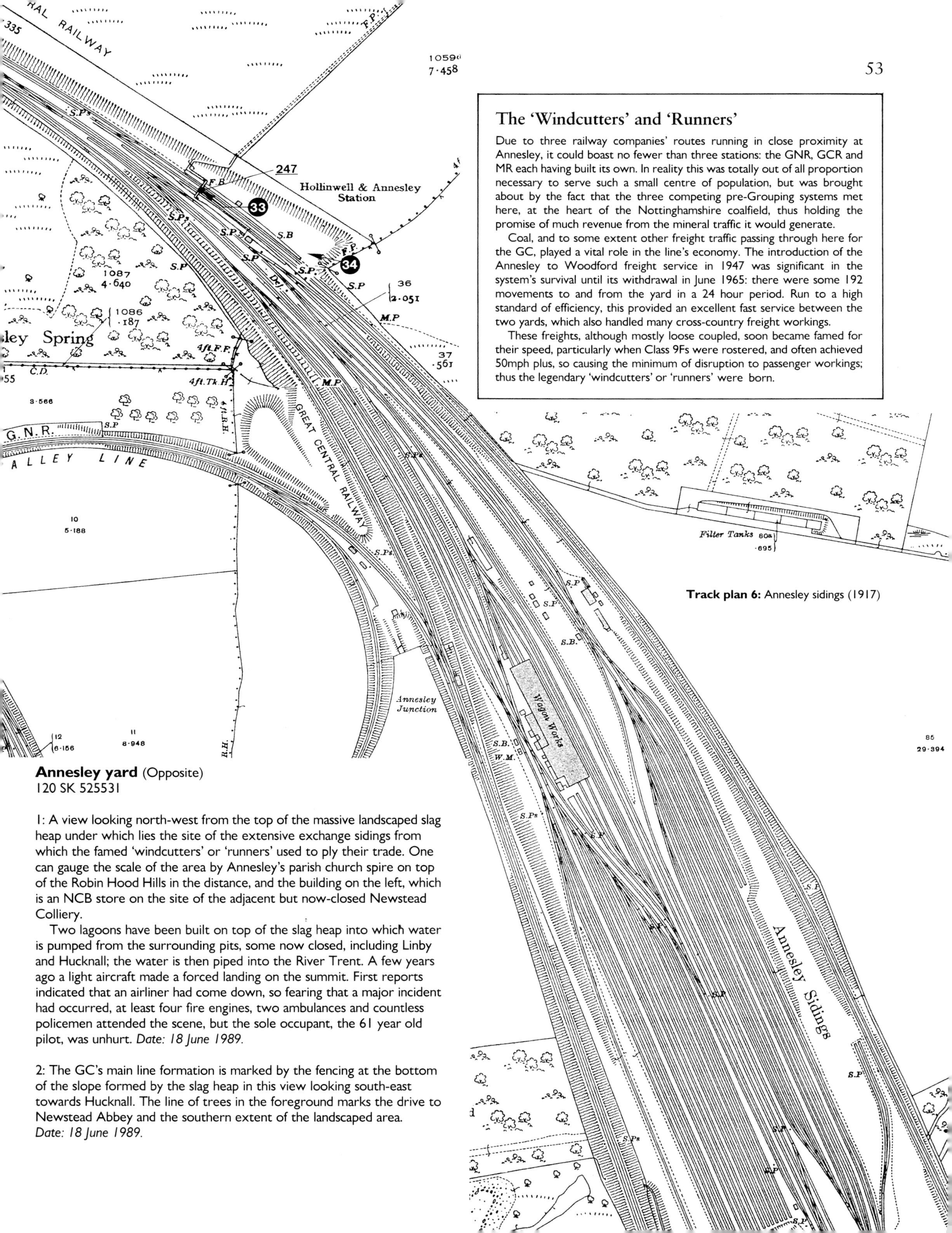
RAL RAILWAY
247
Hollinwell & Annesley Station
33
34
ley Spring
G. N. R.
ALLEY LINE
GREAT CENTRAL RAILWAY
Annesley Junction
Wagon Works
Filter Tanks
Annesley Sidings

Track plan 6: Annesley sidings (1917)

Annesley yard (Opposite)
120 SK 525531

1: A view looking north-west from the top of the massive landscaped slag heap under which lies the site of the extensive exchange sidings from which the famed 'windcutters' or 'runners' used to ply their trade. One can gauge the scale of the area by Annesley's parish church spire on top of the Robin Hood Hills in the distance, and the building on the left, which is an NCB store on the site of the adjacent but now-closed Newstead Colliery.

Two lagoons have been built on top of the slag heap into which water is pumped from the surrounding pits, some now closed, including Linby and Hucknall; the water is then piped into the River Trent. A few years ago a light aircraft made a forced landing on the summit. First reports indicated that an airliner had come down, so fearing that a major incident had occurred, at least four fire engines, two ambulances and countless policemen attended the scene, but the sole occupant, the 61 year old pilot, was unhurt. *Date: 18 June 1989.*

2: The GC's main line formation is marked by the fencing at the bottom of the slope formed by the slag heap in this view looking south-east towards Hucknall. The line of trees in the foreground marks the drive to Newstead Abbey and the southern extent of the landscaped area. *Date: 18 June 1989.*

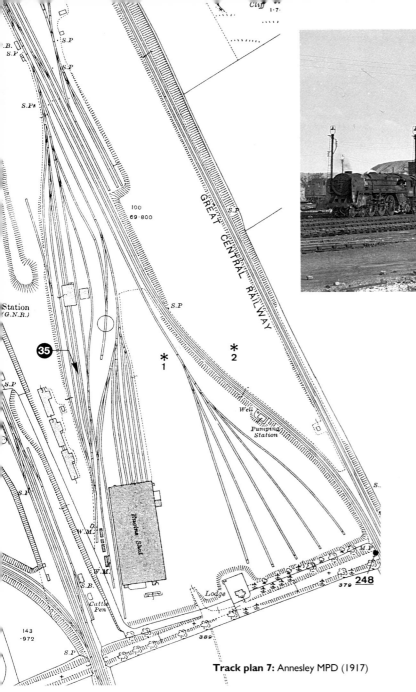

Track plan 7: Annesley MPD (1917)

35
Annesley MPD
120 SK 525530

With less than six months to closure very few engines remain at Annesley. Britannia No 70028 *Royal Star* (without nameplates) and Class 5 No 45416 simmer outside the shed.

Because Annesley depot was far from the major centres of population, engine crews, according to where they lived, were shuttled to and from stations between Bulwell Common and here, by the affectionately named Annesley 'Dido' (an acronym for 'Day In Day Out'), which ran to a regular pattern on a daily basis. During weekdays it would take the Leen Valley line to Bulwell to avoid adding further congestion to the main line, which was only used on Sundays. A variety of engines and rolling stock was rostered for this duty, depending on what was available at any one time, but the coaches used were inevitably old.

Behind the shed an aerial ropeway transports colliery waste from the adjacent Newstead pit to the slag heap, which will grow beyond all recognition within another twenty-five years. *Photo: Tom Boustead. Date: 27 June 1965.*

This photograph was taken from the same co-ordinates, but from about 40ft higher: the shed site is now buried under a mountain of slag — albeit landscaped with top soil. A slight expansion in area has been incorporated on the extreme right as positive proof to the location by the inclusion of the Leen Valley line's formation; and careful study will reveal a bridge spanning the drive to nearby Newstead Abbey, formerly the home of Lord Byron.

From this point much of the GC formation towards Hucknall becomes evident once more. *Date: 18 June 1989.*

A view looking north of Hucknall Central shows the typical layout of the smaller stations constructed on the London Extension which were built on the island platform principle. *Photo: H. C. Casserley. Date: 8 May 1946.*

36
Hucknall Central
129 SK 531485

A down troop special with V2 2-6-2 No 60847 in charge rushes through Hucknall Central, whose weed-strewn flowerbed looks decidedly untidy.

The station was the first on the London Extension south of Annesley constructed to a standard design, which incorporated an island-type platform with the usual associated buildings built thereon. This was a great saving in costs and reduced the staffing levels.

The vast majority of smaller stations between here and Calvert were almost identical in layout, with a few minor variations, particularly with regard to street or road access and platform length, which differed according to local needs and topography. Rushcliffe Halt; Carrington and Arkwright Street stations, having two standard trackside platforms, were the exceptions. *Photo: Tom Boustead. Date: 11 July 1964.*

COMMENT: *Whilst out walking on the infilled cutting to the north of the station I met two ex-Annesley firemen. Alan Attenborough and Lewis Jayes still felt bitter about the railway's demise, even after some twenty-four years, but despite this retained the customary good humour often associated with GC men. Relating to the line's brilliant construction, they pointed to the spire of St Andrew's church in the far distance standing out on a hill in Nottingham: 'All we had to do was to keep in line with that and we would come to Sherwood Tunnel, which passed straight under it – we couldn't go wrong!'*

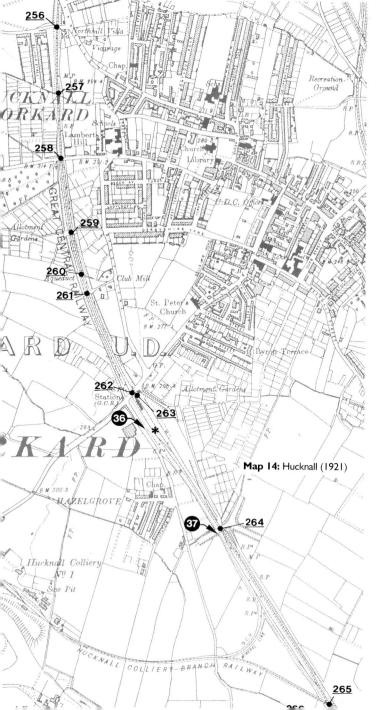

Map 14: Hucknall (1921)

A gale blows with all its fury across the desolate station site, which is now covered by small trees and scrub. Much of the formation through the town has been built on or filled in, including the deep magnesium limestone cutting immediately north of the station.

The station area, although filled to bridge level, has been designated a development site; an old persons' home and flats are planned for here. *Date: 9 September 1989.*

37
Hucknall – Park Drive
129 SK 533482

Approaching the Park Drive road bridge (No 264) is Annesley Class 9F 2-10-0 No 92091 with an empty stock train of eighteen coaches heading north. It is ironic to think that BR's future trains for the Channel Tunnel leaving Rugby are to be comprised of the same number of coaches, proving that little is new.

These sidings were located some quarter of a mile south of the station, with a branch to serve Hucknall Colliery. *Photo: Tom Boustead. Date: 4 July 1959.*

An adjacent dairy has been demolished to make way for the entrance to a modern housing estate. Although the railway bridge survives, the entire section of line here has been built upon. This recent development was built in 1986/7 and is in the Hazelgrove district on the southern outskirts of Hucknall.

Just south of this area the line formation still exists in parts, but only for about a mile or so in the Bulwell direction, where a large housing estate is encountered near to the site of the long gone Bulwell Hall Halt, adjacent to Allcock's Wood. *Date: 18 June 1989.*

Bulwell Viaduct — No 269
129 SK 546457

The 390yd viaduct of twenty-five arches and an average height of 44ft spanned the A611 (Hucknall Lane), the River Leen, the MR's Mansfield–Nottingham line and Bestwood Road, was the longest on the London Extension.

Annesley 'Black Five' 4-6-0 No 45217 passes a down goods as it crosses the viaduct with a special for the south. The springing at the rear of the first coach looks somewhat suspect, if the roof line is anything to go by. *Photo: Tom Boustead. Date: 27 April 1963.*

The viaduct survived in truncated form to the edge of Hucknall Lane until the beginning of 1989, when it was finally demolished; the rubble is piled up on an adjacent site, now dubbed Springfields Park, which is destined for development, and where a Tesco supermarket is to be built. The building on the extreme right is the club house of the BR Staff Association's Bulwell branch, which has considerably expanded its premises since 1963.

The line formation on the north side of the viaduct site has been built on over the last few years, with a mixture of private housing and business developments, as can be discerned in the background. The major portion of the embankment on the south side has been removed since demolition and now forms part of Bulwell Forest recreation park. *Date: 17 June 1989.*

39
Bulwell Common
129 SK 548452

The ex-GN Leen Valley line branched off at Bulwell Forest to rejoin the main line south of the viaduct, having meandered its way southwards from Annesley, passing under the GC once at Linby, and under the Midland line no fewer than three times!

This splendid photograph shows B1 4-6-0 No 61285 coming off the Leen Valley up line with a short goods, and is approaching the junction with the GC. The Leen Valley route's down line, seen on the far side of the main line, passed under the GC fifteen chains north of here, at which point it was some nineteen chains south of the viaduct.

On the extreme right pedestrians and spectators line the fence which forms the boundary of a footpath across the Bulwell Forest golf course from St Alban's Road on the left. *Photo: Tom Boustead. Date: 18 April 1964.*

Map 15: Bulwell Common and South Junction (1938)

COMMENT: *The locals here were very friendly and hospitable. Often being taken into their homes, usually hot and exhausted, I was plied with numerous cups of tea and cold drinks, whilst they showed great interest in my project. Those who were shown a photograph of what their area was like some twenty-five years previously, especially those who did not realise a railway ever existed here, were simply flabbergasted at the change.*

By contrast the glare of a cloudless summer's evening makes any comparison seem futile with this view taken from the same vantage point, where a private housing estate has sprung up over the last few years.

The only reference to the previous photograph to be had is the scrub-covered mound in the background, which once divided the GC from the Leen Valley up line, but the cutting has been partially backfilled and now forms a fairway on the golf course. The adjacent GC formation has been developed for housing, which is now Lema Close. *Date: 17 June 1989.*

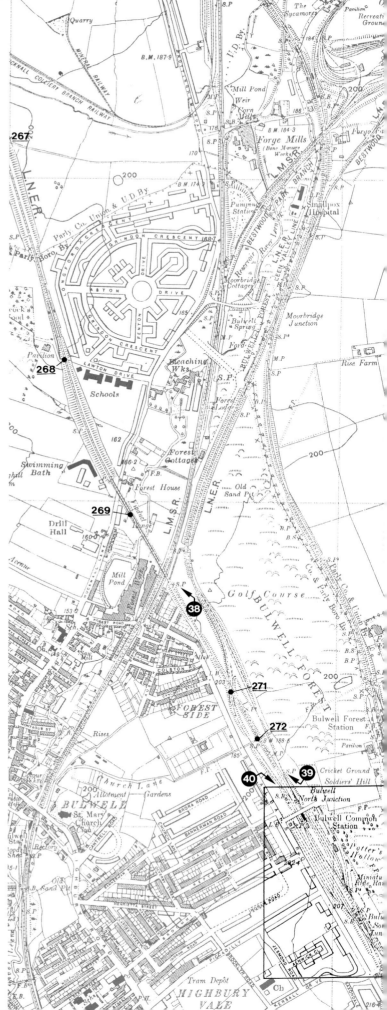

4

BULWELL COMMON — NOTTINGHAM VICTORIA

40
Bulwell North Junction
129 SK 551447

Having left Bulwell sidings, BR Class 9F No 92033 takes the Leen Valley down line at Bulwell North Junction, controlled by the signal box on the right. Bulwell Common station is on the other side of Bridge 273.
Photo: J. F. Henton. Date: c1962/3.

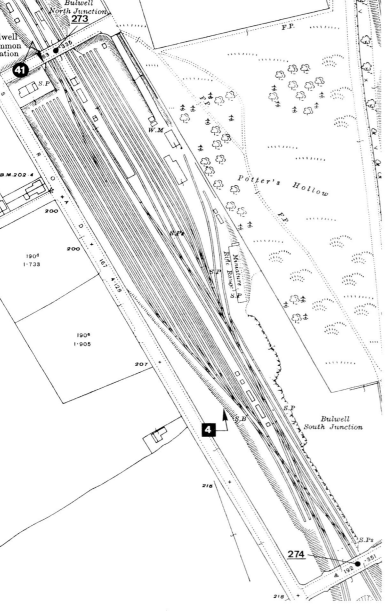

Track plan 8: Bulwell Common (1915)

Once the correct location had been pinpointed, the area was scouted for any identifiable clues to the past. Luckily, the tops of poplar trees, seen in the original photograph, were spotted over a roof in the background — proof positive that the right place had been found. This exciting view of a wall is in Fairway, just off St Alban's Road! *Date: 18 June 1989.*

41
Bulwell Common station
129 SK 548440

A species now extinct: the once ubiquitous Annesley 'Dido' is caught on camera quietly simmering at Bulwell Common during a lull in its duties. Ex-GN 4-4-2 Class C12 No 67363 (introduced in 1898 and finally withdrawn in 1957) has been rostered for this turn.

The sidings, partly obscured by the tree on the right, were extensive and being well placed between two junctions, could handle freight to and from the GN's Derby and Staffordshire line, which was joined via Bulwell South Junction and the joint GC/GN Bulwell South Curve. The junction, with its associated signal box, can be seen in the distance near the bridge in Kersall Drive, linking St Alban's Road with the B683 Hucknall Road. *Photo: A. Laughton. Date: June 1956.*

A total transformation such as this is hard to take in. This view from the surviving bridge parapet adjacent to the Golden Ball public house bears no resemblance to the view from here before, save the houses on the skyline, which identify the area. There is certainly no possibility that trains might ever run through here again. *Date: 21 May 1989.*

COMMENT: *For the householders quietly indulging in a spot of sunbathing in the garden of the bungalow in the foreground to have a 'wot'-type man, armed with photographic equipment, teetering on a pair of steps, to appear over the wall must have been alarming enough, but then to have the good grace to offer to remove the washing from the line to enhance the photograph was a charming gesture, which of course was declined. However, a tree in their garden had to be pruned to obtain this clear view!*

Many surprises to be found in this Bulwell garden: a railway enthusiast has collected these items over the years, many of them from stations on the GC main line. *Date: 21 May 1989.*

Old Basford (1)
129 SK 553442

A footbridge (No 275) between Paton and Gayhurst Road spanned the railway about a ¼-mile south of Bulwell South Junction. Clean-looking Class 9F No 92088 with an Annesley–Woodford freight, mostly comprised of flat wagons, approaches the bridge. *Photo: Tom Boustead. Date: 13 September 1958.*

The houses are unmistakable, but the cutting has been infilled and now forms a paddock. A small development of bungalows has been built on the area immediately north of here as far as the surviving bridge at Bulwell South Junction. The pedestrian bridge no longer remains here, but has been removed to another location in the area and is used as part of a nature walk.

An elderly lady living in one of the houses that backed onto the railway related that during the last war, at the time of the Dunkirk evacuation, if a troop train was checked at the signals, residents would climb down onto the line to offer troops cups of tea brought from their houses. *Date: 21 October 1989.*

COMMENT: *This photograph was taken under extreme stress. Not only was I squatting on top of an odoriferous dung heap to obtain the right aspect, but whilst ensconced thus the paddock's resident horse, 'Blackie', obviously curious about my presence, delighted in inflicting several large, painful and slimy bites on my back! Perhaps Robert Browning's poetic line, 'Boot, saddle, to Horse, and away!', ought to be modified to give the following advice: 'to boot horse and saddle away!'.*

43
Old Basford (2)
129 SK 554440

Just south of the footbridge featured in this view, from which the previous photograph was taken, the line passed behind the houses of Orville Road. With an up local, B1 4-6-0 No 61138 tears under the bridge and is about to skirt the grounds of nearby Basford Hospital, before passing over the former GN Derbyshire and Staffordshire line.

Just west of the GC main line, Basford West and East Junctions on the GN were close to each other and were quite complex: West Junction linked with the GC via Bulwell South Curve at Bulwell Common, whilst East Junction linked with the GC further south at Bagthorpe Junction.

At East Junction, the branch from the GN up and down lines split to avoid unnecessary crossovers when joining the GC; the former passed through a short and height restricted tunnel, known to railwaymen as the

'Rat Hole', under both the main GN and GC formations at the point where they crossed. The up line then rounded the eastern section of Bagthorpe Curve to join the up GC main line at Bagthorpe Junction. The GN down line left Bagthorpe Junction via the western section of Bagthorpe Curve, with Bagthorpe carriage sidings on the right sandwiched between it and the GC, to join the Derby Friargate line at the south side of East Junction. *Photo: Tom Boustead. Date: 12 July 1959.*

The roofs of two houses in Orville Road are visible in the gap between these garages in Mercury Close, off Britannia Avenue, which forms part of an extensive new housing development, but the car is of the same period as the original photograph!

There is no trace of the 'Rat Hole' nor the bridge over which the GC passed the GN line; it has all gone, being flattened during the landscaping work undertaken prior to this housing development being built. *Date: 17 June 1989.*

44
Bagthorpe Junction
129 SK 560433

An unidentified B1 4-6-0 with an excursion from Derby to the East Coast, comes off the eastern section of Bagthorpe Curve to join the up GC main line at Bagthorpe Junction, which was located on top of a large embankment built across a valley previously known as Bagthorpe Hollow.

This view of the junction was taken from the bathroom window of the photographer's former home at 23 Newfield Road, Sherwood.
Photo: Tom Boustead. Date: 15 August 1959.

By the good offices of the present owners, Mr and Mrs Wright, this photograph taken from the same vantage point was made possible today, but presents a somewhat changed scene. The embankment was removed over several weeks in 1980 to make way for this housing estate and only a small portion of it now remains.

During the demolition of Bridge 278 across the A6514 Valley Road, one of the contractor's men was killed when he fell from the parapet whilst it was being cut up and removed in sections by a large mobile crane. *Date: 23 September 1989.*

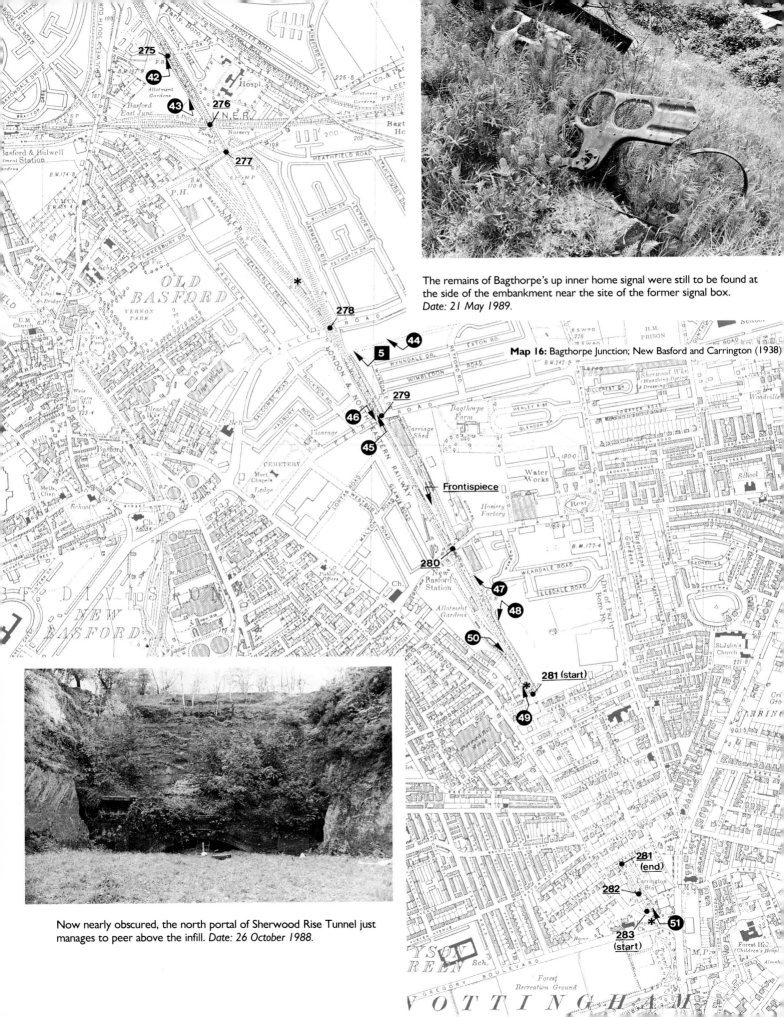

275

42

43

276

277

Hospl.

OLD BASFORD

278

5

44

279

46

45

Frontispiece

280

47

48

50

281 (start)

49

Map 16: Bagthorpe Junction; New Basford and Carrington (1938)

The remains of Bagthorpe's up inner home signal were still to be found at the side of the embankment near the site of the former signal box. *Date: 21 May 1989.*

Now nearly obscured, the north portal of Sherwood Rise Tunnel just manages to peer above the infill. *Date: 26 October 1988.*

281 (end)

282

283 (start)

51

45
Perry Road
129 SK 560431

On a very hazy winter Saturday, O4 class 2-8-0 No 63754 heads an up empty iron ore train through Perry Road cutting. The branch from the GN's Derby Staffs up line swings in to meet the GC at Bagthorpe Junction in the background. *Photo: Tom Boustead. Date: 7 December 1963.*

The bridge (No 279) carrying Perry Road over the railway was removed a few years ago and three new houses have been built on the southerly end of the former cutting, which was filled with surplus spoil from the embankment at Bagthorpe Junction. Heavy plant used the Valley Road bridge to gain access to this site; it is rather ironic to think that this was the bridge's last function.

The houses on both sides of the cutting, especially in Tettenbury Road, have benefited from the infilling, since their gardens have been extended to cover the old line formation. The land abutting the south side of Valley Road is for sale as a building plot. *Date: 17 June 1989.*

46
New Basford carriage shed and sidings
129 SK 560431

Looking southwards from the Perry Road bridge there is a good aspect of the carriage shed and sidings, with New Basford station in the background, beyond which in the distance is the north portal of Sherwood Tunnel. In the early years the carriage shed could even boast its own gasworks for carriage lighting.

With Bagthorpe's down splitting distant signal off, Ivatt Class 4 'Mucky Duck' 2-6-0 No 43091 in charge of a Whit Monday Derby local passes the carriage shed and approaches Perry Road bridge before taking the Derby line at the junction ahead. *Photo: Tom Boustead.*
Date: 18 May 1964.

Many of the houses in the background are easily identifiable, with relatively little new development having taken place. The main area in the foreground is the timber yard of the Stag Furniture Company, whose factory now partially covers the site of the former sidings and carriage shed. Careful study, however, will reveal that a portion of the factory's north-light type of roof on the extreme left survived into the eighties.
Date: 21 October 1989.

47
New Basford station
129 SK 564425

Class B1 4-6-0 No 61275, with an up goods, passes New Basford. Typical in design of the smaller stations on the London Extension, the layout and the island platform can be seen to good advantage; the stationmaster's house is the large building beyond the platform sign.

The distant bridge carries Perry Road over the line and the rear portion of the train is straddling the Haydn Road bridge (No 280), beyond which are the carriage shed and sidings. *Photo: Tom Boustead. Date: 8 June 1963.*

The same vantage point today is the vegetable garden of 11 Linnette Close. The factory building once adjacent to the station, now owned by Messrs Moore & Co, a plastics packaging company, has been extended and borders on the formation of the up line. The ex-stationmaster's house is all that remains from GC days. Haydn Road bridge has long since been removed and only a parapet on the south side survives.
Date: 17 June 1989.

COMMENT: *The kindness of people to consent to such intrusions on their property never failed to impress me. Mr and Mrs Lea were no exception and allowed me to erect my tripod between their rows of peas and potatoes in order to effect this shot!*

48
Sherwood Rise (1)
129 SK 564424

Having just emerged from Sherwood Rise Tunnel and storming through the deep cutting is Annesley Class 9F 2-10-0 No 92072 with a train of coal empties, whilst Class 5 No 44665 from the same shed waits in Basford's goods yard. The yard layout was small by comparison with others, but had a substantial brick-built goods shed. *Photo: Tom Boustead. Date: 8 June 1963.*

A recent development of private housing now occupies the former cutting. It also covers the entire area of the latter-day goods shed and associated sidings. The goods shed survived until this development took place a few years ago. Perhaps rather appropriately, seen from this vantage point, the houses appear to have been shunted into the cutting.

One artefact remains from railway days, which now forms a garden feature: the retaining wall of a recess cut in the bank for the signal box. *Date: 5 November 1989.*

COMMENT: *A further foray was made into a back garden, this time at 27 Camelot Avenue, the home of Mr & Mrs G. Tweedy, where steps had been hewn in the side of the rock cutting, enabling the vantage point to be reached. The rottweiler dog next door resented such an intrusion so close to his territory and treated me to a tirade of abuse!*

49
Sherwood Rise (2)
129 SK 564422

This superb study of New Basford station and its immediate environs, including Sherwood Rise cutting, shows an unusual combination of a double-headed up local with Thompson L1 2-6-4T No 67770 and 'Black Five' 4-6-0 No 44875 in charge, which are about to enter the tunnel.

The large scale of the goods shed can be judged and the station layout with the up and down lines sweeping past on either side of the platform, as portrayed in this view with the carriage serving sidings near the tall chimney. In the distance is the bridge over Perry Road and just discernible beyond is Bagthorpe Junction. *Photo: Tom Boustead.*
Date: 29 September 1962.

This is the rather disappointing vista viewed from the same aspect today. The houses of Camelot Avenue and Linnette Close have been shoe-horned into this small area. Careful study will reveal the signal box recess set in the bank above the garden shed just this side of the factory.

With property values at a premium, maximum utilisation of building land has to be achieved to provide the urban population with the comfortable homes they desire and can afford. It seems a tragedy that it has been at the expense of the GC line here. Had it survived for a few more years, it most probably would have been needed today, especially with the Channel Tunnel in prospect — the reason for building the London Extension some ninety years earlier. *Date: 5 November 1989.*

COMMENT: My natural fear of heights was not helped by the fact that to take this photograph I had to stand right on the cliff edge, made slippery by the autumn rains and rotting vegetation. This was not made any easier by the large amount of brambles and undergrowth that had to be cleared en route, which on two previous visits had prevented me from finding the correct spot.

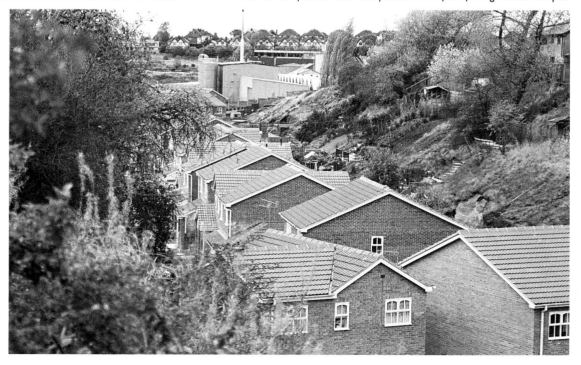

50
Sherwood Rise Tunnel
129 SK 564422

Another fine study of the omnipresent Class 9F No 92072 as it bursts out of Sherwood Rise Tunnel (No 281) with a down 'runner' on its journey back to Annesley. On such duties these locomotives, particularly from Annesley and Woodford sheds, could perform at least two round trips a day, so individual engines became familiar to those living at the lineside. This would perhaps be rather tiresome to train spotters wishing for a 'cop', although they would have plenty of opportunity to secure such with the V2s, B1s, K3s or B16s rostered on the many cross-country fitted freights, such as the York–Bristol, or York–Cardiff. In addition, there were also the fish trains from Hull and Grimsby with destinations such as Plymouth, Swindon or Whitland, often as not hauled by Immingham K3s, and later by Britannias.

The tunnel was 662yd in length and ended at Carrington station, which was built in a cutting between this and Mansfield Road Tunnel. The houses on top of the tunnel here are those in Elton Road North.
Photo: Tom Boustead. Date: 16 May 1964.

From the start of the housing development, some 130yd from the tunnel, a certain amount of backfilling has taken place, which all but obscures the north portal. However, the top of the parapet is exposed and a fraction of the mouth remains open, allowing bats to fly in and out.

Behind the stockade in the foreground is a children's play compound with normal playground equipment, which was provided by local residents. The newly grassed area beyond has been landscaped well and planted with trees. The cutting sides further up on the right are untidy and have been subjected to fly tipping, which has caused much local controversy and resentment. *Date: 5 November 1989.*

51 (Opposite)
Carrington station
129 SK 568416

Built in a cutting between the Sherwood Rise and Mansfield Road tunnels, the station once served the business community in this popular part of Nottingham, but by the time this photograph was taken it had been closed for many years.

With the footbridge spanning the two conventional platforms gone, a good view is had of Class 37 No D6801 as it emerges from Sherwood Rise Tunnel with the 08.30 Newcastle–Bournemouth service, immediately prior to entering the other tunnel under Mansfield Road.
Photo: Tom Boustead. Date: 19 September 1964.

The station cutting has been filled in and the site is to be an office development, pending the ground's settlement. A concrete raft has already been laid at the far end in preparation for the main building to be erected. The large Victorian houses in Clumber Avenue and the 1860s-vintage college building seen in the original photograph provide some continuity, whilst all else has gone. Small access shafts have been built to service the tunnels. *Date: 9 September 1989.*

Proposed Light Rapid Transit system for Greater Nottingham

A feasibility study by the client group of Nottingham County Council, Nottingham Development Enterprise and Nottingham City Council, began in March 1989 to evaluate various schemes for an LRT system for the area. After several potential route corridors were studied, a street option combined with the utilisation of existing BR metals was chosen as part of the initial phase, which would link the north-west outskirts of Nottingham with the city centre and finish at the Midland station.

Another route option seriously considered would have utilised part of the old GC's system under the city via the Mansfield Road and Thurland Street tunnels, then on the remaining viaduct from Weekday Cross to terminate at the Midland station. Like the favoured route it would have started at Hucknall and use existing BR metals (ex-MR's) with a segregated right-of-way through the Leen Valley to New Basford, where it would turn eastward along Wilkinson Street via Noel Street (northbound) and Radford Road (southbound) to meet Gregory Boulevard. The route would also have run alongside Gregory Boulevard on the Forest recreational ground before entering a new cutting and short tunnel to intersect with the existing one under Mansfield Road near Carrington station. It would have then used the old tunnel, save the last 300 metres, and continue through a new section bored at a lower level to dip under the Victoria Centre, where a stop or station would have been built. The LRT route would have continued from under the Victoria Centre to rise to meet the old tunnel under Thurland Street, a little way in from its old north portal, finally emerging at Weekday Cross. Both the Mansfield Road and Thurland Street tunnels were found to be in good condition, although the latter showed some signs of deterioration due to the ingress of water, which was causing the crown to bulge in places; this is partly due to the pipework

from the community heating system running through it. It was discovered to be impractical to run new lines through the underground car park due to the obstacles presented by columns and lift shafts in the Victoria Centre: the only way to achieve this would have been to run the lines separately, given the available space. Initially it had been planned that BR would leave two tracks running through the Centre before it was constructed, however this was not the case. In hindsight, this would have saved a lot of technical problems and considerably reduced the cost. In many respects the GC route from Hucknall, had it largely survived, would have been suitable for an LRT system, (although passenger access to the tunnelled sections would be difficult and therefore have limited the number of stops nearer the city centre) but as it is recent building developments at Sherwood Rise, Basford and Bulwell have prevented this possibility. The planners, some would say lacking foresight, were at least five or ten years too late! In the event the high proportional cost of the tunnel option under the Victoria Centre (estimated at £12 million), effectively persuaded the promoters to go for the on-street option instead.

Although the GC's tunnels are not to be used in the initial phase, they may well be utilised on other route options in the future and have been 'safeguarded' by the local authorities for that purpose, as has the old GN viaduct at Weekday Cross, which might be eventually used if a west/east line is constructed. As it stands, there are proposals in the preferred option to use part of the GC's viaduct from the Midland station, where a terminal stop would be built and which would be linked by a footbridge to the existing BR one over the platforms. A second option would be to continue the LRT system on a new structure built over the station, thus providing direct interchange facilities.

A bill is planned to be set before Parliament in November 1991 and if the feasibility study is found viable both politically and financially, for some private funding will be needed besides a government grant, phase one of the LRT system could be running in 1996.

Carrington station building today is a newsagent's shop, but is threatened with demolition in the near future.
Date: 21 May 1989.

52
Mansfield Road Tunnel
129 SK 573405

Another Annesley–Woodford 'runner': on this occasion with Class 9F 2-10-0 No 92031 in charge enters Nottingham Victoria from the 1,200yd Mansfield Road Tunnel and passes Victoria North box to take one of the outer roads on the eastern side of the station.

The houses above the tunnel are those in Woodborough Lane and on the right, in Huntingdon Street. Note the 70mph speed limit sign at the mouth of the tunnel, which was on a rising 1:132 gradient back to Carrington and at 1:130 through Sherwood Rise Tunnel — perhaps a little optimistic for trains starting from the station, even by GC standards!

The cutting at the north end of the station had a turntable with a short siding set immediately under the cliff in the north-west corner of the complex, and can be seen behind the signal box; the south end was similarly equipped. These turntables being rather small often meant longer engines had to be turned with their tender buffers hanging over the back. *Photo: Tom Boustead. Date: 1 June 1963.*

Now the area is a waste ground extending some 120yd from the tunnel's south portal to the multi-storey car park of the Victoria Centre shopping development, but is not generally accessible to the public. The only train at Nottingham Victoria today is a nondescript class of locomotive painted on the portal's plywood shutter, sanguinely stating its next stop as Nottingham.

A road improvement scheme necessitated the houses above the tunnel being demolished. A few bricks and a couple of bellcranks from the signal box survive in the undergrowth. Behind the bush on the extreme right a signalling telegraph junction box and board still remains, which would have been located behind the cabin seen in the original photograph.

Shrubs and small trees cover the area and in a few years will obscure the tunnel completely. Recently a pair of ducks attempted to raise a family on this site. Tragically, because there was no water available, the ducklings did not survive, despite all efforts by members of the staff at the Victoria Centre. The parent ducks were eventually removed to a safer place to raise another family, and to ensure they did not return here, had their wings clipped. *Date: 20 May 1989.*

Nottingham Victoria station

The construction of Nottingham Victoria station was a monumental feat. Many dwelling houses had to be demolished and some 700,000cu yd of sandstone rock had to be excavated before building could begin. The quarried area covered approximately 13 acres and extended some 650yd from north to south and an average width of about 110yd; a tunnel at each end provided access.

Nottingham Victoria was cavernous. Its cathedral-like roof with three glazed apex sections, spanning the entire width, were divided by station buildings on the two main island platforms. Each had four bays for local services or storage; this brought the total number of platforms to twelve. In addition, passing loops were provided on either side of the outer platforms, in which to hold goods trains, allowing the fast transit of passenger traffic or other freights. The main station building and entrance was located in Milton Street and next to it was the railway company's Victoria Station Hotel.

The station opened on 24 May 1900, over a year after the start of main line services between London and Sheffield, which had commenced on 15 March 1899. The station served both the Great Central and Great Northern railway companies and the name was initially argued over by both companies: the GC wanted to call it 'Central', whilst the GN had initially named it 'Joint'. A compromise was duly reached, and since the station was to be opened on the Queen's birthday, it was decided that henceforth it would be known as Nottingham 'Victoria'.

Map 17: Nottingham Victoria to River Trent Viaduct (1938)

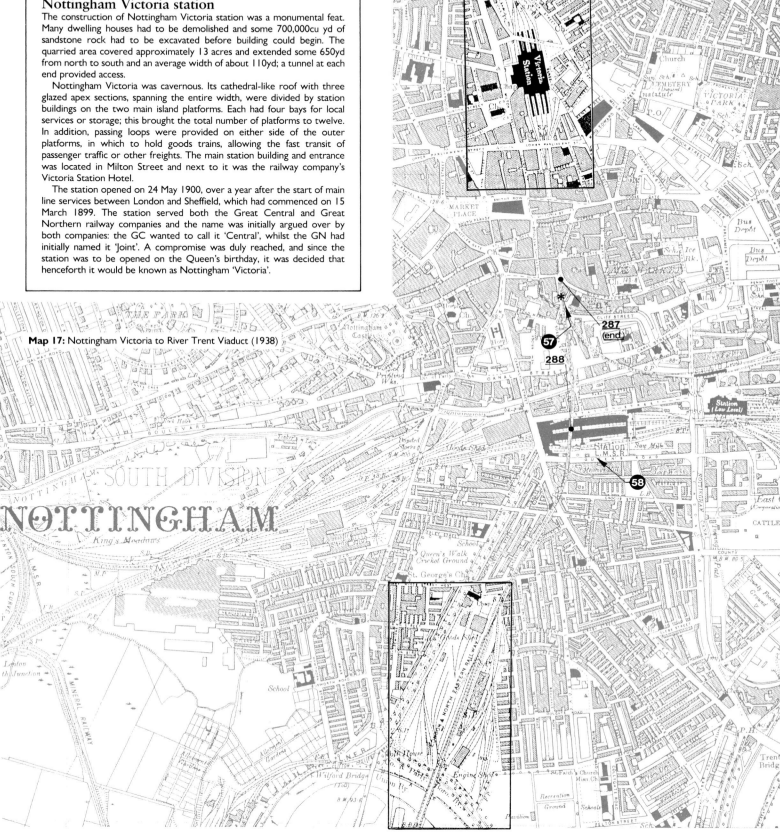

53
Nottingham Victoria station (1)
129 SK 573405

The time by the station tower's clock is 11.05, and a rather special visitor to traverse GC metals passes through Nottingham Victoria en route to Edinburgh: GWR City class No 3717 *City of Truro* heads away from platform 1 as it resumes the journey north.

The neatness of the quarried sides and the scale of the retaining walls can be seen to good advantage. The line on the extreme right led to the north end turntable. *Photo J. F. Henton. Date: 26 August 1959.*

The hideously drab multi-storey car park of the Victoria Centre dominates the background. The station clock tower survives as a centre piece to the shopping centre complex behind. Its aristocratic pinnacle pokes above the concrete jungle around it in a seemingly defiant gesture to this vulgar piece of architecture, recently portrayed by the *Sunday Times Magazine* as one of the worst blights on Britain's cities.

The Victorian brewery building in the original photograph has not been so lucky as the clock tower and has been replaced by a modern office block; however, four of the retaining wall arches underneath do survive from railway days.

Outline planning permission has been granted for this piece of waste ground, which is known locally as the 'Big Hole'. A new car park and bus station may be built here in order that an extension of the Victoria Centre may be constructed to provide more retail space, but this is not likely to happen in the immediate future. Any development will have to take into account the future needs of the proposed LRT system, should an extension be deemed necessary to run into the centre accessed from the Mansfield Road Tunnel.

Although immediately desirable and aesthetically essential, it is conceivable that the demolition and complete redevelopment of the existing Victoria Centre complex, together with the adjoining blocks of flats, might become necessary at some time in the not too distant future, but is unlikely to happen this century. Therefore, given that the proposed LRT system's long-term development options include the operation of trams within the centre, it might then be possible to construct a new station here which could once again link the city centre with the main line – perhaps even with InterCity trains calling here! The chances are remote, but only time will tell. *Date: 9 September 1989.*

54
Nottingham Victoria station (2)
129 SK 574402

Seen from platform 7 the magnificence of Nottingham Victoria's interior can be well gauged from this classic study of Class 9F 2-10-0 No 92042 as it thunders past platform 4 with a down iron-ore train. Although this photograph has been published before, it truly presents the enormous scale of the station, which so often gave the impression of being deserted apart from the occasional small groups of passengers and staff, as seen in this study, who appear to be dwarfed by the sheer size of the structure. *Photo: J. S. Hancock/Ian Allan library. Date: 29 August 1964.*

By careful measurement of large-scale maps, the actual position from which the original photograph was taken is now at the heart of the underground car park of the Victoria Centre. This is the 'inspiring' view now: the piers on the right roughly equate with the edge of platform 4.

Without a doubt, the loss of this station was not only a grievous blow to Nottingham, but also in terms of railway architecture: it must rate as one of the largest and most important stations ever to fall to the axeman. Had it and the line survived for another twenty years, it almost certainly would have been needed in the late eighties; perhaps HSTs could have been offering a profitable 1½hr service, via the Grendon Underwood and Ashendon junctions, to Paddington. Such trains could not have run over the third-rail systems near London on the Metropolitan line and be able to operate through to Marylebone, due to the low ground clearance of Mk3 coaches. *Date: 20 May 1989.*

COMMENT: During the preparation of this book, I often ended up in some unusual situations, but to spend half a day in the basement of a multi-storey car park taking photographs, certainly rates as one of my more eccentric activities and received some bemused looks from most. I also had the good fortune to meet a charming vicar and his wife who had been shopping in the Centre; with a twinkle in his eye he opened a plain brown paper bag to show me his purchase and inside was a copy of The Satanic Verses *. . . 'Thought I'd better see what all the fuss was about!'*

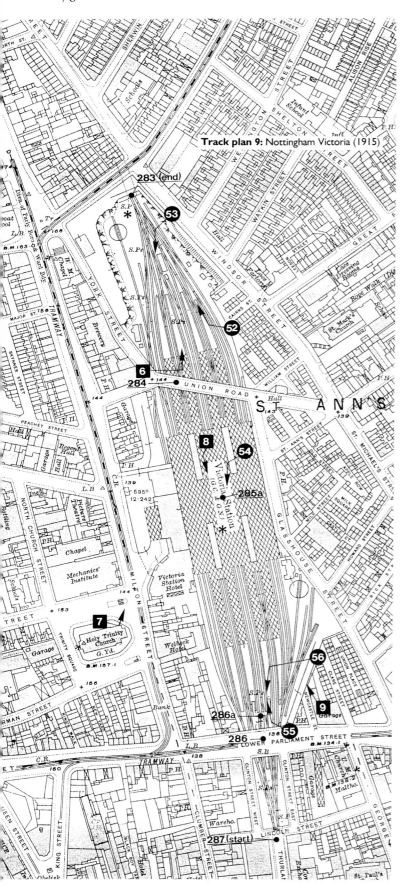

Track plan 9: Nottingham Victoria (1915)

55
Nottingham Victoria station – south end
129 SK 572401

In this fine study B1 class 4-6-0 No 61299 waits at Nottingham Victoria prior to departure from platform 7 with a Derby (Friargate) to Skegness train whilst Standard Class 4MT 2-6-0 No 43154 waits in one of the up bay platforms with a local train. A driver and fireman sit next to two schoolboy admirers and enjoy the sunshine on the southern end of the station, whilst awaiting their turn of duty.

The splendid building of the Victoria Station Hotel and station clock tower behind can be seen to good advantage and dominate the background. *Photo: Horace Gamble. Date: 8 August 1964.*

Another singularly uninteresting view of the multi-storey car park some 230yd south of the previous location. Surprisingly, there was a reminder to be found of railway days, as the retaining walls either side of the station, part of which can be seen beyond the Class 4MT in the original photograph, survive in this section of the car park. *Date: 20 May 1989.*

Taken from above this position, the spectacular Emmett clock inside the Victoria Centre shopping complex is perhaps one of the most redeeming features of the development, although the shops and facilities inside this complex rate among the region's best.
Date: 26 October 1988.

56
Nottingham Victoria station –
Thurland/Victoria Street Tunnel
129 SK 572401

At the southern end of the station, the platforms ended under a road bridge carrying Lower Parliament Street. The lines then converged to enter the 392yd tunnel under Thurland Street, Pelham Street, Victoria Street, Bottle Lane and Middle Pavement, to emerge at Weekday Cross.

In this superbly atmospheric shot it shows the crew of B1 class 4-6-0 No 61089 chatting with another, as the locomotive waits to get under way from the station with a Derby (Friargate) to Mablethorpe train, whilst tender-first Class O4 2-8-0 No 63571 brings a train of ballast hoppers into the down passing loop. The size of the bridge at the end of the station carrying Lower Parliament Street and its associated shops can be judged well in this view. On the extreme left in the background is the entrance to the tunnel out of the station leading to Weekday Cross.
Photo: Horace Gamble. Date: 8 August 1964.

This photograph, taken from the nearest practical point to the original, shows a motorist passing under Lower Parliament Street and looking somewhat camera-shy she leaves the southerly most end of the car park after a shopping trip to the Victoria Centre.

The door in the brick wall at the far end marks the position of the tunnel to Weekday Cross, which now carries the air conditioning and heating pipes from the centre. *Date: 20 May 1989.*

57
Weekday Cross Junction
129 SK 575395

Weekday Cross Junction marked the point where the GC and GN lines to Grantham diverged: the latter running over a series of viaducts for about ¾-mile or so east of this point. The GC similarly was carried on a long viaduct, but due south towards the Midland station, over which it passed on a massive girder bridge.

Seen from the tall signal box controlling the junction, B1 class 4-6-0 No 61159 emerges from the tunnel at Weekday Cross with the up 'South Yorkshireman', to head off on its southward journey across the viaducts carrying the line out of the city, and is set to arrive in London in just over 2½ hours.

Until July 1967 trains to and from the British Gypsum works at Hotchley Hill near East Leake and the MOD depot at Ruddington continued to operate over the single line which remained here, using the tunnel as a headshunt to gain access to the sidings on the Midland line. *Photo: J. F. Henton. Date: 10 May 1949.*

The tunnel is still quite distinctive, but the surrounding area has changed beyond all recognition, apart from one or two buildings which remain. The complex on the left is the Broad Marsh shopping centre set alongside an elevated new road called Middle Hill. The attractive garden in the foreground created on the former trackbed now forms part of the Heritage Centre and provides an excellent facility to the offices converted from adjacent buildings off High Pavement, which are leased to small businesses and to professional persons.

Behind the large retaining wall on the right, part of which recently collapsed, blocking the footpath from High Pavement to Broad Marsh and to Cliff Road, is another attractive garden owned by the corporation. The two footpaths passed under the railway at this point and their walls can be seen in the foreground; the bridges were removed in 1988. *Date: 19 June 1989.*

COMMENT: *To look at the facsimile photograph it would appear quite ordinary; the logistics of actually taking it were somewhat different. The ground level being at least 40ft from the original photographer's position in the now-demolished box, meant a camera had to be mounted on top of a series of interlocking television aerial poles to equate the height. Enlisting help from a passing youth and the proprietor's wife of the nearby Cliffs Garage, I stood on a pair of steps and managed to elevate the camera to about the same height to effect this shot. This feat brought looks of astonishment from passers by, including one professional photographer, who had not seen anything so funny as the spectacle of a 16 stone man wobbling on top of a pair of steps struggling to control a violently swaying camera 30ft above his head!*

A present day view of the GC's long viaduct, which was designated as structure No 288, looking south from Weekday Cross towards the Midland station, just north of which the bridge over the Beeston canal remains as the last survivor of the GC line this side of the Trent. The remnants of the GN's viaduct to link with the Grantham line is on the extreme left of the picture. *Date: 11 September 1989.*

58
Nottingham Midland
129 SK 575391

The GC passed directly over the Midland station via this huge girder bridge, which spanned the main line. Just south of this point was the GC's Arkwright Street station, the platforms of which were built on the viaduct. *Photo: Newton collection/Leicester Museums. Date: c1900.*

The 170ft girder bridge was demolished in the mid-seventies and all that remains is the abutment of the viaduct on the north side of the station.

There is no trace whatsoever of Arkwright Street station, which was the terminus of the truncated Nottingham–Rugby DMU service from September 1967, following the closure of Victoria station, until the final withdrawal of all passenger trains to use this route on 5 May 1969. The area of the station has now given over to a large housing development.

Even the Midland station has changed somewhat, particularly the motive power: an HST set waits in platform 5 prior to setting off to St Pancras. A rash of the modern man's disease fills the car park in the foreground, once occupied by through roads past the station and sidings to a timber yard. *Date: 25 September 1989.*

59
Queen's Walk yard
129 SK 573386

The GC's main goods yard for Nottingham was located just north of the
River Trent in the Queen's Walk and Meadows area of the city. One of
the most modern of its time, it was both spacious and well laid out and
could boast the most up-to-date materials-handling facilities. A large
brick-built goods shed-cum-warehouse was provided, having a large
storage capacity; in addition the company also built both an engine and
carriage shed here, but these were later usurped by Annesley and New
Basford respectively.

Coming off the Nottingham blue brick viaducts out of the city and
about to pass the goods shed with the up 'Master Cutler' is A3 Pacific No
60054 *Prince of Wales*, which will shortly cross over the River Trent. The
line on the extreme right provided access to the carriage and engine
sheds. *Photo: J. F. Henton. Date: 2 March 1949.*

Almost impossible to line up totally accurately, this is the nearest point
able to be plotted from which John Henton would have taken his
photograph. The area is now a modern housing development: Houseman
Gardens is just off Robin Hood Way in the Meadows district of
Nottingham. There is no trace of the railway left at all — even to the
south of this point, where there has been further modern housing and
office development, which totally covers the GC's formation as far as the
River Trent. *Date: 20 May 1989.*

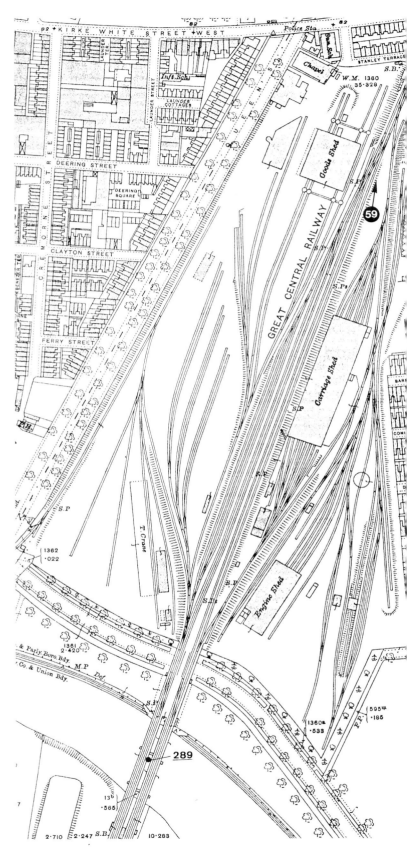

Track plan 10: Nottingham Queen's Walk yard (1915)

River Trent Viaduct – No 289
129 SK 570379

K3 class 2-6-0 No 61809 with an express for Marylebone storms over the impressive girder bridge straddling the River Trent. The steel structure of three 112ft spans weighed about 2,000 tons and carried four lines of way. The two lines on the left facilitated access to and from the yard, the south end of which was controlled by this signal box (Nottingham Goods South).

Just visible on the extreme left and located in the city centre, the dome of the Council House, in which hangs the bell known as 'Little John', is seen. *Photo: J. F. Henton. Date: 28 May 1951.*

The bridge was removed in the last few years. The extent of the modern housing development on the area once occupied by the goods yard can be observed in this study taken from the railway embankment south of the river, from which point the dome of the Council House is still visible in the distance.

On this hazy, still, May evening just the faint but comfortably secure sound of willow striking leather could be heard coming from the match being played on the nearby cricket pitch, followed by typically restrained applause as the boundary was occasionally reached. If this had been accompanied by the distinctive sound of the three-cylinder Gresley beat drifting over the river, one would be in the England now only nostalgically dreamt about by many.

The embankment upon which the railway ran south from here exists intact for a few hundred yards. A few telegraph poles still stand alongside the formation remaining as forlorn reminders of the countless thousands of signalling messages their wires used to carry.

South of the A648 road in West Bridgford, where Bridge 293 has been demolished, the line formation has been bordered by an enormous residential development. Some of the houses even have triple garages — very Yuppy! *Date: 25 May 1990.*

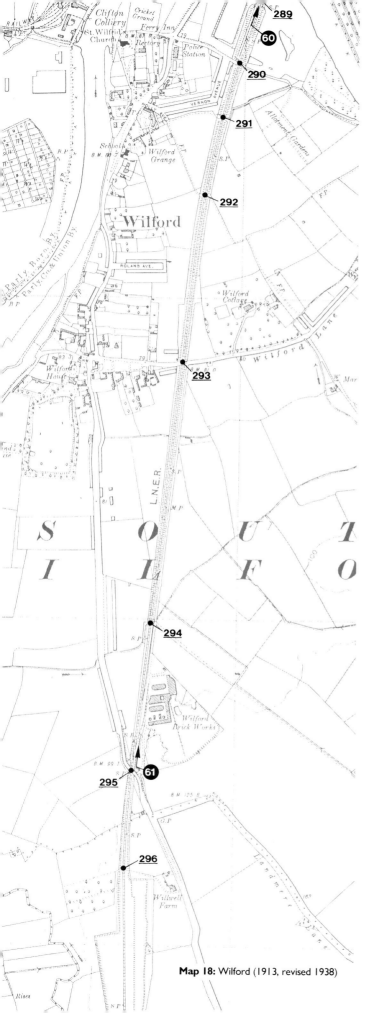

61
Wilford brick sidings
129 SK 567356

B1 class 4-6-0 No 61182 passes Wilford brick sidings with the up 'South Yorkshireman'. The signal box controlled the entrance to the sidings of the Wilford Brick Works. *Photo: J. F. Henton. Date: 7 June 1951.*

The line formation is still well defined at this point, but no trace could be found of the signal box in the undergrowth. The brick works have long since closed and the area it once occupied now forms part of the new Wilford Industrial Estate.

The extensive housing development built near the line north of this point almost reaches back to here, but the formation immediately to the south of here, and just beyond the Ruddington Lane road bridge, has been made into a perfect garden by a local resident. Many wild flowers are also grown on the trackbed and an extensive pond stocked with indigenous species has been built around a spring. All the bridges south from here remain intact. *Date: 19 June 1989.*

62
Ruddington station
129 SK 566332

The station was located on the north-west edge of the village it served and was of the smaller island platform type constructed on the London Extension. Surprisingly, photographs of Ruddington are rare: here 'Black Five' No 44821 gets away from the station with the 13.25 local from Nottingham to Leicester.

A large military ordnance stores and disposal depot was located immediately south of the village, and served by a siding spurred on facing points from the up main line just south of the station near the locally known pedestrian 'fifty steps' bridge (No 299). *Photo: J. F. Henton. Date: 2 March 1963.*

A cloudless summer's evening does not help make this facsimile seem interesting, with shadows casting on the bridge and remnants of the platform.

The weed-strewn down line and a few sidings remain intact since BR serviced the stores depot until its closure some ten years ago. The track was left in situ, extending a few hundred yards north of the road bridge, where it ends. To all intents and purposes, it is the terminal point of the GC line today.

The down line south of here across Ruddington Moor is in fairly good condition, but has become rather overgrown with weeds, but all the structures remain in good condition. *Date: 19 June 1989.*

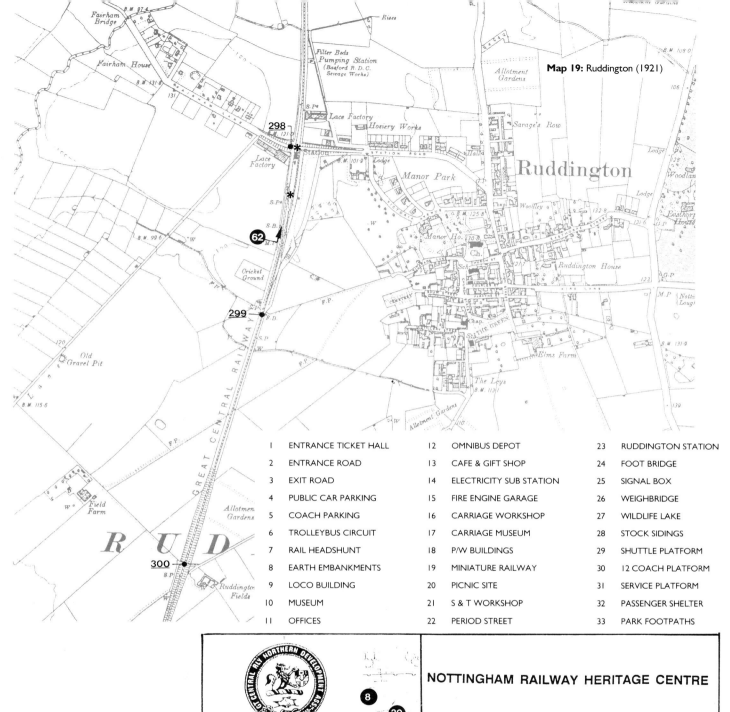

Map 19: Ruddington (1921)

I	ENTRANCE TICKET HALL	12	OMNIBUS DEPOT	23	RUDDINGTON STATION
2	ENTRANCE ROAD	13	CAFE & GIFT SHOP	24	FOOT BRIDGE
3	EXIT ROAD	14	ELECTRICITY SUB STATION	25	SIGNAL BOX
4	PUBLIC CAR PARKING	15	FIRE ENGINE GARAGE	26	WEIGHBRIDGE
5	COACH PARKING	16	CARRIAGE WORKSHOP	27	WILDLIFE LAKE
6	TROLLEYBUS CIRCUIT	17	CARRIAGE MUSEUM	28	STOCK SIDINGS
7	RAIL HEADSHUNT	18	P/W BUILDINGS	29	SHUTTLE PLATFORM
8	EARTH EMBANKMENTS	19	MINIATURE RAILWAY	30	12 COACH PLATFORM
9	LOCO BUILDING	20	PICNIC SITE	31	SERVICE PLATFORM
10	MUSEUM	21	S & T WORKSHOP	32	PASSENGER SHELTER
11	OFFICES	22	PERIOD STREET	33	PARK FOOTPATHS

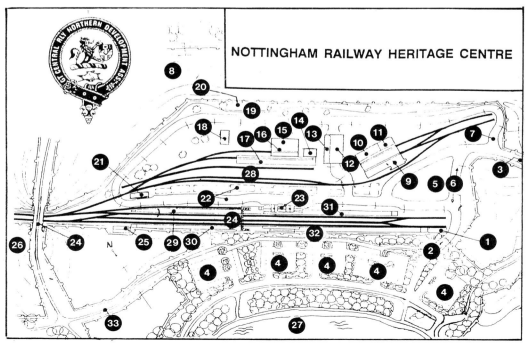

NOTTINGHAM RAILWAY HERITAGE CENTRE

Proposed plan of the GCR's northern
terminus at Ruddington Country Park.

Ruddington station platform and down line as it is today, seen from the road bridge. The compound on the left has been built by the Main Line Steam Trust to house the component parts of a locomotive shed salvaged from Wolverton. *Date: 19 June 1989.*

The remains of a signal post just to the south of the station, and beyond is the 'fifty steps' pedestrian bridge, which spanned the main line. *Date: 19 June 1989.*

Great Central (Nottingham) Ltd

Following the annual general meeting in September 1989 of the Great Central Railway (1976) PLC, it was decided that the management and funding of the proposed northern extension to Ruddington should be run separately from the operation of the existing preserved railway centred on Loughborough. To that end, a splinter group made up of volunteers from the Main Line Steam Trust formed the Great Central Railway Northern Development Association (GCRNDA). This led the way for the formation of an operating company: Great Central (Nottingham) Ltd.

The former MOD storage and disposal depot at Ruddington, extending to some 315 acres, is now owned by Nottinghamshire County Council, which intends to develop the area into Ruddington Country Park and Nottingham Railway Heritage Centre as a leisure attraction, with an area set aside for small industrial units. The Council has given the GC(N) Ltd an eleven-acre site from which to centre its activities; this includes three large industrial and several smaller buildings inside the depot for railway use. A large sum of money will have to be found or granted for this project to succeed, but the railway company's own fund-raising activities will go a long way towards establishing the northern extension to Ruddington.

At the beginning of 1990, volunteers had already started to salvage useful materials from the depot site. The railway will eventually have extensive facilities there, which will also include a two-platform station, engine sheds, turntable, storage sheds and a number of sidings. The site will be linked by a new spur built on the south side of the depot and with the existing access into it from near the station, making a triangle on which engines could be turned if necessary. The former signal box at Neasden will be reconstructed here. Full planning approval was finally granted in May 1991.

The GCRNDA's eventual aim will be to link with the operation at Loughborough, but the bridge will have to be reinstated over the Midland line before this can be achieved. The sums of money involved will be considerable: it is estimated that a new bridge could cost as much as £1½ million. Unless a kind benefactor steps in, the necessary funds will have to be raised by the operating company, GC(N)Ltd. This can only be achieved if the Heritage Centre at Ruddington is successful and with trains operating profitably from there to Rushcliffe or East Leake. Only then would the northern extension warrant connection with the present operation of the GCR(1976) centred at Loughborough, and this may take up to ten years to achieve.

In 1990 limited operations were started by the group in the British Gypsum sidings near Rushcliffe Halt at East Leake. In 1991, trains will be restricted to run on the three-mile section between Ruddington and Rushcliffe, although there is a single track in situ to Loughborough with a connection to the main Midland line, making a total of ten miles. This main line connection will eventually be an advantage, for it would present the opportunity for BR to run excursions to stations on the preserved line, and it may offer the chance for private steam locomotive owners to obviate the need for expensive road transport of their charges when periods are spent working on the railway. Once BR has given the signal that it no longer has a requirement for the seven-mile section of track from Rushcliffe Halt to Loughborough (which also takes in East Leake and Barnstone Tunnel) trains can be run over it.

With enthusiastic support from all the interested parties, including Nottinghamshire County Council and BR, this large project looks set to be assured of an exciting future, which will give much pleasure to countless thousands in the years to come.

63
Rushcliffe Halt
129 SK 552276

Rushcliffe Halt was opened in 1911 and due to the lack of room was constructed with two platforms, but limited facilities were provided. In later years a large British Gypsum works was built here and served by the sidings on the up side, with a spur to the works. In the forties a signal box was built on the down side to control these.

Filthy Class 5 4-6-0 No 44920 enters Rushcliffe with the 11.15 up parcels from Nottingham. This train was in effect the return 'Newspaper', but without passenger accommodation, which had left Marylebone at 01.45. *Photo: J. F. Henton. Date: 5 July 1966.*

Apart from the footbridge (Bridge 307a) the station remains largely intact and the platforms are in reasonable condition. From this point, the old up line remains in situ rather than the down line, save a few hundred yards south of the road bridge, which latterly acted as a siding.

The British Gypsum works were served by BR until a few years ago, but although the line into the factory is still extant, it is not likely that the company will ever wish to move materials by rail in the future. With no such prospect in view, it should not present a great obstacle to the GCRNDA's plan to reopen this section of the line, scheduled to happen in 1991. *Date: 7 October 1989.*

POSTSCRIPT: A few months after this photograph was taken, 1990 saw the arrival at the British Gypsum sidings of locomotives and rolling stock owned by supporters and members of the GCRNDA. An open day was held on 23 June, when Y7 class 0-4-0 No 68088 provided brake van rides for visitors. A Class 08 diesel shunter and a chain-driven Simplex shunter currently make up the motive power kept here; in addition two Mk2 brakes, a few wagons and a seven-ton diesel rail crane are also in residence.

The remains of the signal box at Rushcliffe. *Date: 25 September 1989.*

64 (Opposite)
East Leake station (1)
129 SK 547263

A diesel multiple-unit pauses at East Leake with a Saturdays-only train to Nottingham. They would continue to run over this section for another four years, until final withdrawal of BR passenger services. Note the bridge plate to the right of the unit signifying its number as 312. The multi-windowed structure in the foreground covers the station steps from the roadway below.

East Leake station was set in an attractive wooded area on the western outskirts of the village. The small goods yard being on the north side of the station itself. *Photo: Andrew Muckley/Ian Allan library. Date: July 1965.*

Apart from the buildings having been demolished, everything else is intact, albeit the platform is covered with weeds and wild flowers. The restoration teams would not have too large a task to enable passengers to use this station once again. The bridge plate has gone — no doubt to a private collection. *Date: 9 October 1989.*

Map 20: Rushcliffe Halt to East Leake (1922)
Rushcliffe Halt and sidings shown with pre-war layout

65
East Leake station (2)
129 SK 546262

One of Annesley's rebuilt Royal Scot 4-6-0s, No 46122 *Royal Ulster Rifleman,* departs from East Leake with the 17.15 Nottingham–Marylebone train.

The large and spacious cutting at the southern end of the station signifies the Great Central built these on a grand scale: during its construction some 330,000cu yd of spoil was removed from the 'Big Hill', as it was known locally, and used to create the embankment near the River Soar at Loughborough. Hathern Road bridge (No 313) can be seen in the distance. *Photo: Tom Boustead. Date: 16 July 1964.*

Despite the banks being somewhat overgrown, the cutting still has an air of grandeur about it. The up line is still in good condition, with little attention necessary to bring it back into use. *9 October 1989.*

66
East Leake station (3)
129 SK 546261

Again the 17.15 Nottingham–Marylebone train, but this time with the rather grubby 'Black Five' No 44848 in charge, as it gets away from East Leake. The attractive setting of the station amongst pine trees is seen to good effect in this shot.

East Leake's down inner home signal, like many others on the London Extension, was of the 'approach lit' type and only operated when a train was in the section, which triggered it to indicate its instruction. *Photo: Tom Boustead. Date: 10 July 1964.*

The trees have grown considerably in the twenty-five years that have elapsed, and saplings on the left obscure the signal which still survives. Will it ever cast its lights again upon an approaching train when this section is reopened? *Date: 9 October 1989.*

BARNSTONE TUNNEL —
BELGRAVE & BIRSTALL

67
Barnstone
129 SK 541254

A classic study of a typical down 'runner' hauled by BR Class 9F No 92087 with a very long goods, mainly consisting of coal empties, as it approaches Hathern Road (Bridge 313) between East Leake and the tunnel, the north portal of which is visible in the distance.
Photo: Ivo Peters. Date: 13 May 1964.

The lineside has become overgrown, like most of the section, but the remaining track is relatively clear. East Leake's down distant 'approach lit'

signal stands alone: its companion, the gangers' hut, has been demolished and only a few bricks from its chimney were found in the undergrowth. *Date: 25 September 1989.*

COMMENT: *My late friend Ivo Peters would have been greatly amused at my efforts to secure this photograph. The bank was covered in a mass of brambles and dead rosebay willowherb, which had to be cut back in order that the signal was visible to the camera. At least thirty minutes' hard work with a sickle was involved in laying a 25yd swathe through the tangled growth, only to discover that the signal was still obscured, so further hacking had to be undertaken to ensure its visibility — exhausting work, but good for the figure!*

68
Barnstone Tunnel – north portal
129 SK 538247

Taken from on top of the tunnel's north portal, a clear view is had looking north back to Bridge 313. The oft-seen Class 9F No 92072 storms down the straight towards the 110yd tunnel with an up Annesley–Woodford 'runner', one year prior to the withdrawal of this superb freight service. *Photo: Tom Boustead. Date: 20 June 1964.*

Despite trees obscuring most of the view, some attempt has been made at either end of the tunnel to clear saplings and trees from near its portals. The track here is remarkably clear. *Date: 25 September 1989.*

The north portal of Barnstone Tunnel today. BR designated the tunnel No 314. *Date: 25 September 1989.*

69
Barnstone Tunnel – south portal
129 SK 537244

It is 10.52 on a fine summer's morning and another shot of Royal Scot 4-6-0 No 46122 *Royal Ulster Rifleman*, this time as it emerges from the south portal of Barnstone Tunnel with a Saturday cross-country working. With a down gradient of 1:176 for the next few miles, firemen of engines due to be changed at Leicester took the opportunity to fill the firebox in preparation for the climb between Loughborough and there, in order that they would arrive with a low fire before returning to the shed.

In the next few miles the line curved almost 90° from the south-westerly direction to cross the River Soar near Stanford to head south-east across the river, before turning south again to pass through Loughborough. *Photo: Tom Boustead. Date: 20 June 1964.*

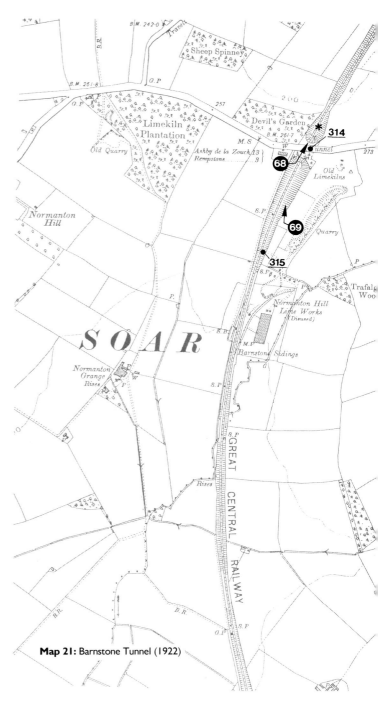

Map 21: Barnstone Tunnel (1922)

The tree line adjacent to the A6006 road which passes over the top of the tunnel has been thinned substantially over the years, but new growth is all too pervasive on the banks. The former up line now rusts quietly, but hopefully and before too long its surface may once again shine from use.

Careful study on the right will reveal a turnbuckle from one of the bracing wires of the telegraph pole, which was nearest the camera in the 1964 photograph. *Date: 25 September 1989.*

COMMENT: *Tom Boustead remarked on the usually poor condition of the 'Scots' during their last years of operation on the former GC line: 'They were like an ancient boxer struggling on until the bitter end.'*

70
Stanford on Soar Viaduct
129 SK 541217

On the northern outskirts of Loughborough, the railway was carried on a steep embankment and then crossed over the River Soar on this 176yd viaduct (No 318). B1 Class 4-6-0 No 61162 hurries over the viaduct with a late-running Bournemouth–Newcastle train on a July day. Judging from the smokebox, it would appear that this engine was not in the best of condition. *Photo: Colin Walker/Ian Allan library. Date: c1962/4.*

The viaduct remains largely intact but vandals, obviously suffering from the all-too-common complaint of Philistinism, have done their usual work for a cheap thrill and cast many of the coping stones from the parapet into the river below. These will have to be retrieved sooner or later to repair the parapets before this section of line is reopened.

Although partially hidden by shadows, and quite by chance, there are two fishermen in more or less the same spots on the river banks as portrayed by the original photograph! *Date: 8 October 1989.*

The Great Central Railway (1976) PLC

In January 1969, with the end of the BR service between Nottingham and Rugby in sight, a group of enthusiasts banded together to form the Main Line Preservation Group, with the ambitious idea of preserving the entire section of the Great Central main line from Nottingham to Abbey Lane sidings, Leicester. This plan was curtailed somewhat by the fact that BR still needed the section between Ruddington, East Leake and Loughborough to operate a freight service, so the group centred its activities on preserving the eight-mile section from Loughborough Central to Belgrave & Birstall on the outskirts of Leicester; the group's efforts would be concentrated first on getting a line operating to Rothley via Quorn & Woodhouse.

Loughborough Central station and the surrounding lands were leased from BR and became the centre of operations. The Group, under the presidency of Lord Lanesborough, through whose lands the railway ran, decided to try and purchase the line: in 1971 the Main Line Steam Trust Ltd was formed with the intention of raising funds for that purpose. The council's abandonment that year of a scheme to link the A6 and A60 roads using the line formation south of the town meant that fund raising could commence in earnest, in order that the track could be purchased eventually from BR. Work also started in gathering locomotives and rolling stock, and in September 1973 the first trains were running to Quorn & Woodhouse under British Rail's supervision.

During the ensuing two years, the British Rail Property Board was putting increased pressure on the Trust to purchase the land. A deadline was set at April 1976, after which date the track would be lifted. The only practical way to ensure that this did not happen was to form a public shareholding company with the specific task of raising a large sum of money, which resulted in the formation of the Great Central Railway (1976) Ltd.

71
Loughborough Midland – Bridge 328
129 SK 544204

The GC crossed over the Midland main line literally at the southern end of the station at Loughborough. Here B1 Class 4-6-0 No 1248, in LNER apple-green livery, crosses the bridge over the Midland line with a down loose-coupled freight. The lines on the left of the fence are the passing loops through the station, also providing access to the Falcon Works of the Brush Company, the traction and locomotive manufacturers, situated adjacent to Loughborough Midland.

Since the closure of the GC main line, a link with the Midland was built to service both the MOD depot at Ruddington and the British Gypsum works at East Leake. A connecting spur from the Midland's up main line, some few hundred yards south of this point, was carried on a newly constructed embankment to join the GC formation near the bridge over the A60 road and some 175yd east of this station. The material for the embankment was gleaned from the GC formation between the canal and the station. *Photo: Neville Stead. Date: c1946/7.*

The missing link: BR removed the original bridge in 1980. If the Great Central Railway Northern Development Association's plan to connect Loughborough with Ruddington is eventually to be fulfilled, the Midland line will once again have to be spanned. There is the possibility that a redundant BR structure could be purchased and re-sited here. Salvaging the disused single-track bridge spanning the A1 at Colsterworth on the High Dyke branch, a former ironstone line, has been mooted. However, the cost of dismantling, transporting and re-erecting it here might prove more expensive than building a new structure. The embankment to the north of the canal will also have to be reinstated, but with the goodwill and help of the GCR (1976) PLC and Charnwood Borough Council, this should be possible.

An HST, with power car No 43094 at the rear, makes a smart getaway from Loughborough with the 11.24 Sheffield–St Pancras InterCity service. The weather conditions were atrocious, with heavy and continuous driving rain making photography extremely difficult, which accounts for the rather dreary result. Note the fencing is unchanged, although now devoid of any enamel advertising signs, much sought after by preservationists today. *Date: 7 October 1989.*

A large publicity campaign designed to raise the necessary funds was immediately embarked upon. In the meantime BR extended the deadline to June, and by May there was enough in the coffers to purchase the track from Loughborough to Quorn. The Borough of Charnwood helped considerably by purchasing the formation, which they then leased to the company for 99 years. Whilst further funding was being sought to purchase the rest of the line by January 1977, which was eventually achieved, BR had graciously left the track in situ to Rothley, but lifted the section south of there as far as Belgrave & Birstall. Due to the quality of track on this section, BR had intended to salvage it for use elsewhere, but for some inexplicable reason cut the rails into 5ft lengths for scrap.

Over the years a large number of locomotives, either individually or collectively owned, and rolling stock has accumulated at Loughborough, with many having been restored to working condition and with others in the process of refurbishment.

The most notable achievement in recent years was the complete rebuilding, once deemed as an impossible task, of the unique BR Class 8P 4-6-2 No 71000 *Duke of Gloucester*, which has been brought up to main line running standards; the latter work was carried out at Didcot. Regular overhauls are also carried out in the company's workshops and outside contracts are often won from other groups and operators.

Locomotive sheds have been built at Loughborough and at Rothley, where the major overhauls and rebuilding programmes are carried out to engines and rolling stock. Visitors to the line will see locomotives representing all the four major railway groups, including an example of an original Great Central Railway passenger engine: LNER D11 class 'Improved Director' 4-4-0 No 506 *Butler Henderson*, built at Gorton in 1919, which belongs to the National Collection and is on loan from the National Railway Museum at York.

The railway has gradually expanded its activities since inception, operating steam and diesel-hauled trains every weekend, summer Wednesdays and bank holidays. The day-to-day operation of the railway is carried out by volunteer workers from the Main Line Steam Trust Ltd, a charitable company which has nearly 2,000 paid-up members, who support the Great Central Railway (1976) PLC, whose responsibility it is to raise funds to ensure the line's profitability; to date nearly £400,000 has been raised from individuals.

With the plans to operate trains on the section between Ruddington and Rushcliffe shortly to come to fruition, and the possibility of linking of the two systems within the next ten years, the original ambition of preserving the section from Nottingham to Leicester may well be fulfilled — albeit probably thirty years after the conception of the idea!

An event of major significance happened in 1990 when Mr David Clarke, a Leicestershire businessman, generously agreed to donate £300,000 for the purpose of doubling the track between Loughborough and Rothley. Original plans had previously restricted this to between Quorn and Rothley, funds permitting. After the tax is reclaimed, the total sum available will amount to £400,000. The first of four annual instalments of £75,000 was handed over during a ceremony at Rothley on 7 July. The first phase, due for completion in 1992, will cover the section between Quorn and Swithland; the second phase, from Swithland to Rothley, is scheduled for completion by 1995. In the longer term there will be double loops and additional sidings and a locomotive shed at Swithland. By the beginning of 1991 track and other materials were arriving here in preparation for the work to commence. Soon the dream of seeing Britain's only preserved section of main line operating on double track will become a reality.

Another landmark occurred in 1990, when on 15 November the first train carrying specially invited guests, including the Reverend W. Awdry, and local dignitaries ran on the newly completed £150,000 extension to Belgrave & Birstall, (now called Leicester North) and the southern terminus of the railway. A new station is being constructed south of the road bridge on the site of the old one. Now that the railway has reached the outskirts of the city, Leicester City Council has allocated funds from its budget to promote tourism on the line. It has promised to help with a number of projects, including the provision of a car park, which may be constructed on the nearby allotments owned by the council, thus offering adequate space to ensure good custom at the Leicester end of the line without encroaching on the trackbed.

Not only have eight miles of the line so far been restored to use, but much restoration work has had to be carried out over the years to the stations at Loughborough, Quorn, and Rothley. A continuous programme of refurbishment and maintenance is undertaken to the highest standards by dedicated volunteers from all walks of life, with a wide variety of skills.

Loughborough shed
129 SK 543197

1: Having spent the summer months of 1989 working on the preserved line, Birmingham Railway Museum's immaculate GWR Castle class 4-6-0 No 5080 *Defiant* undergoes a thorough cleaning and polishing by members of the Main Line Steam Trust outside Loughborough shed, prior to the locomotive's departure by road back to Tysley three days later. *Date: 8 October 1989.*

2: At dusk on a dull autumn evening, a Great Western duo stands near the Empress Road bridge at Loughborough. Modified Hall class 4-6-0 No 6990 *Witherslack Hall* is prepared outside the shed and gets up steam prior to working the 'Charnwood Forester' the following day, whilst GWR Castle class No 5080 *Defiant* stands behind and is methodically cleaned of grime. Alarmingly, as No 6990 was being returned to the shed, the cylinder drain cocks were opened and the blast of steam obscured the newly dug ash pit, into which a volunteer fell as he walked past. Although looking somewhat shaken by this experience, he climbed from the pit unhurt — if a little ruffled! *Date: 7 October 1989.*

3: Loughborough's spacious and well-equipped shed holds a number of locomotives either in the process of being restored or in working order. Among those present are: Merchant Navy class 4-6-2 No 35005 *Canadian Pacific,* which is well under way to being fully restored and is having her motion refitted; behind is West Country class 4-6-2 No 34039 *Boscastle,* of Somerset & Dorset fame, with much of its boiler cladding already fabricated and fitted; Robert Stephenson & Hawthorn-built 0-6-0 side tank No 7597 *Zebedee* occupies the centre road in the background, whilst on the extreme left is Director 4-4-0 No 506 *Butler Henderson.* *Date: 7 October 1989.*

4: With the passing months results are seen from many hours of hard labour. Having completed successful steam trials, Merchant Navy class No 35005 *Canadian Pacific* stands under the Empress Road bridge outside Loughborough shed and in front of LMS Jubilee class 4-6-0 No 5593 *Kolhapur,* a temporary resident; ex-NER Y7 0-4-0 tank No 68088 awaits shunting before being shedded for the night. *Canadian Pacific* entered revenue-earning service on 24 November 1990, following a re-dedication ceremony at Loughborough the day before. *Date: 15 November 1990.*

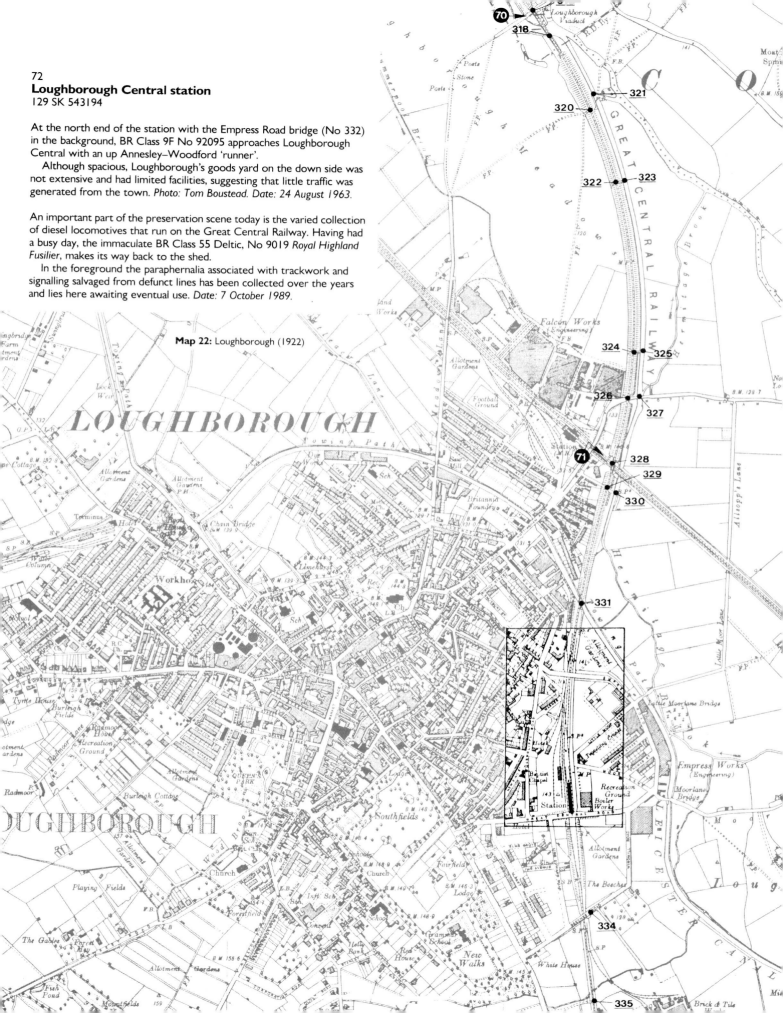

72
Loughborough Central station
129 SK 543194

At the north end of the station with the Empress Road bridge (No 332) in the background, BR Class 9F No 92095 approaches Loughborough Central with an up Annesley–Woodford 'runner'.

Although spacious, Loughborough's goods yard on the down side was not extensive and had limited facilities, suggesting that little traffic was generated from the town. *Photo: Tom Boustead. Date: 24 August 1963.*

An important part of the preservation scene today is the varied collection of diesel locomotives that run on the Great Central Railway. Having had a busy day, the immaculate BR Class 55 Deltic, No 9019 *Royal Highland Fusilier*, makes its way back to the shed.

In the foreground the paraphernalia associated with trackwork and signalling salvaged from defunct lines has been collected over the years and lies here awaiting eventual use. *Date: 7 October 1989.*

Map 22: Loughborough (1922)

1: Standing at the end of platform 2 during shunting operations, GNR N2 class 0-6-2T No 69523, GCR Director 4-4-0 No 506 *Butler Henderson,* and Austerity 0-6-0T No 68009 wait to be hauled back to the shed by a diesel locomotive. With their cylinders dry and devoid of any steam they sounded like three wheezy old ladies suffering from chronic asthma as they were being dragged away in quite an undignified manner for such aristocratic engines — and by a common diesel shunter! *Date: 7 October 1989.*

2: The high standard to which Loughborough Central is kept today can be judged by this study, which shows also Castle class 4-6-0 No 5080 *Defiant* standing at the end of platform 2 and about to be hauled tender-first back to the shed a few hundred yards away. *Date: 8 October 1989.*

3: On the last weekend of working on the line before being moved by road to the Nene Valley Railway, 'Black Five' 4-6-0 No 5231 waits at Loughborough Central prior to departing with the 16.50 to Rothley. *Date: 22 April 1989.*

Track plan 11: Loughborough (1921)

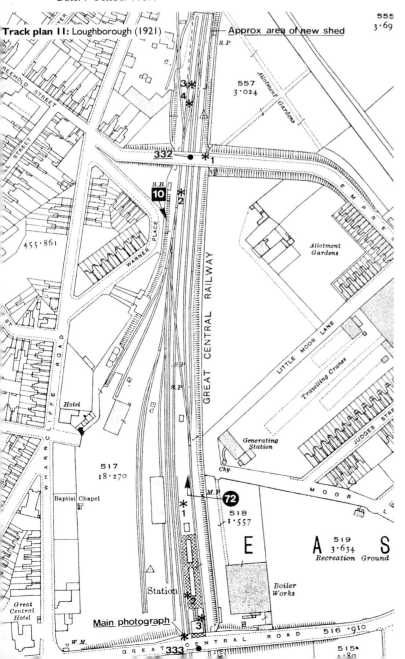

Loughborough Central station – 1990
129 SK 543193

A timeless scene, but this is a modern day view of the station, seen from the bridge on Great Central Road, and shows it in pristine condition, unlike in latter BR days. The island platform is protected by a long multi-section glazed canopy, which gives the station an elegant appearance. The goods shed, just out of camera view, has been severed from the station area and is now used as an industrial unit. The track layout has had to be altered somewhat, the lines on the left being used for the storage of coaching stock.

D11 class 4-4-0 Director No 506 *Butler Henderson* stands against platform 2 ready to take VIPs on to Rothley on the occasion of the opening of the extension to Leicester North (Belgrave & Birstall).

Today's visitor to the railway will not only see many station staff wearing immaculate GCR uniforms complete with white gloves, but with the addition of artefacts from yesteryear gracing the platforms and attractive floral hanging baskets on the canopies and splendidly turned-out locomotives and coaches, which all help to create an atmosphere of a railway with a once proud tradition. The high standard achieved reflects

the tremendous effort put in by individual Trust members in ensuring that at least part of the Great Central Railway lives as one of Britain's best preserved lines for other generations to enjoy in the years to come. *Date: 15 November 1990.*

An unidentified Stanier Class 5 4-6-0 draws into Loughborough Central's platform 2 with an afternoon semi-fast Marylebone–Nottingham train.

The spacious goods yard and shed are seen to good advantage in this view, but there seems to be little activity of note going on.
Photo: Richard Willis. Date: August 1962.

Having returned tender-first with the 13.50 from Rothley, GWR 5205 class 2-8-0T No 5224 pauses at platform 2 with its six-coach train prior to uncoupling and the run-round operation necessary before starting off again with the next scheduled train up the line. *Date: 6 November 1989.*

73
Loughborough – Paget's Farm: Bridge 336
129 SK 545183

With a dramatic leaden sky for a backdrop as a summer storm brews, Stanier Class 5 4-6-0 No 45417 with a mixed-traffic working bursts from under the occupation bridge just over a half-mile south of Loughborough Central station, and is about to duck under the A6 road bridge on its way to Leicester. *Photo: Tom Boustead. Date: 24 August 1963.*

Fireworks day: black-liveried GWR 5205 class 2-8-0T No 5224 has a good head of steam and is working hard as it hauls the 13.00 'Carillon' luncheon service train under Bridge 336 on its journey to Rothley. The train will pause at Swithland reservoir for diners not only to savour their meal, but to enjoy the beautiful scenery. By way of contrast the weather was indifferent and rather dull, so the full glory of trees in their autumn colours would not be seen to advantage by passengers on this trip.

The GWR tank, along with other classes of preserved locomotives, represents types never seen on the former Great Central line which now reside on the railway; but for others like Castle class No 5080 *Defiant*, it is only a sojourn. *Date: 5 November 1989.*

COMMENT: *Surprisingly, four attempts were made to obtain this shot, since it was difficult to identify the correct position. In the event, a sidestep of a yard or so to the left was necessary to avoid the train being totally obscured by the bush, but it is hoped the compromise will suffice.*

74

Loughborough – Woodthorpe Road: Bridge 338
129 SK 545178

Thursday, 18.41 hrs: with two days to go before all through services are withdrawn, Stanier Class 5 No 44984 expends little effort on the 1:176 rising gradient towards Quorn & Woodhouse with the three-coach 18.15 Nottingham–Rugby train, as it approaches Bridge 338, which carries the minor road to Woodthorpe, and is a mile or so south of Loughborough Central.

The A6 trunk road from Loughborough to Leicester passes over the bridge in the background (No 337). A branch from the main line between the distant bridge (No 336) and Beeches Road bridge (No 334), served the brick works whose chimneys are visible in the middle distance.
Photo: Tom Boustead. Date: 1 September 1966.

The permanent way is now singled and the brick works on the right have gone, but little else seems to have changed at one of the favourite vantage points from which to view trains on the Great Central today: this is also one of the more popular photographic locations on the preserved section of the line.

A few minutes after departing spot on time from Loughborough at 13.00, Modified Hall class 4-6-0, No 6990 *Witherslack Hall* charges up the gradient with the 'Carillon' six-coach train and makes plenty of smoke, which usually delights the lineside photographer — if he or she is up wind of it! *Date: 8 October 1989.*

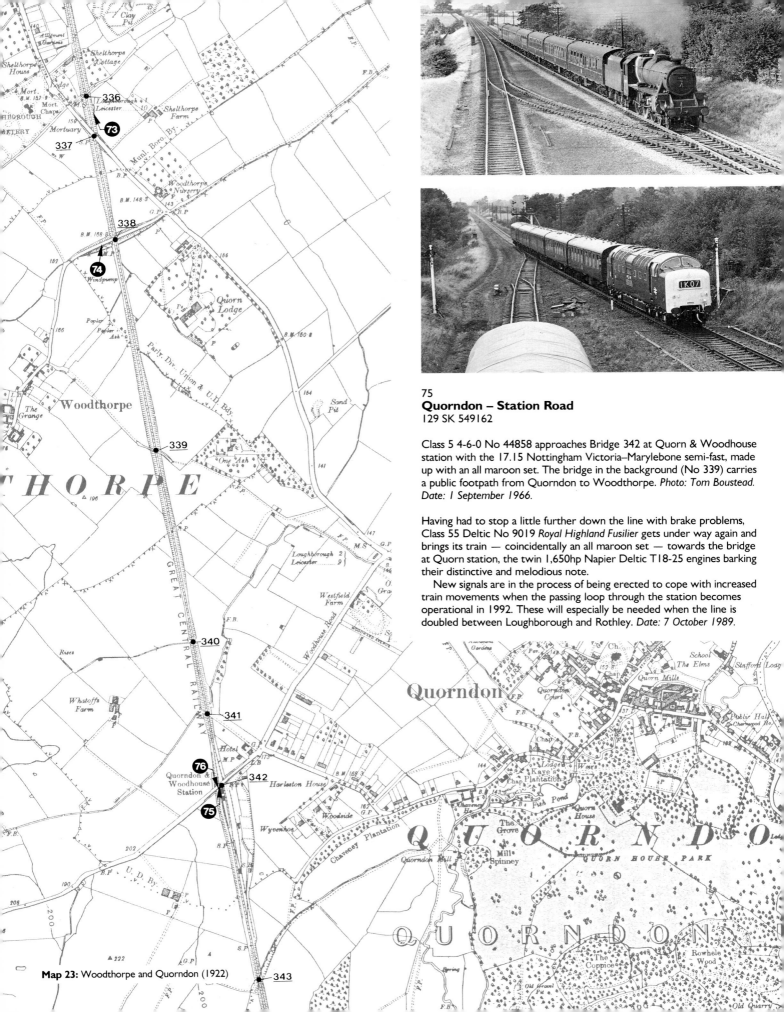

75
Quorndon – Station Road
129 SK 549162

Class 5 4-6-0 No 44858 approaches Bridge 342 at Quorn & Woodhouse station with the 17.15 Nottingham Victoria–Marylebone semi-fast, made up with an all maroon set. The bridge in the background (No 339) carries a public footpath from Quorndon to Woodthorpe. *Photo: Tom Boustead. Date: 1 September 1966.*

Having had to stop a little further down the line with brake problems, Class 55 Deltic No 9019 *Royal Highland Fusilier* gets under way again and brings its train — coincidentally an all maroon set — towards the bridge at Quorn station, the twin 1,650hp Napier Deltic T18-25 engines barking their distinctive and melodious note.

New signals are in the process of being erected to cope with increased train movements when the passing loop through the station becomes operational in 1992. These will especially be needed when the line is doubled between Loughborough and Rothley. *Date: 7 October 1989.*

Map 23: Woodthorpe and Quorndon (1922)

76
Quorn & Woodhouse station
129 SK 549162

A sequential shot of Class 5 No 44858 as it passes the station of Quorn & Woodhouse, which had closed to passengers in 1963. The humble but functional buildings, now minus their canopies, on the island platform of this typical London Extension country station can be seen to good effect. As with most other stations, plenty of provision was made for an extensive goods yard, but its two sidings were little utilised. Some years later this space would be much needed by the railway preservationists.

One of the stipulations that the former Lord Lanesborough made to the Great Central in exchange for allowing the passage of the railway through his lands was that any train could be stopped at Quorn when his lordship wished to travel on the line to and from his nearby country seat at Swithland Hall. It was not unknown for the driver of such a train, especially an express not scheduled to stop at Quorn, to receive a tip from his important passenger at Marylebone. This landowner's privilege was not confined to the noble lord, for King Edward VII was said to have alighted here by request when he travelled to ride with the famous Quorn hunt!

This stretch of line was probably one of the most scenic parts of the route towards London; the splendour of the countryside particularly around Charnwood Forest and Swithland reservoir was appreciated by many a traveller. Near the site of the proposed station at Swithland there were a few sidings and a half-mile branch on the up side to serve the nearby quarry, once owned by the Mountsorrel Granite Company. *Photo: Tom Boustead. Date: 1 September 1966.*

The modern day sequence: now running a few minutes late with the 13.00 ex-Loughborough, Class 55 *Royal Highland Fusilier*, with the immaculately restored maroon set, gets away from Quorn and will shortly cross Swithland Viaduct over the reservoir before reaching Rothley.

Although taken on a dismal and wet Saturday, the tidy condition of Quorn & Woodhouse is evident from this view, which also shows the signal cabin rescued from Market Rasen in 1984, now erected at the southern end of the goods yard. Carriage stock is temporarily stored on the down loop.

In the autumn of 1990, having been salvaged during the re-signalling of the Chiltern Line, the former 92-lever signal box at Neasden was moved here; the top portion being stored in the yard together with 22 tons of signalling equipment, including the frame. The box will eventually be reassembled and sited at the end of the station in the Heritage Centre at Ruddington. *Date: 7 October 1989.*

On a disappointingly dull afternoon, GWR Hall class 4-6-0 No 6990 *Witherslack Hall* with the 14.30 train from Loughborough passes over one of the two viaducts at Swithland reservoir on the way to Rothley, a mile or so distant. Note: the permanent way gang are out in force busy maintaining the track, an operation which never stops. *Date: 8 October 1989.*

77
Rothley – Bridge 354
129 SK 568122

In far from ideal photographic conditions on this thoroughly wet and bleak Monday afternoon, a very grubby 'Black Five' 4-6-0, No 44865, with the eight-coach 17.15 Nottingham–Marylebone train, approaches the B5328 road bridge adjacent to Rothley station. During the line's final three years of operation trains usually were made up of only four coaches, except this service, which usually consisted of seven. *Photo: Tom Boustead. Date: 19 August 1966.*

A complete contrast in the weather on a bright October afternoon some twenty-three years later shows No 6990 4-6-0 *Witherslack Hall* approaching the bridge on the down passing loop with the 'Carillon' train from Loughborough. *Date: 8 October 1989.*

Map 24: Swithland and Rothley (1927)

78
Rothley station
129 SK 568122

Another in a sequence: the photographer dashes over the road to the other side of the B5328 bridge to capture Class 5 4-6-0 No 44865 passing Rothley station with the 17.15 train as it heads off towards Belgrave & Birstall, a little way down the line.

At first glance there is little or no difference between this and Quorn station. One could easily be confused as to the location, because the southward views are also very similar, except Rothley had a slightly more extensive goods yard, with sidings off the up line and one on the down side, which was later made into a loop. *Photo: Tom Boustead. Date: 19 August 1966.*

A busy scene at Rothley as GWR Hall class No 6990 *Witherslack Hall* runs around its train prior to returning to Loughborough Central with a late afternoon service. The engine is no stranger to the line, having regularly worked on it during the 1948 locomotive exchanges.

No 6690 is just passing by the new shed which is nearing completion, whilst on the right beyond the train SR Merchant Navy class Pacific No 35025 *Brocklebank Line* which awaits long-term restoration. *Date: 8 October 1989.*

1: This is what a preserved line and working steam railway is all about: *Witherslack Hall* pauses briefly during run-round operations at Rothley station, to be admired by passengers representing all generations, young and old alike. A proud father explains the intricacies of No 6990's motion to his offspring, whilst others look on. The gathering clouds signify that the heavens are about to open; the resulting hail storm will send the passengers scurrying back to their seats on the train. *Date: 21 October 1989.*

2: The first passenger train conveying a hundred specially invited guests on the new extension to 'Leicester North' (Belgrave & Birstall) starts off from Rothley with ex-GWR 5700 class 0-6-0PT No 7760 gently pushing the two-coach train through the tape placed at the southern end of the station, whilst Director No 506 *Butler Henderson* whistles in salute. *Date: 15 November 1990.*

79
Belgrave & Birstall station (1)
140 SK 587084

Viewed from bridge No 363 carrying Station Road, and having climbed from Leicester on the ruling 1:176 gradient, BR Class 9F No 92033 brings the 16.30 Woodford–Annesley 'runner' through Belgrave & Birstall on its journey northwards.

Unlike many others of the type, the station managed to retain a portion of its protective canopies until the closure of the line. Set at the end of a deep cutting, the station was located near a golf course on Mowmacre Hill on the northern outskirts of Leicester, which can been seen in the distance. *Photo: D. Holmes. Date: 15 August 1962.*

In this view ballast for the new extension from Rothley, the track of which has already been laid, lies ready for use and covers the remains of the island platform. By March 1990 the job of ballasting had been completed, including being tamped along the entire extension from Rothley to here by a private contractor. Note by way of contrast from the previous view how the high-rise blocks of flats dominate the Leicester skyline today. *Date: 8 October 1989.*

1: Class 5700 0-6-0PT No 7760 leaves Belgrave & Birstall, soon to be called 'Leicester North' and the new southern terminus, with the first passenger train on its return journey to Rothley. *Date: 15 November 1990.*

Leicester North Station

During the autumn of 1990, Belgrave & Birstall became the southern terminus of the preserved line from Loughborough. The investment by Leicester City Council of approximately £150,000 towards the £250,000 project enabled work to commence on the construction of an entirely new station, to be named Leicester North. By May 1991 the contractors, Messrs Paul John Construction of Leicester, had dismantled the old island platform, and the new one, some 250 metres long, on the golf course side was already taking shape, with the edging and face nearing completion. This had necessitated the removal of some of the banking. The other platform on the up side is to be considerably shorter, but may be extended as funds allow. Some 197,000 engineers' blue bricks have been used in the construction of the two platforms and backing walls.

The modified track layout will include a central release road to allow locomotives to run-round their trains; in addition, modest servicing facilities will also be provided. The new platforms will be connected by a concourse at the southern end and will have a full range of visitor reception facilities housed in a brand new building, which will be sited at the end of the access road. Entrance to the proposed car park for the terminus will be made from the top end of the link road and is expected to be built on land previously used for allotments to the east of the formation.

The first train to Leicester North ran on 3 July 1991 in the rehearsals for the 150th anniversary celebrations of Thomas Cook Ltd.

2: A somewhat different view from the road bridge, taken a week or two before the first train was scheduled to run into the new station, shows work on the down platform at Leicester North nearing completion and the new lines being laid by Trackwork Ltd well advanced along its length. What a contrast to the 1989 views! *Date: 11 June 1991.*

3: This impressive aspect, looking north towards the bridge from the access road, gives some idea of the scale of the project and the intensity of the work being carried out to finish on schedule. *Date: 11 June 1991.*

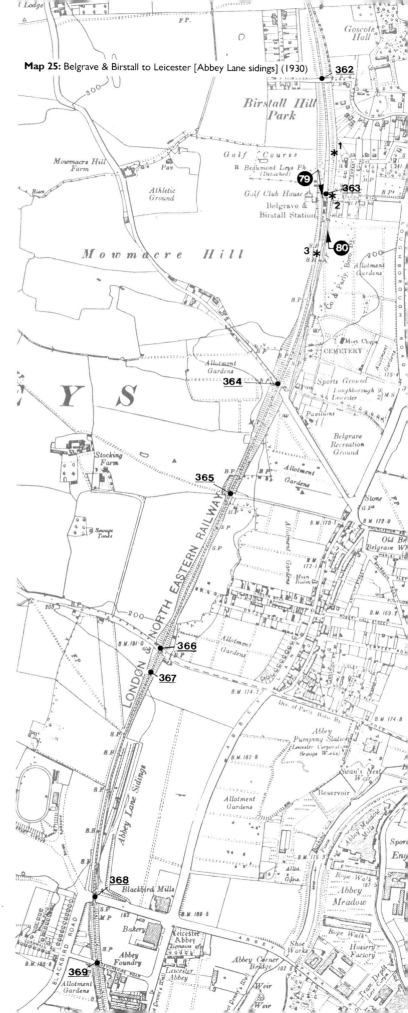

Map 25: Belgrave & Birstall to Leicester [Abbey Lane sidings] (1930)

80
Belgrave & Birstall station (2)
140 SK 588083

One of the last cross-country workings for which the line was famous was the Newcastle–Bournemouth service, and on this occasion hauled by Brush Type 4 (Class 47) No D1896, is seen passing the derelict buildings and platform of Belgrave & Birstall station. The covered staircase from Station Road onto the island is well portrayed here.

The station had neither sidings nor goods handling facilities.
Photo: Tom Boustead. Date: 1 September 1966.

Although the bridge (No 363) is in good condition, the graffiti 'artists' have been unable to resist daubing their childish slogans on its face. The staircase arch remains firmly bricked up.

The bridge and much of the embankment about a quarter of a mile south of the station have been removed to make way for the Leicester northern link road, but the council has constructed a steep spur from it to a point just short of the southern end of the platform for access. A little further south and towards Abbey Lane sidings, some of the formation survives, but is under constant threat from development. *Date: 9 October 1989.*

1 (Opposite)
Sheffield Victoria
110/111 SK 361880

Class B1 4-6-0 No 61127 waits in the centre road whilst on pilot duty at Sheffield Victoria. In the early sixties, regular trainspotters became used to seeing engines of this class on such station duties. A particular B1 from Retford shed often seen here, No 61212, became a firm favourite and was duly christened the 'Retford Rocket'. *Photo: Colour-Rail. Date: 1954.*

The trackbed between the former platforms has been filled in, leaving little to indicate that this was once a station. The boundaries of the Victoria Hotel's new car park are marked by the fence line and coincides with the platform edge, the post holes having been dug along its length. A desolate scene set to depress any railway enthusiast.
Date: 24 September 1989.

2
Killamarsh
120 SK 448808

Class D11 4-4-0 Improved Director No 62660 *Butler Henderson* rounds the curve just south of Killamarsh station with an up local train; the next stop will be Renishaw Central. *Photo: Colour-Rail. Date: September 1960.*

3
Chesterfield – Horns Bridge
119 SK 387706

Having passed Chesterfield Central and seen emerging from the tunnel under the town, Class O4 2-8-0 No 63827 in charge of a mixed freight approaches Horns Bridge, where three railway systems crossed. The train is about to duck under both the main Midland line and the viaduct carrying the former LD&EC line, which was already disused, having closed five years earlier. By this date the Chesterfield loop itself was only a few months from closure and the weeds are already evident on the trackbed.

Note Chesterfield's unique landmark, the crooked spire of St Mary's church. *Photo: Colour-Rail. Date: 1962.*

4
Bulwell Common yard
129 SK 550448

In the last days of operation of the line, Class 8F 2-8-0 No 48185 shunts some coal empties in the spacious yard at Bulwell Common. Could this be the final clearing operations before closure? The station is seen in the background; and just beyond the bridge to its right, is the Golden Ball public house distinguished by the large orb on its roof, visible from miles around. *Photo: Great Central Railway collection. Date: September 1966.*

Not exactly an inspiring comparison, but this illustrates some of the problems in effecting facsimile photography. The only indication that this is the same spot is the tree on the left in the background. Although the banks are covered in young trees and undergrowth, the trackbed itself is reasonably clear and used by both walkers and off-road motorcyclists. The large retaining wall which was obscured by the train on the up side of the line is still in good condition, as indeed, is *Butler Henderson*, which now resides on the preserved Great Central Railway at Loughborough! *Date: 23 September 1989.*

Quite a transformation: the A61 Chesterfield inner relief road now cuts through the area and no trace is to be found of the GC route, save a portion of the abutments or retaining wall near the site of the former bridge under which it passed the Midland line.

Despite the other changes, St Mary's church has stood the test of time.
Date: 23 September 1989.

This shot had to be taken through a hedge in the garden of a house on St Alban's Road. The only way to recognise the location is by the three poplar trees in the left background and the Golden Ball public house, which still proudly proclaims its presence.
Date: 21 May 1989.

5
Bagthorpe Junction
129 SK 560432

On a hazy spring day, B1 class 4-6-0 No 61210 passes Bagthorpe Junction with an up coal train and straddles the bridge (No 278) over Valley Road. The connections to and from the former GN's Staffordshire and Derbyshire line with the GC's main line can be seen clearly in this view, which was taken from the garden of 5 Newfield Road.
Photo: Tom Boustead. Date: 1 May 1965.

6
Nottingham Victoria (1)
129 SK 573405

Class B1 4-6-0 No 61036 emerges from Mansfield Road Tunnel to enter Nottingham Victoria with a York–Bournemouth train made up of a 'blood and custard' set. An engineers' wagon has been shunted up against Victoria North box, which looks in a dirty condition, but hardly is surprising, considering its proximity to the exhaust smoke of engines starting from the station.
Photo: Colour-Rail.
Date: 19 September 1956.

7
Nottingham Victoria (2)
129 SK 572403

The splendour of Nottingham Victoria's main station building with its fine clock tower fronting Milton Street is seen well in this view taken from a multi-storey car park opposite. A corner of the Victoria Station Hotel is visible on the extreme right. *Photo: Colour-Rail. Date: 12 May 1966.*

Taken from the same spot the outlook is somewhat different today. It is hard to comprehend that such changes are possible in the relatively few years since the demise of the railway. In the middle distance a wholesale grocery cash-and-carry has been built on the remaining portion of the GC's embankment, whilst a new housing estate has been built on the other side of Valley Road where it has been cleared to ground level.
Date: 24 September 1989.

Hardly a scene to inspire the railway fraternity. The only view to be had of the tunnel today is from the Victoria Centre car park; it is a potent illustration on how the emphasis has changed in the mode of transport over the last few decades.
Date: 20 May 1989.

Definitely a rose amongst thorns. By good fortune, the planners decided to retain the clock tower as the focal point to the Victoria Centre, but hardly blends in with its surroundings and looks positively threatened by them. Date: 19 June 1989.

COMMENT: Preoccupied, imagine my surprise when I heard an inquisitive voice behind me say: ' Scuse me sir, would you mind telling me what you're doing?' It was the law: alarmingly, two policemen were approaching me. It transpired the staff of the bank thought I was casing the joint. My hurried explanations accepted, they went on their way, as did I, thinking it not appropriate to wait another twenty-four minutes for the clock to read the right time . . . that would have been too much stress for the bank to bear!

8
Nottingham Victoria (3)
129 SK 574404

This night-time shot of Nottingham Victoria embodies all the essential ingredients to make a classic scene of a main line station in the steam days. It is 8.20pm and Britannia Class 7MT, No 70054 *Dornoch Firth* blows off furiously, having arrived some minutes before.

Britannias made a brief return to the line in the autumn of 1965 to supplement other classes, including the 'Black Fives', which provided the mainstay of the few remaining services. No 70054 was of a batch with high-sided tenders, which were needed to avoid unnecessary re-coaling, as Annesley was the only GC shed still open to service them. *Photo: Colour-Rail. Date: October 1965.*

9
Nottingham Victoria (4)
129 SK 575402

Viewed from over a high wall in an alley off Clare Street on the south-east side of the station, Nottingham Victoria is a hive of activity. B1 class 4-6-0 No 61264 has its water supply replenished before departing for Mablethorpe with its train, whilst Class 4MT 2-6-0 No 43142 is on station pilot duty and prepared to move some coaches from alongside platform 7. An unidentified Class 5 4-6-0 in the immediate foreground awaits its next duty in one of the sidings near the turntable road, whilst an Austerity 2-8-0 waits to proceed with a goods train in one of the loops. *Photo: Colour-Rail. Date: June 1963.*

10
Loughborough Central
129 SK 542196

Class 5MT No 44941 leaves Loughborough Central with the three-coach 16.38 Marylebone–Nottingham semi-fast during the last remaining months of through services.

The sidings in the goods yard have already been removed and the remaining sleepers are devoid of their rails, whilst others lie in untidy heaps. A sure sign that all is not well. *Photo: Colour-Rail. Date: June 1966.*

In the perpetual gloom of the underground car park at the Victoria Centre, there is no longer the smell of oil and steam in the air to ginger the nostalgic senses. Only the obnoxious odour from car exhausts hangs in these modern-day catacombs to assault the nostrils, making one's head throb. Oh, lackaday, lackaday! *Date: 20 May 1989.*

Is it the same place? One small clue as to the location is the wall just discernible at the bottom right-hand corner of the photograph and on which the camera was resting in order to effect this shot, showing part of the service and administration section of the Victoria Centre. *Date: 20 May 1989.*

Not so gloomy now, despite the derelict-looking 0-4-0 saddle tank in the foreground awaiting restoration sometime in the future. In the last light of an autumn evening, GWR Modified Hall class 4-6-0 No 6990 *Witherslack Hall*, having worked the last service of the day and uncoupled from its train, reverses back to the shed for the night. Waiting on the other road are Castle class 4-6-0 No 5080 *Defiant* and GWR 5205 class 2-8-0T, which are about to be taken back to the shed by one of the line's resident diesel shunters sandwiched between them. Loughborough sees more movements today than it did in latter BR days. Good news indeed. *Date: 8 October 1989.*

11
Leicester Central
140 SK 582045

Stanier Class 5 4-6-0 No 45215 pulls away with its four-coach train from Leicester Central with the 12.30 semi-fast ex-Nottingham for Marylebone. The driver keeps a sharp lookout, but the dangling 'fag' in his mouth gives him a look of nonchalance, as much as if to say, 'I've done this a thousand times before'. Some sixteen months hence he probably would be wishing he could do it a thousand times again! *Photo: R. C. Riley.*
Date: 4 May 1965.

12
Rugby Viaduct – No 451
140 SP 156756

BR Class 9F 2-10-0 No 92132 with an up Annesley–Woodford 'runner' storms across the viaduct over the West Coast main line at Rugby.

As part of the wayleave agreement with the LNWR when this viaduct was built in 1897, the Great Central had to provide and maintain at its own expense a massive gantry of signals, each set being duplicated. It was erected on the east side of the viaduct for controlling the southern approach to Rugby Midland station. The gantry was finally dismantled in 1939 after electric colour-lights were installed. *Photo: Colour-Rail.*
Date: October 1964.

13
Rugby Central station
140 SP 515744

Receiving admiring looks from would-be enginemen, Class 6P 4-6-0 Jubilee No 45666 *Cornwallis* stands at Rugby Central before proceeding with the 08.15 Nottingham–Marylebone semi-fast.

The situation of the booking hall and main building on the Hillmorton Road bridge is clearly visible in this view. Rugby Central was a fairly modest station, as illustrated by the canopy over the waiting rooms, providing scant shelter for passengers standing on the platform.
Photo: Colour-Rail. Date: August 1962.

This is what the former station site looks like now on a weekday and Saturdays. The car park is found to be very convenient by people who either walk to their places of work in the city centre, or to the shops.

The last weed-strewn remains of the bay platform can be seen dividing the lines of cars in the background. Little else relates to the previous photograph except two chimneys near the trees on the extreme right in the background, which also can be spotted in the 1965 view. *Date: 24 May 1990.*

Just two sections of the viaduct are left spanning the West Coast main line. BR decided that to dismantle these would cause too much disruption to the rail traffic on the busy route; and since the spans have been found to be in good condition, they are set to remain for some time to come as a memorial to the LNWR's former rival.
Date: 15 August 1989.

The removal of the building on the Hillmorton Road bridge created an ugly scar in the shape of an exposed red-brick wall on the parapet and out of kilter with the rest of it. However, the platform remains in good condition having received attention from an MSC restoration scheme. *Date: 15 August 1989.*

14
Rugby Central goods loops
140 SP 514740

Passing the long goods loops just to the south of Rugby Central is BR Class 9F 2-10-0, No 92010 in charge of a long ballast train heading south towards Woodford. The water tower on the down side of the line was quite a feature of this section, appearing in many photographs. *Photo: Michael Mensing. Date: 22 July 1961.*

15
Catesby Tunnel – south portal
152 SP 534568

B1 class 4-6-0 No 61360 storms out of Catesby Tunnel with a train for Marylebone. Soon it would probably be 'taking a dip' in the Charwelton water troughs a few hundred yards up the line. *Photo: Colour-Rail. Date: 10 August 1961.*

16
Woodford Halse station
152 SP 541523

Class B1 No 61206 stands at Woodford before departing with an up local. The symmetry of the island platform and its building's canopy is apparent in this view. It was not unusual in the dying days of a railway to see more staff than passengers on the station, as is evident from this view, although closure was five years away. *Photo: Colour-Rail. Date: 31 August 1961.*

From the same vantage point the water tower, if it still existed, would surely now be obscured by the growth of trees and shrubs on the bank; however, the oak trees near the houses, seen in the 1961 view, are the only recognisable features to identify the location. *Date: 15 August 1989.*

At rest: will Catesby see Channel Tunnel traffic in the years to come? *Date: 24 October 1989.*

COMMENT: *Caught just in time! An exhausting half hour was spent hurriedly hacking back the dead rosebay willowherb so that the tunnel could be viewed and photographed before the sun disappeared on this late autumn day.*

There is nothing that corresponds with the former scene in this view of the showmen's caravan park; just the occasional trace of the platform edge foundations remain exposed. *Date: 24 October 1989.*

17
Woodford Halse – Eydon Road: Bridge 498
152 SP 541517

A number of enthusiasts had already gathered on the bridge and at various locations on the lineside to witness the passing of this special train from Waterloo to Stratford, hauled by the newly restored LSWR Drummond Class T9 4-4-0 No 120, coupled ahead of N class Mogul No 31790.

Woodford Halse station can just be seen in the distance through the left arch of the bridge. *Photo: Barry Hilton. Date: 12 October 1963.*

18
Woodford Halse – Bridge 499
152 SP 542518

LMS Class 5 4-6-0 No 45342 passes under the S&MJ line bridge (No 499) with a Bournemouth–Bradford train. The former South Junction was located between this bridge and the one seen in the background (No 500), a mile and a half beyond which was Culworth Junction.
Photo: Colour-Rail. Date: 29 August 1964.

19
Banbury branch – Thorpe Mandeville: Bridge 15
151 SP 516451

The 'Banbury Motor' at work: Class 4MT 2-6-4T No 42082 passes underneath the Wardington Road bridge near Thorpe Mandeville with the local service train that shuttled between Banbury and Woodford. The bridge spanned a long and deep cutting about halfway between the two locations, which was a favourite place for photographers to gather, offering them the best view on the seven-mile branch. *Photo: R. C. Riley. Date: 12 October 1963.*

As can be judged, the bridge is in generally fine fettle and seemingly ready to welcome its next customers to pass beneath its central arch. Who knows what may happen in the years ahead?
Date: 24 October 1989.

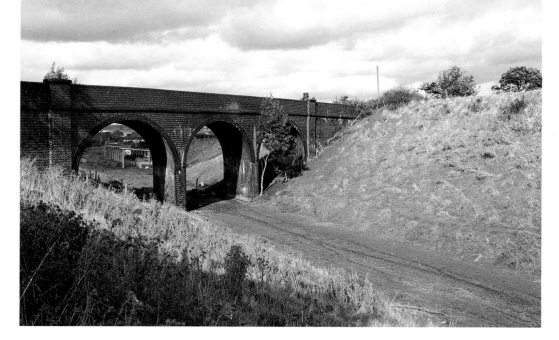

The cutting here has been cleared of bushes in the last year or so by the owner of the nearby piggery. He intends to create several paddocks here for the pigs that are allowed out of their pens to rootle around the area, so this is probably the best condition the banks are likely to be seen in years to come!
Date: 24 October 1989.

Now covered by numerous bushes, the overgrown banks provide excellent homes for an infinite variety of wildlife. The parapet of the bridge is only just visible, since it has been backfilled on its east side; the far bank has also been built up a little in the process.
Date: 17 August 1989.

20
Brackley – Northampton Road:
Bridge 525
152 SP 590379

B1 class 4-6-0 No 61106 stands at the end of the platform at Brackley Central and is about to set off with its train towards Woodford Halse and Nottingham. The embankment on the down side beyond the A43 road bridge has been set on fire by a previous train, but poses little threat at this time of year. Lineside fires were a common occurrence in the days of steam during long, dry periods. *Photo: Colour-Rail. Date: 24 March 1961.*

21
Aylesbury
165 SP 817134

During the summer and autumn of 1961, running trials were conducted over GC metals of the futuristic-looking 2,750hp English Electric 4-6-0 GT3 experimental gas turbine locomotive, seen here approaching Aylesbury with a nine-coach test train. The photographer, standing on the footbridge at the northern end of the station, wisely is not positioned over the engine, as the efflux of exhaust gases would have surely singed his eyebrows! The very hot exhaust was one of the problems experienced with this locomotive, which caused fire damage to a number of wooden footbridges and signalling equipment as it passed underneath. *Photo: Dr G. C. Farnell. Date: September 1961.*

22
Marylebone
176 TQ 275824

On a glorious September afternoon, the penultimate day of through services, Stanier Class 5 44872 leaves Marylebone with the 16.38 semi-fast for Nottingham Victoria, and passes the Rossmore Road bridge before entering the three tunnels under St John's Wood, just a few hundred yards north of the station. *Photo: Roy Hobbs. Date: 2 September 1966.*

The trees on the right provide the only clue as the A43 road bridge has long since been removed and the greater portion of the cutting beyond it has been filled in. *Date: 18 August 1989.*

Very few trains operate over this section north of the station today, but with the building of the Networker-Turbo depot to the western side of the line here, this situation will change over the next year or two.

In this comparison photograph the layout is very similar, save a few minor alterations and engineers can be seen employed at the pointwork in preparation for linking the new depot, still to be built at this date, to the main line. *Date: 6 November 1989.*

Not such a glorious September afternoon: dull and overcast with thunder rolling in the heavens, a Chiltern Line DMU enters Marylebone. The track layout has only altered slightly over the years, but at least one of the buildings along Rossmore Road has been demolished. *Date: 13 September 1989.*

COMMENT: *Crawling through some prickly bushes carefully avoiding treading on indescribable things flung into them from flats built on the site of the former goods depot, to stand under a high wall topped by a mesh fence, I had to dismantle the camera and work the components through the wire before being reassembled to take this shot. Unable to see the tracks I had to guess the line-up. Apologies for capturing an arriving rather than a departing train!*

7
LEICESTER —
ASHBY TUNNEL

Leicester Central station

The approach to the station was made on a viaduct constructed from near the junction of Abbey Gate and Harrison Street (in 1899 on the northern outskirts of the city), which continued for 35 chains with intermediate girder spans over the River Soar (No 374), Slater Street, the Leicester arm of the Grand Union Canal, Northgate Street, and finally to a bridge over Soar Lane, at which point the island platform of Leicester Central was reached.

All Saints' Road passed under the station, at which point the viaduct was some 190ft wide; the supporting structure was suitably heavy to withstand the enormous weight imposed upon it. The island platform was 1,300ft long and 85ft wide, with two bays provided at either end for local services; each was about 430ft in length, in addition to which a parcels dock, often referred to by railwaymen as the fish dock, was located adjacent to the main building on the east side. Passing loops and carriage sidings were built on either side; a few standing sidings and a turntable were provided on the south-east of the station adjacent to Great Central Road.

The station had three main buildings on the island, all of which were protected by a canopy which extended some 830ft along the platforms. The facilities included the usual waiting rooms, offices, refreshment bar and a restaurant — a kitchen, cellars, stores and further offices were built underneath.

Entrance to the station was gained from both sides at street level some 20ft below, but the booking hall, parcels office and cab rank were on the east side, above which the main building was situated: although it was a fairly modest red brick structure, it was built to the highest standards. During the station's construction, a Roman pavement was unearthed near Jewry Lane and a glass-light covering was placed over it for protection, at great expense to the railway.

From the end of the platform the viaduct continued for another 28½ chains to span Welles Street, Bath Lane, the River Soar again, the junction of St Augustine and West Bridge Street, the old River Soar course where the viaduct ended, the line then entering Leicester North Goods yard on an embankment.

The station site and the line formation from Thurcaston Road was sold by British Rail in the mid-seventies. Today, the GC's formation from Thurcaston Road is still fairly distinct in parts, but under constant pressure from development which borders close to it; most of the site around the former sidings at Abbey Lane has already succumbed. The series of viaduct arches near the A6 dual carriageway at St Margaret's Pasture survived until recently, although the steel girder bridge over the River Soar had been removed, as had the ones over both the Grand Union Canal and Northgate Street, which were cut up and sold as scrap. The abutments survive in Soar Lane as does the bridge in All Saints' Road, under the station.

23 (Opposite)
Marylebone
176 TQ 276822

Class 4MT 2-6-4T No 42086 backs out of the station to await its next duty. Rossmore Road bridge situated off the end of the platforms at Marylebone provides a good backdrop to the array of signals placed on the northern end. In the left background B1 class 4-6-0 No 61106 stands on the turntable and powers itself around; shortly No 42086 will require turning. *Photo: Roy Hobbs. Date: June 1961.*

A Class 115 DMU departs from Marylebone with the 17.58 service for West Ruislip. The signals will not survive much longer and will soon be replaced by electric ones, but the turntable's future is undecided. The plastic netting in the foreground cordons off part of the platform upon which contractors' portable cabins are placed whilst the station undergoes refurbishment and its layout is altered. *13 September 1989.*

Map 26: Leicester Central, North and South Goods; Leicester [GC] shed (1931)

Leicester – River Soar: Bridge 374
140 SK 580053

Having just started out from Leicester Central on its journey northwards towards Nottingham with the 16.38 from Marylebone, and seen traversing the long viaduct north of the station, Stanier Class 5 4-6-0 No 44835 crosses the River Soar on a girder bridge, which was one of several constructed on this elevated section of line through the city.
Photo: M. Mitchell. Date: 12 July 1966.

The girder bridge became a casualty a few years ago, being dismantled and removed for scrap. The small industrial buildings on the left have remained largely the same, save a few minor alterations and the addition of a water tower, which obscures the signal post seen in the original photograph and which still survives to this day.

The bridge in St Margaret's Way can be spotted between the trees on the left and the viaduct's abutment. *Date: 24 May 1990.*

The signal post stands alone on the viaduct in splendid isolation, its duty done for ever. *Date: 24 May 1990.*

Track plan 12: Leicester Central (1930)

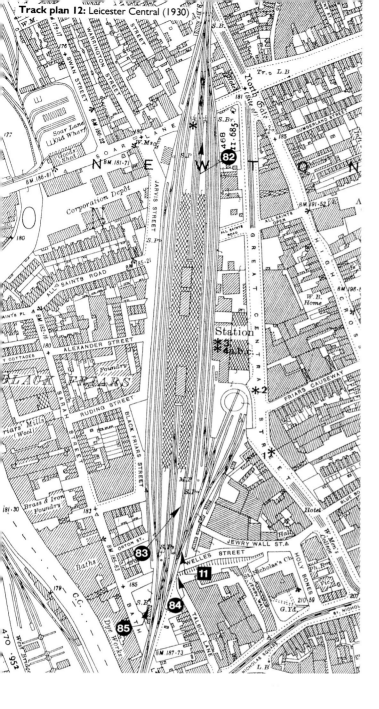

82
Leicester Central station (1)
140 SK 582048

With nationalisation just a few months away B1 class 4-6-0 No 1153, still proudly sporting its LNER livery, enters Leicester Central's up platform from the north with a Marylebone-bound train. The two lines on the immediate left are those for the island platform's northern bays.

Being one of two sited at the station, Leicester Passenger North signal box, seen here, controlled the movements at this end of the complex. One of the handsome signal gantries for that purpose can just be spotted beyond the girder bridge in the background, which spanned Soar Lane.

A prominent landmark at Leicester Central, with its name spelt out in large white letters on its roof, was the modest Great Central Hotel. Although lacking the grandeur of its namesake at Marylebone, the hostelry undoubtedly played host to many a weary traveller to the city. *Photo: H. C. Casserley. Date: 14 July 1947.*

Today much of the former station area has been given over to industrial units; the north end is now used as a lorry-cum-trailer park by a transport and distribution company. The Great Central Hotel has been demolished, but the chimneys of an adjacent building, seen above the engine's cab and tender in the original photograph, can be observed in the centre of this view.

Together with the section of the viaduct that separated them, the girder bridge over Soar Lane has long since been removed, as has the one which skewed across Northgate, where a similar but much larger and imposing steel structure was also erected.
Date: 24 May 1990.

A view looking north taken from the abutments of the Soar Lane girder bridge shows no obvious sign of the railway having ever existed here, but the new industrial units built beyond the parked cars in the storage compound below perhaps provide the only clue to its route out of the city. *Date: 24 May 1990.*

83
Leicester Central station (2)
140 SK 581045

On a fine summer's afternoon K2 class 2-6-0 No 61753 prepares to depart from Leicester Central's platform 6 with an up train, whilst two GWR Halls, No 4970 *Sketty Hall* and No 5916 *Trinity Hall* wait in the sidings near the turntable.

From 1963, until displaced by Class 37 diesel-electrics, Halls frequently worked the section between Oxford and Leicester of the Bournemouth–York cross-country service that ran via Banbury, and from there over GC metals to Woodford: a facility no longer available today, since they now all run via Derby. The Halls usually returned from Leicester on a Woodford local, departing at 15.20. *Photo: Barry Hilton. Date: 16 August 1958.*

The whole of the area once taken by the standing sidings and turntable is used as a car park, which is filled to capacity during weekdays by commuters, and on Saturdays by shoppers going to the city centre. The main station building survives in reasonable condition and is used by small businesses. *Date: 22 April 1989.*

(Opposite)
1: The main station office building and covered cab stand near the main entrance, as seen from Great Central Road in 1989. Today Leicester Central station buildings enjoy listed status and limited development is only allowed by the businesses which now own or rent its premises. *Date: 22 April 1989.*

2: Close-up of the gateway and façade to the parcels offices. *Date: 22 April 1989.*

3: The subway to the station in the main booking hall as it is today, which, with the left luggage offices, is used by a company manufacturing specialised cookers for Chinese restaurants. The ceiling plaster and ornate coving around the skylight had only just been removed, due to the fact that it was deemed unsafe. *Date: 22 April 1989.*

4a, b & c: Poignant reminders of bygone days: an old timetable which shows the 'South Yorkshireman's' departure time from platform 6 at 1.17pm still adorns a wall in the booking hall; nearby a notice advises the final withdrawal of all services between Nottingham Arkwright Street and Rugby Central, whilst another in the left luggage office lists charges and conditions.
Date: 22 April 1989.

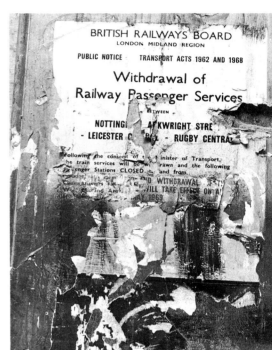

BRITISH RAILWAYS LEICESTER CENTRAL 15th Jun
13th ber in
TRAIN DEPARTURES
WEEKDAYS

RAILWAYS BOARD LE LUGGAGE
ARGES AND CONDITIONS

Leicester Central station (4)
140 SK 581044

Seen from the south side of the Welles Street bridge, Stanier Class 5 4-6-0 No 44717 leaves Leicester Central with the 11.15 Nottingham–Marylebone. The lines curved quite sharply out of the station and converged near the south signal box some 200ft from the end of the platform.

By this date the preponderance of ex-LMS and BR Standard class locomotives was obvious; the ex-LNER types were gradually displaced and seldom seen after the spring of 1963, following transfer of control from the Eastern to the Midland Region in February 1958. *Photo: Horace Gamble. Date: 29 August 1964.*

In the fading light of a spring evening this photograph, taken from a pair of steps placed in the car park of the Private Patients' Plan office in Talbot Lane, shows a remaining buttress of the bridge over Welles Street, the steel deck having since been removed for scrap. The main station area has given way to a series of industrial units constructed in its centre, but the last remains of the platform's southern portion survives near the willow tree on the left.

South of this location the bridge over the junction of St Augustine and West Bridge Street has been removed, as has the one over Corah Street. The southern abutment of the latter marks the commencement of The Great Central Way, a cycle path and walkway created from the formation of the line, which extends from here to the city boundary at Blue Bank lock on the Grand Union Canal. Access at the northern end is made from steps off Duns Lane onto the remaining portion of the viaduct. The girder bridge over Western Boulevard survives and is surprisingly painted in various shades of green, blue and cream. *Date: 19 May 1989.*

A view looking north through the girder bridge over Western Boulevard to a point abutting Corah Street, which marks the northern limit of The Great Central Way. *Date: 25 October 1988.*

85
Leicester Central station (5)
140 SK 581044

A classic panorama of the station taken from Leicester South Passenger signal box shows V2 class 2-6-2 No 60961 collecting some vans from one of the bays, as it prepares the 11.15 Nottingham–Marylebone train.

In the background the Maxim buildings of G. Stibbe & Co Ltd were a familiar backdrop in many photographs taken at Leicester Central. The Welles Street bridge is in the immediate foreground.
Photo: Horace Gamble. Date: 20 June 1964.

Travelling back in time is relatively easy from this office — and an everyday occurrence, right round the clock! The office has been built on the trackbed immediately south of Welles Street in Talbot Lane and is occupied by Private Patients' Plan, the health care specialists. Note the old station offices and the Maxim buildings are just visible through the windows. *Date: 19 May 1989.*

COMMENT: *The office staff of PPP could not have been more helpful and co-operative, having to endure the inconvenience of a tripod-mounted camera placed at or on their workstations, whilst various attempts were made to secure this shot.*

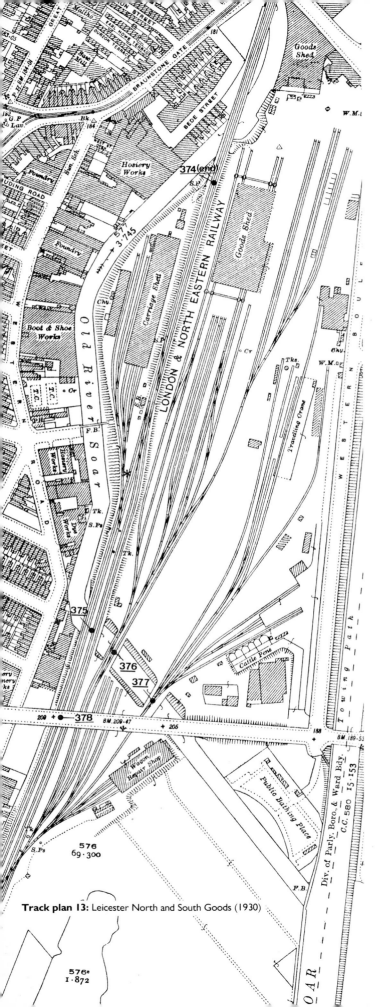

Track plan 13: Leicester North and South Goods (1930)

Leicester North Goods yard
140 SK 579036

The former Leicester North Goods yard is now the location of Vic Berry's well-known scrapyard, which takes up the greater portion of it. The company is one of the largest breakers of British Rail locomotives and rolling stock in the country. Access to the site is gained via a spur from the Leicester to Burton line, which links in with one of the old sidings near the former Leicester Central shed.

This sad photograph taken in rapidly failing light shows locomotives looking like no more than discarded toys; various classes of diesel-electric locomotives are stacked to form a tidy pile, as if to form a funeral pyre, whilst they await the breaker's torch. The types represented include Classes 20, 25, 26, 45 and a DMU power coach. Note the former railway goods shed and warehouse beyond; this is a building which has been listed as desirable for retention when the area is to be redeveloped, as has the old wagon repair shop to the south of Upperton Road. *Date: 25 October 1988.*

Postscript: Vic Berry's scrapyard forms the northern part of an area known as Bede Island, which was scheduled for redevelopment over the course of the next few years, but the plans put forward in 1990 have been shelved for the foreseeable future, due to the depressed economic climate. If redevelopment plans eventually go ahead, Berry's yard would relocate and the company has, in principle, agreed to a move to an alternative location. The company has bought a 117-acre green field site at Newton Unthank, near Desford, some seven miles from here and is near the former Desford Junction, where the Leicester–Swannington line met the Midland's from Knighton Junction. However, the scrapyard is unlikely to move over the course of the next two or three years at least; any plans for such were not helped when a severe fire occurred on their premises in April 1991, believed to be caused by arson perpetrated by children.

The Bede Island area extends to some 86 acres from Western Boulevard in the north, to the proposed Evesham Road/Saffron Lane link road in the south, provisionally programmed to be constructed in 1995/8. The area's proposed redevelopment planned a mixture of residential properties, retail outlets and industrial units, but a portion of it would have been devoted to providing an attractive local recreation area using the Grand Union Canal and River Soar as an important feature. In addition, the creation of a variety of leisure activities, like an entertainment complex and sports hall facilities, would have formed part of the scheme. The Great Central Way is likely to remain largely unaffected by any future redevelopment, save an underpass constructed where it would cross the proposed southern link road.

Leicester South Goods Junction
140 SK 577032

Access to Leicester Central shed was made from points off the goods loops near the Leicester South Goods signal box, located roughly halfway along the 26 chains that separated Upperton Road bridge on the north side, and the Midland's Leicester–Burton line in the south. The rear of the shed itself overlooked the junction of the Grand Union Canal and the River Soar.

One of the two rebuilt Jubilee 4-6-0s, No 45735 *Comet*, crosses the goods loop running parallel to the main line and leaves the shed sidings. The end of Leicester South Goods signal box is just visible on the extreme right, whilst the shed can be seen in the background behind the large pylon, which featured in many photographs of the shed area. Note the coaling stage, known to enginemen as 'hungry hill', seen over the engine's tender. *Photo: Horace Gamble. Date: 2 November 1963.*

Although the pylons have remained untouched by the passage of time, very little else seems to be the same, especially on the skyline. The coal gasworks has gone, as have the two gasometers, which have been replaced by a single but much larger one. The expansion of Gimson's timber yard is evident: many hundreds of 'sets' now cover the area and encroach on the former sidings.

Between the hedge and the timber yard fence, is the spur from the MR Leicester–Burton line, leading to Vic Berry's scrapyard. The two cyclists are riding on The Great Central Way's path, which has been laid directly over the course of the old up line. *Date: 9 October 1989.*

87
Leicester Central shed
140 SK 578029

The photographer catches a quiet moment outside Leicester shed, where Jubilee 4-6-0 No 45594 *Bhopal* is caught basking in the sun, awaiting another turn of duty. The brick-built shed was small by comparison with others on the GC: it had four roads and was 300ft long by 97ft wide, with the offices, stores, mess room, smiths' and machine shops taking almost half of its area. A turntable was located immediately on the south side of the shed, the siding of which was sandwiched between the coaling stage and the shed roads.

Depending on size, the normal complement of the shed was twenty-one locomotives, which worked mainly local freights and passenger trains, including the express workings between Leicester and Marylebone. From the earliest days, the standards achieved by crews were consistently high and such was the skill of many Leicester enginemen that their reputation was second to none. The shed closed in July 1964. During the last year of its life, it was coded 15D. The code under the Eastern Region was 38C, but changed to 15E when the Midland Region assumed control in 1958. *Photo: Horace Gamble. Date: 21 June 1963.*

This view of the two pylons was obtained by the good offices of the Gimson Timber Group, which now owns the site of the former shed and much of the associated area. As the area had been completely given over to their storage, the yard foreman kindly arranged for a sideloader to remove several sets of timber in order that the pylons could be viewed through the camera.

Although the shed and various artefacts, including the turntable, remained when Gimson's bought the site following closure of the line, today there is no trace of it or anything else left; the only items that are visible are the few air raid shelters adjacent to it, that were constructed during the war. *Date: 24 May 1990.*

88 (Opposite)
Leicester South Goods
140 SK 577029

Seen from Bridge 379 carrying the MR's Leicester to Burton line over the GC is the immaculately turned out A3 Pacific No 4472 *Flying Scotsman* as it restarts the Stephenson Locomotive Society's 'Great Central Rail Tour' train, after taking on water at Leicester South Goods. The water column can be observed near the group of people standing about halfway along the train on the down passing loop. On the extreme right in the middle distance is Leicester South Goods box, just beyond which is the spur to the shed and coaling plant. Upperton Road bridge (No 378) can be seen in the distance, under which the South Goods sidings passed, terminating on the canal bank just beyond. The wagon repair shop was located off a spur this side of the Upperton Road bridge.

The building on the extreme left is an iron foundry. The houses that back on to the line are those in Western Road, the residents of which often complained about the smoke created by engines making typically rapid Great Central type starts as they accelerated away from Leicester: this covered any washing which might have been hung out to dry with black soot. These complaints sometimes prompted the more mischievous drivers to encourage their firemen 'to lay it on a bit thick' as they passed here! *Photo: Horace Gamble. Date: 18 April 1964.*

The extent of the path that now forms The Great Central Way can be gauged by this study. Leicester City Council has done a fine job in providing such a pleasing amenity created from the former line, which is considered an advantage by local inhabitants who either wish to cycle in safety, or to walk almost into the city centre from the outskirts.

The foundry and the houses in Western Road have changed little, and Upperton Road bridge remains untouched. Plans are in the offing to re-introduce passenger workings on the Leicester to Burton line, but this is not likely to commence before 1992. *Date: 9 October 1989.*

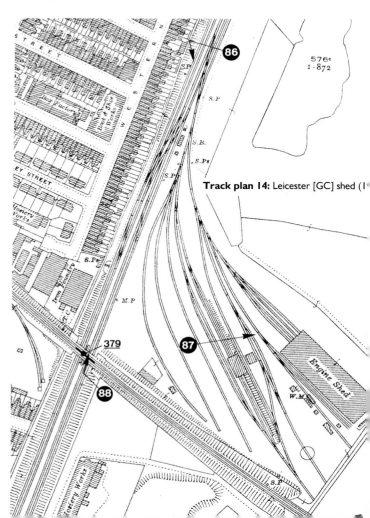

Track plan 14: Leicester [GC] shed (1

89
Leicester – Marlow Road: Bridge 380
140 SK 575025

Leaving the South Goods yard, the line passed through a shallow cutting which extended to the outskirts of the city near to the point where it re-crossed the River Soar at Aylestone.

This shot taken from Evelyn Drive/St Mary's Hill road bridge (No 381) shows BR Class 9F 2-10-0 No 92068 with an up 'runner' for Woodford Halse, seen passing under the bridge carrying Marlow Road, and it is about to cross over the trailing points that signify the end of the goods loop and sidings that stretched from Leicester North Goods. This was a modification to the original layout, since both the lines on the right were constructed as sidings with buffers located just beyond the bluff in the foreground; at that time the main line was only rejoined adjacent to the South Goods box, some 39 chains north from this point.

No 92068 was withdrawn from service in January 1966.
Photo: Barry Hilton. Date: 23 May 1957.

The only remaining clues to the location are the terraced houses in Marlow Road. The cutting has been filled in and the well-lit path of The Great Central Way weaves between the two bridges, which survive, although only the parapets are visible. The bridge to the south of this position marks the point at which Evesham Road crossed the line, and it is from here that a new link road is planned to meet with Saffron Lane, just over a half-mile or so to the east.

The link road will have a spur from it to provide southern access to the proposed Bede Island development. This will be laid using part of the Great Central's formation — the cutting having been re-excavated here — and will extend beyond Marlow Road, which will involve the demolition of a small industrial development, then passing under the Leicester to Burton rail bridge, just seen in the original photograph.
Date: 9 October 1989.

90
Aylestone – Bridge 386
140 SK 568009

Just south of Leicester, the line crossed the Soar Valley on a ¾-mile bank, and the penultimate crossing of the Grand Union Canal was made here at Aylestone. This was one of the more aesthetically pleasing locations to photograph trains on the GC's London Extension, this photographer being no mean exponent.

Crossing the canal with the 17.15 Nottingham–Marylebone semi-fast train is Stanier Class 5 4-6-0 No 45289, which is making a fair amount of smoke as it accelerates towards Whetstone, where it will start the long haul up the 1:176 bank to Ashby Magna station and the summit beyond. In less than a month, with the imminent cessation of all through services, the children on the river bridge near the canal will no longer be able to enjoy the spectacle of steam engines plying their trade on the line. For the next few years the only regular passenger trains that will run past here will be DMUs operating the service between Nottingham (Arkwright Street) and Rugby Central. *Photo: Horace Gamble. Date: 16 August 1966.*

Although the embankments of the formation are somewhat overgrown on either side, the bridge remains in very good condition and now carries The Great Central Way southwards towards Whetstone, where it terminates at Blue Bank lock on the Grand Union Canal, which marks Leicester's city boundary.

Caught in the last glimmers of the evening's light — and by sheer coincidence — two children stopped on the bridge close to the position adopted by those in 1966, to enjoy a rest whilst out cycling on the canal's towpath; photographer's luck more than good judgement! *Date: 5 November 1989.*

Proposed light railway system for Leicester city

In May 1990 Leicester City Council announced that it had commissioned a feasibility study into providing the city with a light railway system or tramway which would link the centre with both the northern and southern outskirts.

The initial study included looking at the possibility of using much of the Great Central's formation to carry the railway towards the heart of the city. The plan included the creation of a park-and-ride station near Junction 21 of the M1 motorway at a point just north of Blaby and Whetstone. From a point just south of Aylestone the light railway would have then utilised the GC's route to a point near the former North Goods yard, before diverting towards the city centre using public roads. After passing through the heart of the city it would have rejoined the old line formation at a point near Blackbird Avenue, having come from the centre via St Margaret's Way. The light railway would have then continued along the formation with a view to terminating at Belgrave & Birstall near the site of the station on the preserved portion of the Great Central, which is being rebuilt as 'Leicester North'.

The study was completed by the late autumn of 1990, but the LRT scheme was subsequently found not to be viable for a variety of practical and political reasons, so the idea was abandoned for the time being. The most important reason for its abandonment was the unlikelihood that any Central Government finance would be made available for a light railway, as several similar schemes had been refused financial help (it was only after a long delay caused by political indecision that Sheffield finally got the go-ahead and some government funding for its LRT system). In addition, there were logistical reasons which prevented what remains of the Great Central's former route being used, particularly on the northern parts of the city, due to much of its removal and the difficulties that would be encountered in getting wayleave rights. It is therefore likely that The Great Central Way will remain as it is for many years to come and, sadly, not destined to see trains run over part of its former route through Leicester — at least in the foreseeable future.

Map 27: Aylestone (1904)

91
Whetstone
140 SP 556977

After leaving Aylestone, then passing through a series of short cuttings south of the village, the GC was carried on girder bridges over the River Sence, and for the last time, the Grand Union Canal. Having crossed the canal and river, the GC passed over the Midland's (ex-LNW) Leicester–Nuneaton–Birmingham line, situated just to the north side of Whetstone, at which point it climbed for the next seven miles at 1:176.

Whetstone, a pleasant village on the southern outskirts of Leicester, was blessed with its own station — again of typical London Extension design and similar in most respects to many others on the line. Goods handling facilities were of moderate size, with fairly extensive sidings located off both the up and down sides. Coal and latterly cement were the chief commodities handled here; the station's goods yard was also initially provided with both cattle and horse docks.

Seen entering Whetstone from Leicester is B1 class 4-6-0 No 61186 with the 12 noon service to Woodford. Note the substantial stationmaster's house on the right of the picture. *Photo: M. Mitchell. Date: 25 March 1961.*

This new development has a typically twee eighties name of Spinney Halt — off Station Road, of course! At first glance there is nothing to which one can relate to yesteryear's scene: certainly no B1 nor island platform remain, but close inspection will reveal the chimney stacks of the former stationmaster's house poking above the new white-painted house on the right.

The estate covers all of the station site, plus the goods yards; another casualty was the bridge over Station Road (No 398) which has been demolished and not even the abutments remain, although the embankment north of it does and provides walking facilities for local people and their dogs. *Date: 24 May 1990.*

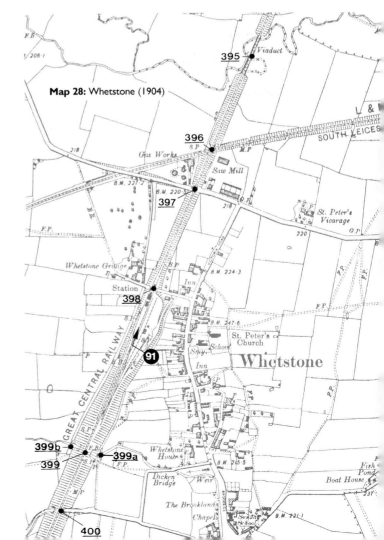

Map 28: Whetstone (1904)

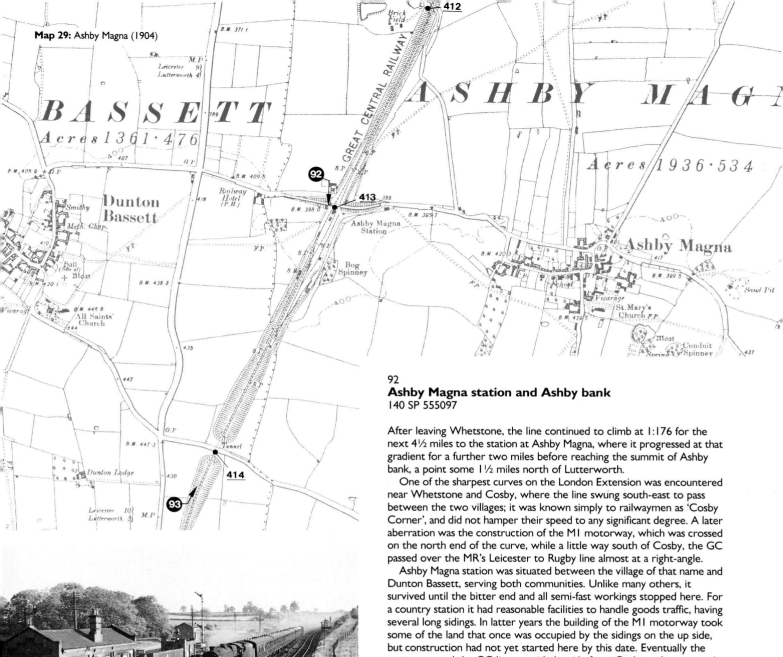

Map 29: Ashby Magna (1904)

92
Ashby Magna station and Ashby bank
140 SP 555097

After leaving Whetstone, the line continued to climb at 1:176 for the next 4½ miles to the station at Ashby Magna, where it progressed at that gradient for a further two miles before reaching the summit of Ashby bank, a point some 1½ miles north of Lutterworth.

One of the sharpest curves on the London Extension was encountered near Whetstone and Cosby, where the line swung south-east to pass between the two villages; it was known simply to railwaymen as 'Cosby Corner', and did not hamper their speed to any significant degree. A later aberration was the construction of the M1 motorway, which was crossed on the north end of the curve, while a little way south of Cosby, the GC passed over the MR's Leicester to Rugby line almost at a right-angle.

Ashby Magna station was situated between the village of that name and Dunton Bassett, serving both communities. Unlike many others, it survived until the bitter end and all semi-fast workings stopped here. For a country station it had reasonable facilities to handle goods traffic, having several long sidings. In latter years the building of the M1 motorway took some of the land that once was occupied by the sidings on the up side, but construction had not yet started here by this date. Eventually the motorway and the GC line ran side by side from Cosby to Lutterworth: a distance of 5½ miles.

Seen arriving at Ashby Magna is a Stanier Class 5 4-6-0 with the 16.25 Marylebone–Nottingham train. Obscured by the signal box in the background is the smoke-filled Ashby Tunnel. *Photo: M. Mitchell. Date: Spring 1961.*

The same view even taken on a fine spring day does little to enhance this bleak scene. The outline of the platform foundations are clearly visible in the paddock formed from the station site. The timber company of Coltman Bros, seen in the background, occupies the site of the goods yard and straddles the main formation; the company manufactures various types of fence panels and farm gates. The cutting to the tunnel beyond the mill is used for storing sets of timber.

The bridge over the railway, carrying the minor road to Ashby Magna from Dunton Bassett, has been backfilled and the parapet on the southern side demolished. A magnificent garden has been created on the trackbed north of the bridge, for a residence that once abutted the railway line here. The formation up Ashby bank to this point remains more or less intact, albeit rather overgrown. Most of the bridges have survived the passage of time, but the underbridge (No 411) at grid reference 140 SP 558914 has been demolished. *Date: 28 October 1988.*

93
Ashby Tunnel
140 SP 551898

Although officially named Dunton Bassett Tunnel, railwaymen knew it as Ashby Tunnel and seldom referred to it in any other way. The tunnel (No 414) was short, being only four chains long, and went under the minor road from Dunton Bassett to Gilmorton.

Having passed through Ashby Magna station, seen beyond the far portal, Class 37 diesel-electric No D6747 emerges with the 10.08 York–Bournemouth cross-country working. *Photo: Tom Boustead.*
Date: 19 June 1965.

Now surrounded by trees and undergrowth which have been allowed to mature over the past twenty-five years, the tunnel is in remarkably good condition and used for the storage of timber by Coltman's. The cutting and the formation south of here towards Lutterworth are reasonably clear and most of the bridges survive intact save Nos 418 and 420, both of which carried minor roads to Gilmorton from the A426. A few yards north from the site of the former, the steps from the up distant signal for Lutterworth are still to be seen at the side of the line's formation.

Although hemmed on either side by the growth of trees and bushes, it is still quite easy to see the route of the GC from the motorway.
Date: 22 September 1989.

LUTTERWORTH — RUGBY

94
Lutterworth — Bridge 422
140 SP 548850

BR Standard Class 5 No 73004 with the 14.38 Marylebone–
Nottingham semi-fast approaches Gilmorton Road bridge north of
Lutterworth station, which is seen in the background. Already some
of the sidings have been lifted, a sure sign that the closure of the line
is imminent.

The newly completed M1 motorway has yet to see any traffic
pass over it. Little did its builders realise the nightmare proportions
of the volume of traffic that would relentlessly course its way along
it some twenty-five years later. Perhaps if the Great Central line is
reborn in the mid-nineties it will take a little of the heavy goods
traffic away from the M1. *Photo: Michael Mensing.*
Date: 22 May 1965.

From the same vantage point today the motorway is partially
shrouded by shrubs and trees, but the sign indicating the turn-off for
Junction 20 is just visible. The factory of Freudenberg (Engineering)
Ltd, which manufactures vibration dampers for the motor industry,
now occupies much of the site of the former goods yard. A large car
park that has been provided for staff, also spans the line formation.
Date: 22 September 1989.

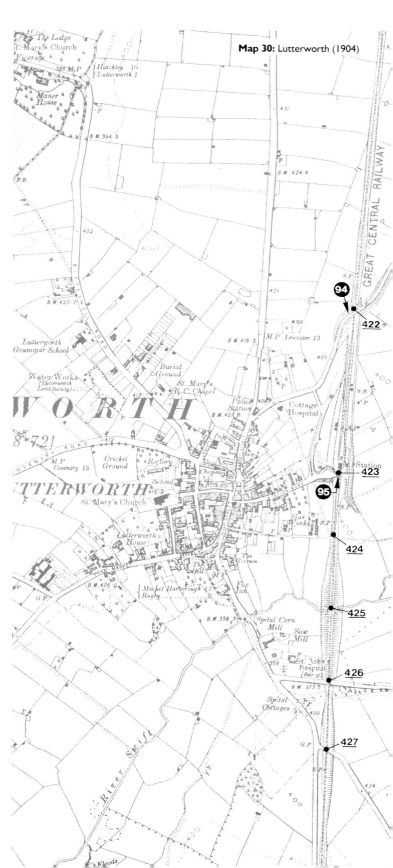

Map 30: Lutterworth (1904)

95
Lutterworth station
140 SP 548843

A view looking north from the end of the platform at Lutterworth station clearly signifies its rather dilapidated condition six months prior to the line's closure. All the sidings in the goods yard have been removed, but a hotch-potch of sheds has been erected on either side of the shunters' cabin.

The steel latticework on the extreme right surrounds the gap between the two spans of Bridge 423, from below which access to the station was gained. *Photo: Andrew Muckley/Ian Allan library. Date: March 1966.*

A housing development that has taken place over the last few years now occupies all of the station site and backs onto the Freudenberg factory. The last vestiges remain of the platform ends either side of the bridge's lattice surround, which still survives.

The line formation immediately south of this point is used by local people walking out with their dogs. Beyond, Bridge 425 over the River Swift still stands, but is not in the best shape. Bridge No 426 over the A427 motorway link road has been demolished: this was of restricted headroom and tall lorries would have had some difficulty in passing under it, if not finding it impossible!

At Shawell the formation is still fairly distinct, although a certain amount of infilling of shallow cuttings has been done in isolated places. Just to the west of Shawell, Flaxleys Bridge (No 433) carrying the minor road to the village from Gibbet Hill on the junction with the A5, has been demolished, but the handsome three-arch Coles Bridge (No 434), just to the south, survives. The trackbed along this stretch is quite walkable, although often wet under foot, as far the demolished bridge (No 437) over the A5 (Watling Street). *Date: 8 September 1989.*

COMMENT: *On seeing a strange man lurking in the bushes, the lady in the house was plainly intrigued as to why her home was being subjected to such close scrutiny, and a rapid explanation was necessary. No doubt she thought my reasons plausible, as the police were not sent for!*

96
Newton (1)
140 SP 533788

A Sunday working in winter: having passed Shawell box on the 1:176 descent towards Rugby, B1 4-6-0 No 61192 approaches a small occupation overbridge near Newton with the 09.30 Sheffield–Swindon service.

The train has just crossed over the A5 road bridge, and in the distance Bridge 434 at Shawell is just visible. *Photo: M. Mitchell. Date: 14 January 1962.*

This sad scene is all too indicative of modern thinking on transport policies. Constructed in the late sixties and early seventies, the M6 cut clean across the GC's formation, leaving only a small reminder of the line in that a well-grazed portion of the trackbed is the only evidence, and that disappears under the motorway embankment. On the right, the stunted bush has grown somewhat, in front of which a remnant of a boundary fence post remains.

From the appearance of the heavy transport hurtling along the northbound carriageway — 'Fido' the dog will be lucky and get his dinner on time, and his master will also have his 'sunshine breakfast' delivered!

It is likely that near this point will be located the roll-on roll-off terminal to serve the Midlands, if the Central Railway Group's plan to reinstate the line goes ahead. *Date: 22 September 1989.*

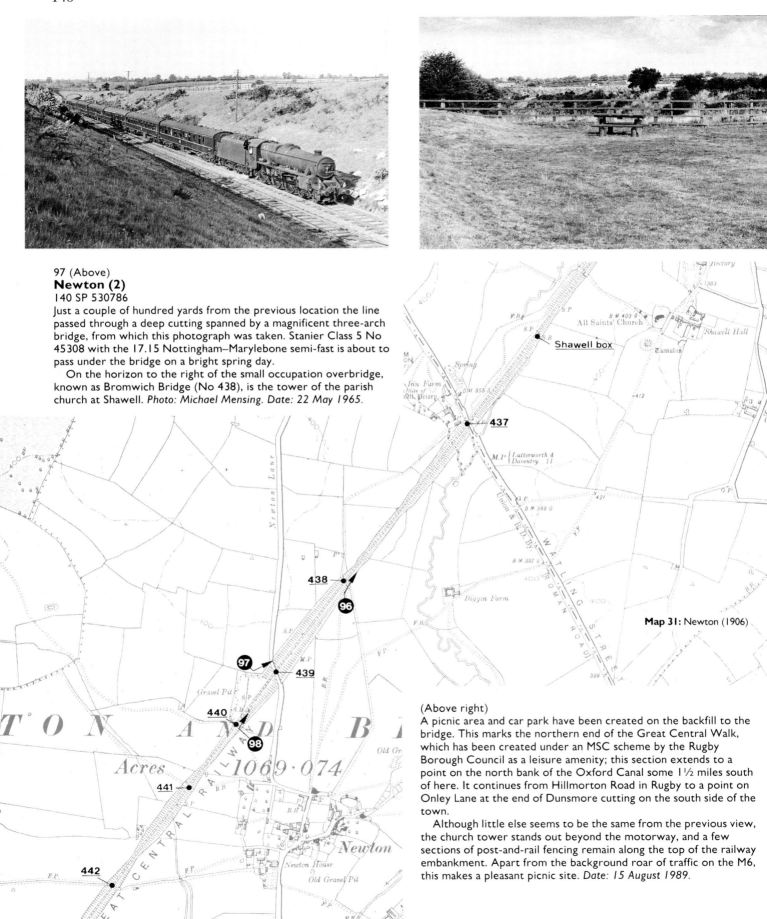

97 (Above)
Newton (2)
140 SP 530786

Just a couple of hundred yards from the previous location the line passed through a deep cutting spanned by a magnificent three-arch bridge, from which this photograph was taken. Stanier Class 5 No 45308 with the 17.15 Nottingham–Marylebone semi-fast is about to pass under the bridge on a bright spring day.

On the horizon to the right of the small occupation overbridge, known as Bromwich Bridge (No 438), is the tower of the parish church at Shawell. *Photo: Michael Mensing. Date: 22 May 1965.*

Map 31: Newton (1906)

(Above right)

A picnic area and car park have been created on the backfill to the bridge. This marks the northern end of the Great Central Walk, which has been created under an MSC scheme by the Rugby Borough Council as a leisure amenity; this section extends to a point on the north bank of the Oxford Canal some 1½ miles south of here. It continues from Hillmorton Road in Rugby to a point on Onley Lane at the end of Dunsmore cutting on the south side of the town.

Although little else seems to be the same from the previous view, the church tower stands out beyond the motorway, and a few sections of post-and-rail fencing remain along the top of the railway embankment. Apart from the background roar of traffic on the M6, this makes a pleasant picnic site. *Date: 15 August 1989.*

Newton (3)
140 SP 529784

Another Sunday working: passing under the other side of the tall three-arch Bridge No 439 at Newton between Shawell box and Rugby, rebuilt Royal Scot 4-6-0 No 46111 *Royal Fusilier* heads towards Marylebone with the 10.10 working from Nottingham.

The bricked recess on the right was designed for housing a signal box to control this section, but in the event it was not used for many years before being demolished.
Photo: M. Mitchell. Date: Spring 1962.

The area is now the northern extremity of the Great Central Walk. The bridge still survives, but like the northern side, was backfilled some years ago and a ramped path now zig-zags down from the road, on the far side of which is the car park and picnic area. In the bushes on the left by the sign is a most attractive pond with a wooden footbridge across it. This has created a small enclave which is a haven for a variety of wildlife, and which local people can enjoy. The walk along the trackbed heading south is easy going for both the able-bodied and disabled as far as the Oxford Canal.

The recess still survives, but there is a subtle difference from the previous view: an extra course of bricks has been laid by the MSC team under the large coping stone. *Date: 22 September 1989.*

Rugby Viaduct – No 451
140 SP 516756

Situated on the north side of Rugby, the girder bridge carried the Great Central over the West Coast main line, which is just visible on the left of the photograph. Seen passing through the bridge, is Standard Class 5 4-6-0 No 73157 returning light engine to Woodford.

Three chains south of the bridge, points led to a couple of sidings, one of which was provided with pens for the unloading of cattle. The beasts would then be driven down Chester Street to the nearby market in the town.

The viaduct beyond the bridge spanned the flood plain of the River Avon and Oxford Canal. The line was then carried north on a high embankment to a massive girder bridge of 110ft spanning the canal. *Photo: P. H. Wells. Date: 17 October 1964.*

The tarmac area in the foreground, which was once garden allotments, now forms part of the playground of St Andrew's Church of England Middle School.

Two spans of the bridge still survive over the West Coast main line; the bridge was recently surveyed and passed fit to carry heavy goods traffic. In latter years it has become known to many as the 'Birdcage', but was by all accounts not referred to as such by GC railwaymen, to whom it was simply known as the 'girder bridge' — at Rugby. The term 'birdcage' was, however, frequently used to describe a similar bridge on the Midland line in Leicester, so it is likely that the two were confused at some stage. In any event, it is a simple case of 'a rose by any other name'!

The viaduct and embankment as far as the canal on the north side of the bridge have recently been demolished and the area vacated now provides space for a small industrial estate. The roofs of two factory units built there can be seen on the left; these are in Great Central Way, so the line is remembered and not totally forgotten. *Date: 15 August 1989.*

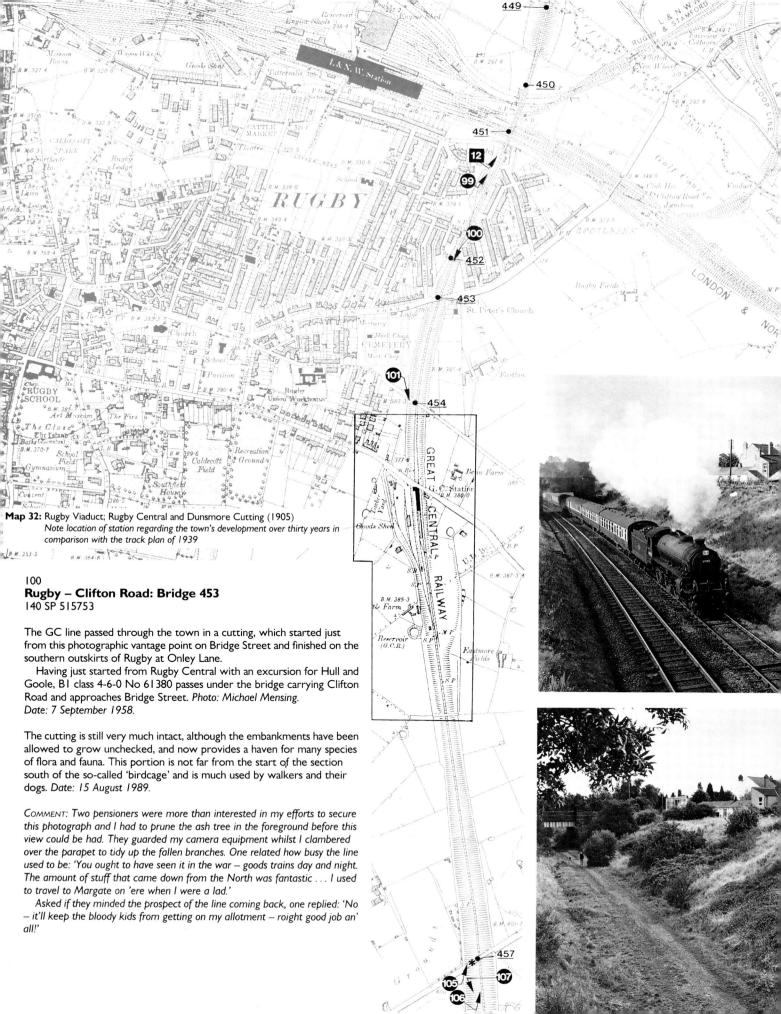

Map 32: Rugby Viaduct; Rugby Central and Dunsmore Cutting (1905)
Note location of station regarding the town's development over thirty years in comparison with the track plan of 1939

100
Rugby – Clifton Road: Bridge 453
140 SP 515753

The GC line passed through the town in a cutting, which started just from this photographic vantage point on Bridge Street and finished on the southern outskirts of Rugby at Onley Lane.

Having just started from Rugby Central with an excursion for Hull and Goole, B1 class 4-6-0 No 61380 passes under the bridge carrying Clifton Road and approaches Bridge Street. *Photo: Michael Mensing. Date: 7 September 1958.*

The cutting is still very much intact, although the embankments have been allowed to grow unchecked, and now provides a haven for many species of flora and fauna. This portion is not far from the start of the section south of the so-called 'birdcage' and is much used by walkers and their dogs. *Date: 15 August 1989.*

COMMENT: *Two pensioners were more than interested in my efforts to secure this photograph and I had to prune the ash tree in the foreground before this view could be had. They guarded my camera equipment whilst I clambered over the parapet to tidy up the fallen branches. One related how busy the line used to be: 'You ought to have seen it in the war – goods trains day and night. The amount of stuff that came down from the North was fantastic . . . I used to travel to Margate on 'ere when I were a lad.'*

Asked if they minded the prospect of the line coming back, one replied: 'No – it'll keep the bloody kids from getting on my allotment – roight good job an' all!'

Rugby – Hillmorton Road: Bridge 455
140 SP 513749

Passing between the two bridges of Hillmorton Road in the background and the one over Lower Hillmorton Road from which this shot was taken, is Class 5 4-6-0 No 45215 with the 14.38 Marylebone–Nottingham Victoria semi-fast.

Rugby Central station is in the background and accessed from the road. The main station building was built on the bridge and a cab rank was provided at its entrance in the form of a small lay-by. *Photo: Michael Mensing. Date: 24 April 1965.*

Despite the weather being vile and pouring rain making lighting conditions difficult for photography, it is still easy to see that the cutting between the two bridges is remarkably clear of obstructions, save for the bushes on the embankment. Conversely, the view from the other side of the bridge looking north is not so good, as there is a considerable amount of undergrowth and trees on the cutting sides.

The platform of Rugby Central station in the background is in pristine condition, having been done up under an MSC scheme. A ramp for the disabled, providing easy access to the trackbed from Hillmorton Road, was also constructed. *Date: 7 November 1989.*

The view looking back towards Bridge 454 from Hillmorton Road, and the access point to the cutting on the north-west corner of the bridge. *Date: 7 November 1989.*

102
Rugby Central station
140 SP 515744

A good view of Rugby Central is to be had in this shot, which shows the layout of the station quite clearly. The platform was 600ft long and extended just a fraction beyond the A428 Hillmorton Road bridge, on top of which the station booking office was built. Entrance to the goods shed, seen in the background behind the water column, was gained via sidings on the down side; the points were set some 11 chains south of the platform end, where a crossover also facilitated access from the up side. The line in the foreground was the only siding-cum-loop provided on the up side and extended from points on the north face of the bridge for twenty-four chains south, where it was exited.

With steam leaking from all joints, filthy Class 5 4-6-0 No 45126 waits in the down passing loop, having deposited its passengers shortly after its arrival from Nottingham with a local train.
Andrew Muckley/Ian Allan library. Date: March 1966.

The platform is in remarkably good condition, having received recent attention under an MSC scheme. The Borough Council deemed it wise to reinstate the edging and resurface the platform to lessen the chance of pedestrians using the Great Central Walk hurting themselves should they trip on an uneven and broken tarmac surface. *Date: 16 August 1989.*

COMMENT: *Whilst photographing here, an ex-Midland Region driver stopped to chat. His latter duties included driving the Rugby Central–Nottingham DMU service from 1966 to 1969, when it ceased; he then retired. One of the problems experienced was the remoteness of this station in relation to any help, should the DMUs ever have trouble. In the winter, as a precaution against drivers being unable to start the engines the following morning, they often saw fit to leave them running all night long. A sure temptation for vandals, but apparently nothing untoward ever happened.*

1: Rugby Central station site as it was in August 1987 before the MSC scheme restored the platform to the condition it is in today, but the old goods shed and warehouse still proudly proclaims its origins. A timber company now uses the building and adjacent site.

2: A present-day view of the station from the site of the booking office on Hillmorton Road clearly shows the good condition of the platform. The area on the down side has been allowed to fill with water and now is well stocked with pond life. An officer of the Nature Conservancy Council is seen making a study of the species that now live there. *Date: 16 August 1989.*

3: Close-up of former goods shed. *Date: 16 August 1989.*

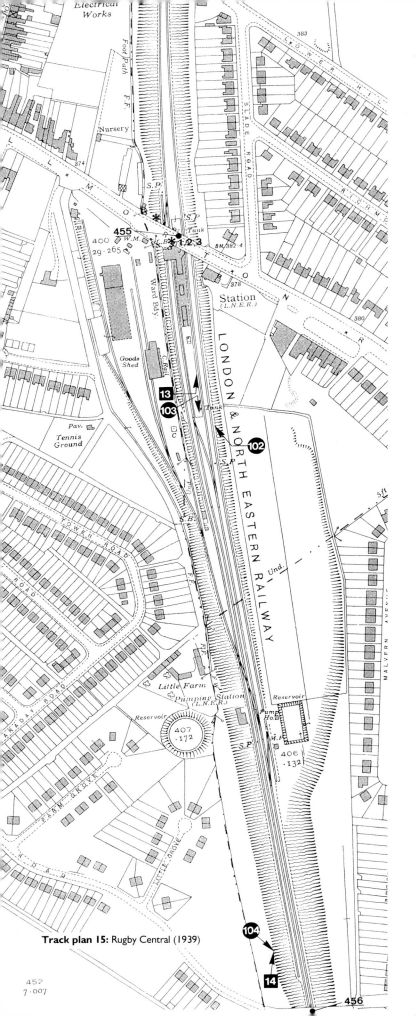

Track plan 15: Rugby Central (1939)

103
Rugby Central goods yard
140 SP 515744

A superbly atmospheric photograph taken from the end of Rugby Central's platform looking due south along the goods yard sidings towards Bridge 456 some 27 chains distant, carrying the footpath between Pytchley Road and Catesby Road. A prominent feature at Rugby was the large brick-built water tower supporting a steel reservoir tank, seen on the right.

This unhurried scene shows a Leicester–Woodford pick-up goods with Class J39 0-6-0 No 64747 in charge, having waited in the up loop for a 'runner' to pass, hauled by Annesley 9F class 2-10-0 No 92033 seen disappearing into the distance beyond the bridge. A Class B1 4-6-0 waits in the down loop prior to its next turn of duty on an 'ord': a term used by GC railwaymen for a long-distance stopping train. Meanwhile a ganger uses a lid from one of the enamelled cans as a receptacle to sample some water, which is to be delivered by the guard of the pick-up goods to the signalman at Braunston & Willoughby box which had no mains supply of its own. *Photo: Dr G. C. Farnell. Date: September 1961.*

A total contrast on a foul autumn day twenty-eight years later. Rain clouds blow in from the south-westerly direction and unleash their entire contents as if to unburden themselves solely upon the photographer, doing nothing to facilitate the task in recording this rather dismal scene. However, a few mature trees in the distance, the tennis court fence and the roofs of the houses in Malvern Avenue signify that the area is the same.

Given fine weather, the walk along the trackbed from here is most enjoyable. There is plenty to see in terms of wild flowers, also a large variety of butterflies and birds that the area now attracts.
Date: 7 November 1989.

104
Rugby – Bridge 456
140 SP 514740

Bridge 456 near the Browns Estate marked the southern end of the goods yard. The white paint was daubed on the parapet to aid a driver's view of the signals placed at the end of the up loop and siding.

Class 9F 2-10-0 No 92120 drops down the 1:176 grade to duck under the bridge with a long part-fitted freight, which included several steel flats. *Photo: Michael Mensing. Date: 22 July 1961.*

This shot illustrates some of the problems involved in facsimile photography. Although not apparent from this view, the bridge is totally intact — even to the white paint still adorning its northern parapet. Careful study will reveal a chimney of a house just to the right of the oak tree, which has grown somewhat over the years. *Date: 24 October 1989.*

105
Rugby – Dunsmore cutting: north end
140 SP 515732

On the extreme southern outskirts of Rugby, a magnificent view is had from Bridge 457 carrying the B4429 road to Dunchurch and shows the splendour of the deep cutting through which the GC line ran.

Seen approaching the bridge on a fine Whit Monday afternoon is 'The Fish'. This previously published photograph portrays one of the more appropriately named freight workings on the line, being the Hull–Plymouth fish train, hauled as usual by an Immingham K3 class 2-6-0, on this occasion K3/2 No 61950.
Photo: Michael Mensing.
Date: 26 May 1958.

Despite the view now being partly obscured by the tree on the left, the cutting between the two bridges is remarkably clear from 'jungle growth' and is easily accessible to the public wishing to perambulate the Great Central Walk via a series of steps from a car park provided on the south-east side of this bridge.

The houses on the right are those in Percival Road.
Date: 16 August 1989.

A view taken in August 1987 of Dunsmore cutting from the centre of the bridge, looking north towards Bridge 456.

Rugby – Dunsmore Road: Bridge 457
140 SP 516730

Class O1 2-8-0 No 63780 brings a long rake of coal wagons for Woodford down the 1:176 gradient through Dunsmore cutting about ¾-mile south of Rugby Central and passes under the splendid three-arch bridge. *Photo: Michael Mensing. Date: 7 November 1956.*

The long shadows of a late summer's afternoon cast across the trackbed, now well trodden by countless pairs of leather-clad feet, rather than the tyres of coupled steel wheels. The bridge, like all those through Rugby, remains as solid as the time it was built. Perhaps a modern generation of trains will one day pass under its central arch, again to fulfil its original purpose. *Date: 16 August 1989.*

107
Rugby – Dunsmore cutting: south end
140 SP 516731

Some of the most successful engines used on the London Extension for express duties, were the Gresley A3 Pacifics. They responded reasonably well to the GC style of 'brisk' driving, which was a legacy dating back to early days, when the tight timings of express trains demanded much from engines and their crews.

Although GC men lamented the A3s' departure from the route in 1957, their stable mates with which they had shared these duties, the Gresley V2 2-6-2s, had already proved their worth; with their smaller driving wheels they were probably better suited for the fast accelerations that traditionally were part of the driving style associated with the line. B1 4-6-0s appeared on expresses at the same time as the V2s; both were later supplemented by Stanier Class 5s and latterly by BR Standard Class 5s, which also performed well on the semi-fasts and were generally liked by crews.

Looking in the opposite direction from the previous photograph, the 1:176 rising gradient through Dunsmore cutting poses little problem to Class A3 4-6-2 No 60059 *Tracery*, which makes light work of its train of seven coaches and a van as it approaches Rugby Central with the 12.15 Marylebone–Manchester express on a bright autumn afternoon. Bridge 458 can be seen in the distance at the end of the cutting to the rear of the train. *Photo: Michael Mensing. Date: 7 November 1956.*

Although few features, apart from the cutting itself, are instantly recognisable, the two tall trees in the original photograph can be identified and, as one would expect, have grown in stature over the years.

The line formation south of this point is well defined and those using the Great Central Walk will find easy access at Onley Lane, where Bridge 458 has been demolished. Apart from the small Cornbridge occupation underbridge (No 459) a few yards further south, most of the others towards Willoughby remain, including Bridge 460a over the M45, just over a mile from here. *Date: 16 August 1989.*

108
Willoughby Wharf
151 SP 523681

After Dunsmore cutting the line was carried on an embankment to the county border, where it passed from Warwickshire into Northamptonshire at Rains Brook in Onley Fields, and after about a ½-mile further south it crossed over the latter-day M45 motorway on Bridge 460a. The line then skirted an army depot constructed during the war which had its own sidings controlled by a flat-topped signal box; a small WD steam locomotive was used for shunting purposes. At this point, the line ran parallel with the Oxford Canal for 1¼ miles to Willoughby Wharf, where the two diverged.

Approaching Willoughby on the long straight from Rugby is Jubilee 4-6-0 No 45565 *Victoria*, with the 12.25 Nottingham–Marylebone train and is about to pass under Bridge 466 adjacent to the wharf. The course of the Oxford Canal is behind the hedgerow on the extreme right of the picture.

Braunston & Willoughby's distant bracket signal is just visible to the rear of the train. The neatness of the track ballast and concrete drainage covering on either side of the running lines is evident in this photograph. With easy grades and long straights, fast running was generally the norm on this section. *Photo: M. Mitchell. Date: 8 July 1961.*

Not so neat and tidy now, but the line formation, although covered in tall marsh grasses, is quite distinct as far as the eye can see in the distance towards the former army depot, which is now a Borstal for young offenders.

The drainage system here has survived and still efficiently channels water, but most of its covering has been lost or removed: garden walls and pathway material perhaps? A surprising survivor is the bracket signal post, which has defiantly withstood the ravages of time. Will its eventual demise come if the railway is re-laid and it is replaced with a modern electronic equivalent? It would be sweet irony if that were to be the case. *Date: 24 October 1989.*

109
Braunston & Willoughby station
151 SP 524672

The station was situated between the two villages it served on the southern side of the A45 trunk road. Like Culworth and other stations in rural areas, it never enjoyed good trade and was an early casualty, closing on 29 September 1958.

Approaching the dilapidated station with the 16.25 Marylebone–Nottingham semi-fast is K3 2-6-0 No 61973. Although closed three years previously, the station sign has not yet been removed, nor purloined for a private collection. At some time in the past the platform staff had obviously made an effort to ensure that the station looked at its best for passengers, as the remnants of a rose arch are evident surrounding the General Waiting Room door. The weed-strewn sidings and the loading gauge were dismantled shortly after this photograph was taken. *Photo: M. Mitchell. Date: 26 August 1961.*

Not a trace left: the station site is devoid of any railway artefacts and is now a paddock in which these heifers temporarily reside. The line formation for 50 chains south of here to the site of the former 12-arch viaduct over the River Leam is well defined and kept grazed, either by livestock or rabbits. The bridge (No 468) over the A45 Daventry road has been removed and only a portion of the abutments remain. *Date: 24 October 1989*

COMMENT: *The bovine residents were very curious about my presence when I first entered the paddock, and upon spotting a ring through the nose of what appeared to be a well-fed young Angus bull approaching at a rapid trot, without a moment's hesitation I turned tail and made a beeline for the nearest gate at a gallop, vaulting over it to cock a snook and utter expletives at my pursuer in safety. I then realised, much to my embarrassment, these insults were being directed at no more than a cow fitted with an anti-suckling device in her nose . . . so much for my calumny! The offended 'lady' in question is third in the line-up.*

> 'Tis Autumn time in Braunston
> And now the forager swears;
> The cattle rise and listen
> In the valleys far and near,
> And blush at what they hear.
>
> *After Hugh Kingsmill (1889-1949)*

Still remarkably complete, Braunston & Willoughby's up distant signal post still stands beside the formation. *Date: 26 October 1988.*

COMMENT: *A family canal holiday was interrupted, amid much protest from the crew, whilst a quick dash was made up the line formation to take this photograph of the signal post on a dank autumn morning.*

Map 33: Willoughby Wharf and station [Braunston & Willoughby] (1901)

110
Wolfhampcote
151 SP 525649

The passage of the GC through a few miles of East Warwickshire was marked by the beautiful countryside and some notable structures built on this part of the line. These included the viaduct over the River Leam and one near Staverton Road on the border with Oxfordshire, where a signal box was also sited to control the block sections between Rugby, Braunston and Charwelton. The views to be had from the surrounding hillsides in the area provided

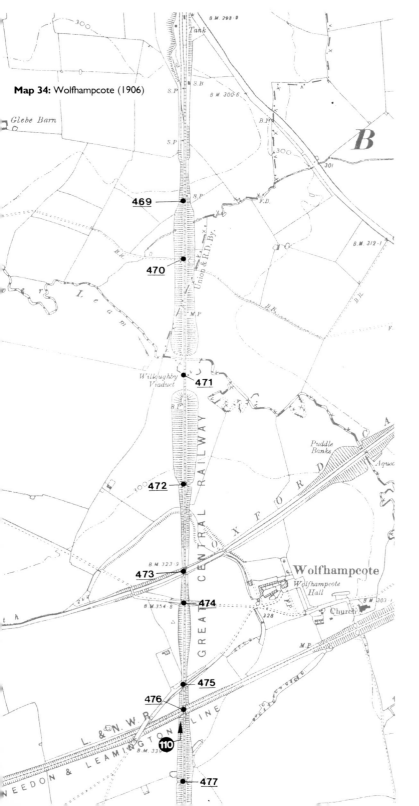

Map 34: Wolfhampcote (1906)

splendid vantage points from which to observe the railway at work and were exploited by many photographers.

Just a mile or so south-west of Braunston village, the line crossed both the Oxford Canal and the former Weedon–Leamington branch of LNWR at Wolfhampcote, noted for its church that holds a service but once a year at Christmas when worshippers even have to bring their own chairs. The area does not have the population to warrant the church's being used more.

With two miles to go before it passes Staverton Road box, BR Class 9F 2-10-0 No 92087 storms up the 1:176 gradient with an up 'runner' for Woodford about to pass over Bridge 476 spanning the defunct Weedon–Leamington branch. It has just crossed the Oxford Canal beyond occupation Bridge 474 in the background, which was rebuilt during the fifties and, rather surprisingly, was fitted with brackets for supporting overhead wires in preparation for possible electrification of the route. Soon the train will be entering the impressive Catesby Tunnel, some 3½ miles from this point. The summit of the climb from Braunston will be reached at Charwelton on the far side of the tunnel, where most express engines 'took a dip' from the water troughs situated on a level stretch of a mile before the 1:176 descent to Woodford Halse. *Photo: M. Mitchell. Date: 20 April 1965.*

Whilst Bridge 474 remains intact, those over the public road to Wolfhampcote from Flecknoe and the branch railway have been removed, together with the embankment in between, enabling a bigger field to be created. Note the dead tree on the right, which has remained standing since the original photograph was taken twenty-four years previously . . . obviously the local farmer is not short of firewood! Staverton Viaduct has been demolished, but the trackbed in the locality is well defined and in generally very good condition.

This area is one of the most tranquil of locations, being fairly inaccessible from the main highway. Protected by cattle grids on the approach roads, animals are allowed to roam freely around much of the parish, so care has to be taken when motoring along the lanes, many of which are unfenced. *Date: 24 October 1989.*

111
Catesby Tunnel (north portal)
151 SP 525596

Half a mile on the northern approach to
Catesby Tunnel a 12 arch viaduct (No 486)
spanned the infant River Leam. Being 3,000yd
in length, the tunnel was the longest on the
London Extension and was built on a rising
grade from north to south at 1:176. An
estimated 30 million bricks were used in its
construction, which was governed by various
restrictive covenants imposed by local
landowners, regarding certain design
parameters, which forced the railway
company to build a tunnel although a cutting
would have been feasible. However, the
contractors, Messrs Thomas Oliver, had little
difficulty in building it and took just over two
years to complete the task. The tunnel was
prone to being rather wet, and water ingress
was occasionally the cause of unwary train
crews poorly protected by open cabs
receiving an impromptu bath, especially if an
engine was running tender-first!

This photograph of the north portal was
taken a year or two before the line was
opened and only a contractor's railway had
been laid through the tunnel to service it.
Although the façade surrounding the portal
has yet to be built, it shows that the tunnel
has already been lined with the Staffordshire
blue bricks that were used to face its roof
throughout. In the background is the historic
Catesby House, which was the meeting place
where the Gunpowder Plot was hatched,
being one of several houses used by Guy
Fawkes and his fellow conspirators.
Photo: Newton collection/Leicester Museums.
Date: c1897/8.

The portal, although partly obscured by trees in this view, is in
remarkably good condition. Following a spell of wet weather, water
can be heard cascading from the roof some way back inside the
tunnel; conversely on a fine sunny day, the far portal can be seen
quite clearly. Catesby House can just be observed through the
trees.

In recent years BR was forced to restrict entrance to the tunnel
and protect the portals with wire barriers to prevent young
persons riding motorcycles through it. On one occasion, a teenage
girl rode her pony through the tunnel, but the animal stumbled into
a drain and caused the rider injury. The parents of the girl
complained to BR about the fact that she was able to ride through
here, which directly resulted in her being injured. BR was obliged to
act and make some effort to ensure that this did not happen again.

The lowest occupation overbridge (No 488), known to BR as
Attenborough No 2, on the line was situated a few chains north of
the tunnel, and still bears the scars of fire irons left on full tenders of
engines, especially having coaled at Leicester, striking the north
arch on the up side. A little way further north Catesby Viaduct still
stands, so far escaping demolition. *Date: 23 October 1989.*

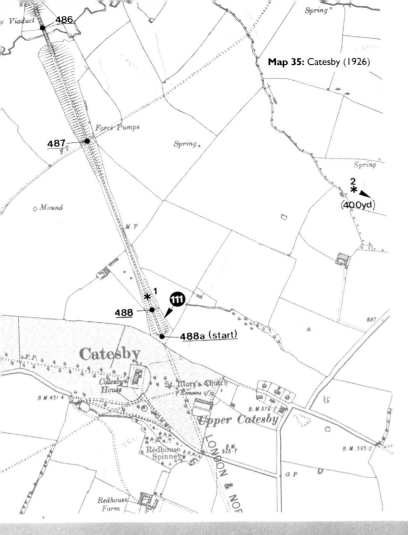

Map 35: Catesby (1926)

1: Bridge 488, the lowest on the line, with the north portal of Catesby Tunnel in the background. Careful study of this photograph, although taken in appalling conditions with heavy rain, will reveal the chipped arch of the bridge. *Date: August 1987.*

2: Set in the heart of glorious countryside on the Northants border, Catesby Viaduct still has a purposeful look about it. Note Shuckburgh Park house in the distance, which is just in Warwickshire. *Date: 25 May 1990.*

Catesby Tunnel (south portal)
152 SP 533569

Class O4 2-8-0 No 63841, in early BR livery, enters the south portal with a down goods train. This photograph is full of interesting detail: note the wonderful variety of tools and implements, including old-fashioned scythes, hanging on the rear of the platelayers' hut. The banks surrounding the tunnel are notably kept trimmed and tidy, topped by a neat post-and-rail fence: a credit to the section's linesmen and more worthy of a country house garden or park than of a railway.
Photo: H. Weston/Ian Allan library.
Date: 14 May 1949.

How things have changed since then! The tunnel mouth is now surrounded by trees and undergrowth. A soggy mass of dead rosebay willowherb covers the embankment in the foreground. The portal itself is in remarkably good condition and the date of its origins still proudly proclaimed above its gaping mouth. Will it be able to gorge on a feast of new trains in the years to come? *Date: 24 October 1989.*

The south portal from the trackbed. Careful study, in the lower left segment of the gate and just below the crossmember, will reveal a chink of light at the other end of the tunnel some 1¾ miles away.
Date: 24 October 1989.

113
Catesby Tunnel cutting (1)
152 SP 534568

What must arguably be one of the finest photographs ever taken on the line shows rebuilt 'Royal Scot' 4-6-0 No 46160, *Queen Victoria's Rifleman* storming out of Catesby Tunnel with an up FA Cup Final special. The match to be held at Wembley that day was between Leicester City and Tottenham Hotspur. The engine has been cleaned for the occasion and even the buffers have been given a coat of white paint.
Photo: T. E. Williams/NRM collection.
Date: 6 May 1961.

Map 36: Charwelton (1900)

In high summer when trees and shrubs are in full leaf, the tunnel mouth is partly hidden by the proliferation of growth in the cutting, but the air shaft on the hill behind still stands clear of obstructions in a field, and will never see smoke billow from its tower again.

British Rail has sold practically all the land it once held on the defunct line, but still retains a few chains between the main A361 road to the tunnel, in order that access can be had to undertake any necessary maintenance for which it is still responsible. However, if somebody is willing to undertake this burden, BR would willingly dispose of the tunnel and sell the remaining few hundred yards of trackbed involved.
Date: 16 August 1988.

114
Catesby Tunnel cutting (2)
152 SP 535565

Another classic study by Ivo Peters, rated by most enthusiasts as the doyen of railway photographers. Unfortunately he paid little attention to the GC and concentrated most of his efforts in recording the Somerset & Dorset line during the last two decades of its existence. He stopped here and at Charwelton only on the one occasion to take a few shots of 'runners' at work whilst on the way to photograph the ironstone lines in the east Midlands.

This photograph shows one such train, as Annesley Class 9F 2-10-0 92091 comes through the cutting from the tunnel with a 'runner' and approaches Charwelton's up outer home signal, which also controlled the loop, and is about to pass under Helidon Road (Bridge 489), beyond which is Charwelton station. The siding on the left was used as a headshunt for the goods yard beyond the bridge. *Photo: Ivo Peters. Date: 7 October 1964.*

Twenty-five years on. At first glance there is nothing much to see, apart from the tethered goat peacefully grazing in the foreground. This is not BR's latest weapon to combat the unchecked growth of the banks, but belongs to a happy band of travelling folk, who had taken up residence in the cutting. Parked on the trackbed near this spot was a fifties-vintage ex-London AEC bus and an old Bedford coach, which many enthusiasts would have appreciated.

Careful study of the photograph will reveal the torched remains of the signal post at the foot of the shadow on the extreme right; also the air shaft tower can just be spotted to the right of the tree on the left. *Date: 24 October 1989.*

COMMENT: *I found this small band of Christian travelling people most hospitable, peaceful and content with their life. Although one does not necessarily agree with their lifestyle, I could not help but sympathise with them regarding the hostility and harassment they receive from the general public, who tar them all with the same brush. Not true.*

115
Charwelton station
152 SP 535563

B16 class 4-6-0 No 61475 passes
Charwelton with a Woodford–
York fitted freight.

The station was again typical in
design of those on the line and
access was gained from Bridge 490
carrying the main A361 road; a
few chains further south was
Bridge 491, just beyond which the
line was on a level stretch where
the water troughs were sited.

The siding, gained from facing
points on the down line opposite
the signal box and branching off to
the right, led through a gate past
Charwelton Hall to an ironstone
quarry some distance away. The
goods yard was provided with
quite extensive sidings to cope
with this traffic, but were not used
in latter years, the quarry having
been worked out.
*Photo: M. Mitchell. Date: 27 May
1961.*

The station area has been
completely cleared of all railway
artefacts, but remains surprisingly
free of rubbish and undergrowth.
Bridge 490 has been demolished
and the A361 road flattened out
and widened in this area.

The line formation just south of
the road is still fairly distinct and
between Bridges 491 and 492,
which still stand, the remnants of
the water trough drainage
channels can be seen. Just beyond
the short cutting south of Bridge
492, a small building and water
troughs' tower still stand; this is at
the northern end of what was
Woodford's 'new' yards, which
now forms two large fields. *Date:
23 October 1989.*

A view looking north from the site
of Woodford's 'new' yards today.
Note the remains of the water
troughs' tower in the distance.
Date: 25 May 1990.

116

Woodford Halse MPD

152 SP 542531

The extent of the shed area can be gauged well from this atmospheric photograph taken during a lull in activities. Austerity class 2-8-0s seem to predominate: those present include Nos 90299 and 90297. Also on shed is B1 4-6-0 No 61368, in addition to which two K3 class 2-6-0s, Nos 61843 and 61960, are in residence. An unidentified ex-LNER L1 class 2-6-4 tank lurks behind the squat building being the dry sand bin, beyond which is an engineers' machine shop. Just visible on the extreme left is the carriage and wagon repair shop, at the north end of which a traverser was located to facilitate handling in and out of the works, behind which the up and down main lines ran. *Photo: Ivo Peters. Date: 25 May 1963.*

The area the shed and wagon repair shops once occupied now is a small modern industrial estate. The bridge over Byfield Road (No 496) has been demolished and access to this estate is made via a new road named 'The Great Central Way' entered from the position once occupied by the former bridge, whose abutments have also been removed.

On the south side of Byfield Road the area covered by the former exchange sidings of the old yard is now a plantation: thousands of young trees and shrubs have been planted over several acres and have taken the place of many hundreds of coal and freight wagons which were handled here daily.

Not a single item from railway days could be found, apart from a small section of rough ground on the estate upon which some ballast and coal slack remained. The line immediately north of here has been wiped off the map and turned back into farmland. *Date: 23 October 1989.*

Woodford Halse

The coming of the railway saw Woodford's emergence from a small sleepy Northamptonshire village in central England to a thriving railway community of some considerable proportions. The line's construction brought jobs and prosperity to the area; it also brought many newcomers who were directly employed by the railway company and settled here, effectively doubling the population, which peaked in 1931 to 1,700. New homes were constructed to house them and terraced cottages, more often associated with the style of those found in the North, soon became a feature of Woodford.

Being centrally located geographically, with connections to the Great Western's Paddington–Birmingham Snow Hill main line reached at Fenny Compton through Byfield via a junction with the ex-East & West Junction Railway (later to become Stratford & Midland Junction Railway), and a little further south, a junction at Culworth with a double-tracked branch to Banbury, Woodford's role as a major cross-country interchange point for freight and some inter-regional passenger workings was assured.

A large shed sufficient to house thirty locomotives, with provision for thirty more, was built, together with all the necessary accoutrements to service and handle them, such as a turntable, triangle, coaling plant and water towers; in addition, commodious carriage and wagon repair shops were constructed. Located between the locomotive shed and station, extensive exchange sidings and yards were laid on a massive embankment formed by using the spoil excavated from Catesby Tunnel.

Late as 1941 further yards were laid north of the shed to help cope with the enormous increase in freight traffic generated by the needs of war. These were dubbed the 'new yards' and were controlled by Woodford No 1 signal box. No 2 box controlled the north loop of the old yard and entrance to the shed. Woodford had no fewer than four signal boxes to control the yards and junctions.

The station itself was fairly modest and built on the usual island platform principle. Access was gained from the Woodford to Hinton road that ran under the railway. A wooden platform, replaced in 1956 by a concrete version, but thereafter still referred to as the 'wooden platform', was constructed on the down side to handle the local trains to Banbury and Byfield, until these services were withdrawn in 1964. A small goods yard with two sidings and a warehouse was located on the up side adjacent to the main platform.

1. The bricked-up station entrance to Woodford Halse.
Date: August 1987.

2. The former Woodford 'old yard' is now this scrubland planted with trees. *Date: August 1987.*

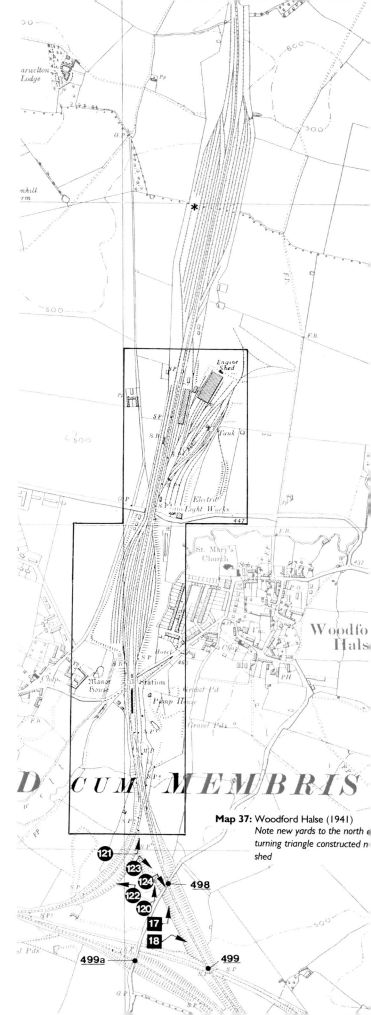

Map 37: Woodford Halse (1941)
*Note new yards to the north
turning triangle constructed n
shed*

117
Woodford Halse exchange sidings and yard
152 SP 541524

A portion of the old yard is seen from the north end of Woodford's platform. An 08 class diesel shunter has caught the eye of the photographer's wife, who raises her camera to record its passage across Bridge 497 with two wagons as it goes about its duties in making up a fitted freight, probably to be hauled by the ex-GWR Class 28XX 2-8-0 No 2857, which waits patiently in the goods loop near the gantry signals before coupling up to its train.

Woodford No 3 signal box, whose roof is seen above the shunter, controlled the old down yard and was only 150yd or so from No 4 box, also known as Woodford Central, situated just off the southern end of the station, which controlled the junction to the S&MJ line and trains received into the section from Culworth.

The large LNER-type coaling stage sited near the MPD dominates the skyline in the background and was a significant landmark in the area. The terraced cottages on the right are those in Sidney Road.
Photo: Dr G. C. Farnell. Date: September 1961.

GWR 2-8-0 No 2857, having spent 11 years and 11 months in Woodham's scrapyard at Barry, has survived the ravages of time and is preserved on the Severn Valley Railway.

However, little else here has been so lucky: the tracks were lifted through Woodford Halse between the late spring and early summer of 1967 and the last vestiges of the platform were removed a few years ago by the present owners of the site. The coaling tower was reluctant to be toppled, and the demolition charges only succeeded in lifting it like a Saturn rocket clear of the ground, before it promptly settled back down again!

Today Bridge 497 remains over the road, although it has lost some of its brickwork on the west side parapet; this was obscured by the wooden hut in the original shot. Beyond the fencing part of the aforestation on the former exchange sidings can be seen. The houses in Sidney Road are now obscured by young trees which over the years have been allowed to grow. At road level the former entrance steps to the station have been bricked up and backfilled to platform level.

Woodford folk still lament the railway's passing and many people remain bitter about its demise. The railwaymen's social club in the village, an imposing building which was formerly the Hinton Gorse Hotel, also known to locals as the 'Goss', still thrives and the casual visitor can still hear members talk affectionately of GC days. They may return yet — albeit in a different form — and that *would* give them something to talk about. *Date: 17 August 1989.*

COMMENT: *This view was totally obscured by elder and ash saplings growing near the bridge parapet, so some difficult pruning had to be undertaken here which necessitated standing perilously on a pair of steps to lean through the top two strands of a barbed-wire fence with a pair of 8ft long pruners. Considerable housing development during 1993/4 at Woodford Halse has encroached the site of the former sidings and yard near the road bridge.*

118 (Opposite)
Woodford Halse station (1)
152 SP 540523

Ivatt Class 4MT 2-6-0 No 43144, yet to have its headlamp code transferred to the tender, waits at Woodford's down platform with a special Woodford–Calvert working, due to leave at 15.05. Engineering works at Aylesbury meant that through trains were being routed via Banbury.

The platform was fairly modest and only some 375ft in length, but was provided with the usual waiting rooms, booking office and lavatories, which were covered by an adequate canopy to protect passengers. A footbridge at the north end gave access to and from the local services platform on the down side.

Close scrutiny of the photograph will reveal the tower of Woodford's parish church, St Mary the Virgin, the top of which is only just visible between two roof vents of the carriage immediately to the right of the station sign. *Photo: Neil Sprinks. Date: 10 May 1963.*

The station site is now a winter home for travelling showmen, whose caravans and vehicles are kept in a compound, which is surrounded by wooden post-and-rail fencing fronted with young cypress trees planted to screen the area.

Although there is no resemblance to the previous view, the church tower can be seen immediately to the rear of the lorry.
Date: 7 November 1989.

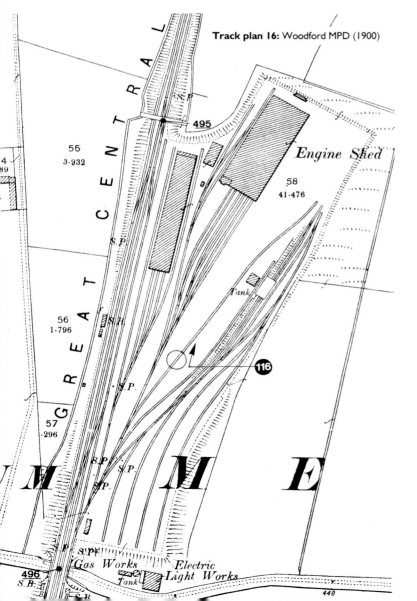

Track plan 16: Woodford MPD (1900)

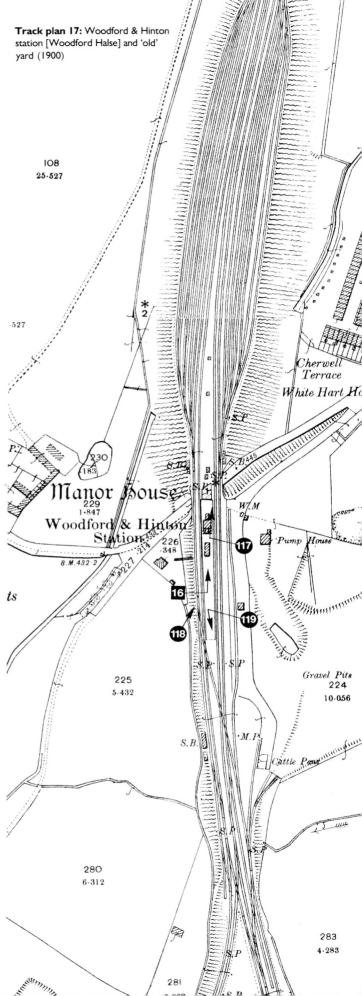

Track plan 17: Woodford & Hinton station [Woodford Halse] and 'old' yard (1900)

119
Woodford Halse station (2)
152 SP 540523

In this view taken from the south end of Woodford's platform, WD Austerity 2-8-0 No 90337 stands in the goods loop on the up side of the station, whilst it waits for the signals to clear before starting off with its train to take the S&MJR line, seen branching to the right a few hundred yards beyond the station.

The main line passed under the handsome three-arch Eydon Road bridge (No 498), which is just visible in the background beyond the locomotive's smokebox. *Photo: Dr G. C. Farnell. Date: September 1961.*

When standing in the same position now, one is at the south end of the showmen's caravan compound, marked by freshly planted trees and tall post-and-rail fencing, but Bridge 498, albeit in shadow, can just be seen between the cypress and the defunct ERF tractor unit. Remnants of the platform foundations are still to be spotted amongst the grass in the foreground and the torched-off base of the bracket signal was found beyond the fence. The odd assortment of private sheds and garages on the edge of the former goods yard on the up side of the station, are also still extant. *Date: 17 August 1989.*

COMMENT: A roaring gale made photography difficult enough, particularly with tree movement, but if it had not been for my travelling companion, fellow author Robert Robotham, holding a cypress back whilst standing out of sight behind the lorry, the bridge would not have been seen at all!

WOODFORD HALSE — HELMDON AND THE BANBURY BRANCH

120
Woodford North Junction (1)
152 SP 541519

Although not officially named as such, but was in effect, Woodford North Junction marked the spur off the main line to Byfield and swung sharply through 120° to join the S&MJ line at Woodford West Junction a few chains round the curve. The junction was controlled by Woodford No 4 box, seen in the background, beyond which a short goods train waits in the down loop near the local platform for the signals to clear before proceeding to Woodford's yard.

Having deposited its goods train in one of the yards, GWR Hall class 4-6-0 No 5992 *Horton Hall* ambles past the junction along the GC's main up line towards Eydon Road bridge, under which it is about to pass on the way back light engine to Banbury via Culworth Junction 1½ miles south-east of this point.

The extensive expanse of the old yard, with hundreds of wagons in the sidings, can be gauged beyond the station in the background.

Above the engine the coaling plant tower sticks out like a sore thumb against the horizon. The dramatic sweep of the main line through the wide cutting past the junction and through the station belied the fact that normal line speed limits applied and that trains did not have to slow down through here. *Photo: Ivo Peters. Date: 25 May 1963.*

Despite the passage of time, the history of the area is still evident as the formation's sweep towards the former station is remarkably well defined.

The pig unit was built in the shadow of the bridge in 1988, so is a relative newcomer to the scene and is farmed as a 'clean' area, so visitors are asked to stay away, especially if they have been near farms with other pigs. In the background the showmen's compound is clearly defined on the site of the station, but in a few years the trees will obscure it from view altogether. It is interesting to note how some of the deciduous trees in the vicinity have grown over the past twenty-six years. *Date: 17 August 1989.*

121
Woodford Halse – North Junction (2)
152 SP 541520

An early view looking towards the junction, with its fine array of signals, taken from the embankment near the S&MJ curve and shows the station in the distance, with the goods yard and warehouse featured in the centre of the photograph. The slow shutter speed of the camera has captured a blurred image of an express train, which is about to enter the station, having come from the south along the GC line and is seen sweeping in from the right.
Photo: Newton collection/Leicester Museums. Date: c1900.

The locality is unmistakable. Friend and fellow author, Robert Robotham, marks the position where he found the sawn-off remains of the telegraph pole, which was on the extreme left in the original photograph. A few spoil heaps, now covered with grass, mark the point of the junction with the main line. *Date: 17 August 1989.*

COMMENT: *Shortly before this shot was taken we were caught by a heavy shower, and took shelter under a prickly blackthorn bush growing on the trackbed of the S&MJ curve to avoid being completely soaked, if not being a little spiked in the process!*

122
Woodford Halse – S&MJ curve
152 SP 540519

GWR Hall class 4-6-0 No 7927 *Willington Hall* swings round the curve from the S&MJ line towards the GC main line with a goods train from the Western Region, having come from the Stratford-on-Avon direction. Woodford West Junction, whose signal box is partly obscured by a tree, is in the background, originally controlled not only this spur, but the southern connection with the GC line at South Junction.

The connection with the GC at South Junction was intended to provide a direct link between Marylebone and Stratford-on-Avon using the S&MJ line through Byfield, but was an early casualty; although the date of its severance from the main line is unclear, it is thought to have been removed during the twenties. Although the points to the GC were taken out, the rails remained in situ and acted as storage sidings off the S&MJ. *Photo: Ivo Peters. Date: 25 May 1963.*

Another example of how pervasive undergrowth can be when trying to take facsimile photographs. The trackbed of the curve is generally well defined, but has a fair amount of growth on its surface. The former West Junction is similarly endowed with vegetation; the whole area is now a haven for scores of rabbits which breed almost unchecked, except for the occasional bouts of myxomatosis which inevitably occur from time to time to control their numbers.

Reference to the area can be judged by the hedgerow lines on the hillside in the distance. *Date: 24 October 1989.*

123
Woodford Halse – Eydon Road: Bridge 498
152 SP 541520

Passing under the central arch of Bridge 498 that carries Eydon Road, Austerity 2-8-0 No 90486 approaches the north junction at Woodford with a down coal train on a cold day in early spring. Ivo Peters' great friend and fellow photographer, Norman Lockett, stands on the embankment and also captures the 'Aussie' on film.

This bridge has been referred to, in typical railwaymen's euphemistic style, as the 'Marble Arch', which would be a most fitting title for this elegant structure, as it is well placed to act as the triumphal gateway to the GC's own Hyde Park Corner. However, there is considerable doubt as to the validity of the name being applied to this particular bridge which has been the cause of much argument at Woodford. Authoritative sources state that the term

was in fact affectionately accorded by railwaymen to a structure at Thorpe Mandeville on the Banbury branch, where it kept company with other bridges referred to by Banbury men as 'Faith, Hope and Charity'. Whatever the mythological answer, the name was not official and therefore it matters little. *Photo: Ivo Peters. Date: 26 March 1963.*

Cast against the light with its north face in shadow, but nevertheless looking every inch a triumphal arch, having stood the test of time, the bridge still stands proudly, not over weed-free railway lines, but over a well grazed cutting. No longer to be heard is the clank of the Austerity's coupling rods, the squeal of flanges or the smell of steam as it rounds the bend to Woodford — only the squeal of pigs, whose contented grunts and a somewhat different odour fill the air today! *Date: 24 October 1989.*

Woodford Halse – Bridge 499
152 SP 541519

A view looking south from the parapet of Bridge 498 on the Eydon road, shows Stanier Class 5 4-6-0 No 45454 crossing over the GC on the bridge carrying the S&MJ line, as it heads a goods train towards Towcester. The long-defunct South Junction was situated a few chains beyond the Bridge 499 in the background. A signal box was built to control it, and a bricked recess constructed to house it on the up side of the main line, but the box was later demolished.

The S&MJ line was upgraded in its latter years to handle heavy goods and steel traffic that threaded its way cross-country from Scunthorpe and Consett via Stratford-on-Avon and Fenny Compton to the finishing mills in South Wales, thus avoiding the bottlenecks of either Banbury or Birmingham. Crews performing such duties on trains carrying steel ingots used to refer to the roster as 'working the door knockers'. The gradients of 1:107 at Byfield and 1:98 near Aston-le-Walls occasionally proved the downfall of some freight engines, particularly the Austerity 2-8-0s, due to their propensity to slip, especially when in charge of a heavy freight up such banks. This occurrence sometimes led to a train being 'lost' in the section for anything up to three hours, and somebody would then be dispatched to look for it! *Photo: Dr G. C. Farnell. Date: September 1961.*

In this view, the cutting embankments between these two bridges have recently been cleared of undergrowth by a local farmer, who has started to fence sections of it to enable his pigs to enjoy a chance to rootle about on the sides, when they are allowed outside. Note how relatively little the oak tree on the left has changed. The steel deck of the S&MJ bridge has long since been removed and scrapped, but Bridge 499a remains: a magnificent three-arch brick structure that carries the Eydon road over the S&MJ/GC link to the former South Junction. The site of South Junction is well defined a few chains beyond Bridge 499's abutments in the background, although wet under foot; the recess for the signal box is still extant — even after all these years.

From here the formation south towards the former Culworth Junction is remarkably clear due to its use as a farm track. The occupation bridge (No 500), which was positioned at 137 miles 57½ chains from Manchester London Road station, is still standing, as is Bridge 501 carrying the Preston road just beyond; and apart from Bridge 502 over the minor road between Eydon and Canons Ashby, whose abutments only are left, all other bridges to the site of Culworth station survive. Just south of Bridge 502's abutments the remains of Woodford's down distant signal still stand at the side of the formation, but leans at an alarming angle, having been used as a cattle scratching post during the intermediate years! The last vestiges of the signal box at the well-defined site of Culworth Junction can be found on the up side trackbed. *Date: 17 August 1989.*

The concrete post of Woodford's down distant signal leans at an alarming angle, as seen from this shot looking north towards Bridge 501 in the background. *Date: 25 May 1990.*

125
Banbury branch – Thorpe Mandeville (1)
151 SP 512451

The tall and spindly footbridge in the background is widely believed to be the candidate for the title, accorded by GC railwaymen, 'Marble Arch'. It was situated in a deep cutting some 1½ miles west of Thorpe Mandeville village about two-thirds of the way along the branch from Culworth Junction towards Banbury Junction. Was the road bridge in the foreground dubbed 'Charity' by the Banbury men of old, being the third of the virtuously named trio, as railway folklore suggests, of road bridges encountered on the long climb from the junction? The others, of course, being 'Faith' and 'Hope'.

The summit of the six-mile climb from just north of Banbury station was reached in just under 1½ miles from this point and was between the platform halts of Eydon Road, serving Thorpe Mandeville, and Chacombe Road, which served the village of that name. The halts closed on 2 April 1956 and 6 February 1956 respectively.

The well-known link service on the branch between Woodford and Banbury was the domain of the 'Banbury Motor', which is seen here passing under 'Marble Arch' with the typical combination of an ex-LNER L1 class 2-6-4 tank in charge of a two-coach set; this particular train was the 17.00 service from Woodford. These engines were sometimes referred to on the Eastern Region operating out of Liverpool Street on local services as 'Stortford Pacifics', since their wheel arrangement justified the accolade when working bunker first! *Photo: M. Mitchell. Date: 14 April 1962.*

The bridge still stands in reasonable shape — and probably will do so for the next hundred years. There has been a certain amount of backfilling beyond, but it does not extend for more than a few yards. The footbridge has been demolished and no trace whatsoever remains; even the abutments have been removed for some reason.

Note the repaired section of the bridge's parapet, which is still much in evidence: a road vehicle must have damaged it at some time in the past. This wound is probably destined to be visible as long as the bridge stands. A local landowner has cut a track on the embankment in order that farm vehicles can negotiate the cutting with relative ease.

The linesmen's hut seen between the two bridges in the original photograph survives in a dilapidated state at the side of the formation, but the trackbed towards Culworth Junction is well defined, although covered by bushes and trees in parts. *Date: 23 October 1989.*

Map 38: Thorpe Mandeville (1921)

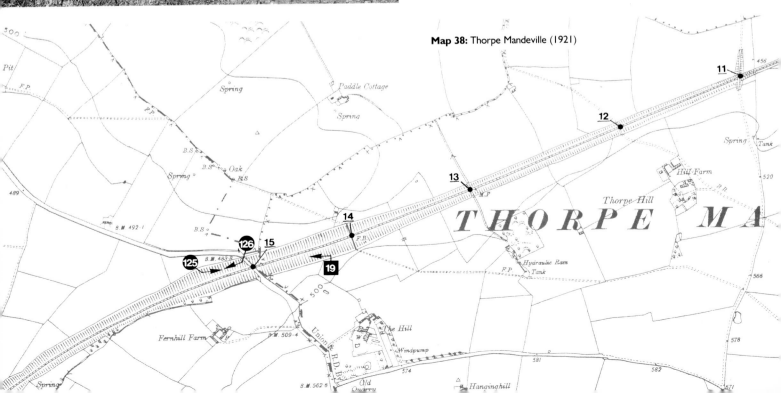

126
Banbury branch – Thorpe Mandeville (2)
151 SP 512451

This view looking in the opposite direction from the same position as the previous photograph depicts the dramatic sweep of the line through the cutting, which shows BR class 9F 2-10-0 No 92000 climbing up the 1:100 gradient from Chacombe Road with a load of coal empties bound for Woodford. *Photo: M. Mitchell. Date: 20 April 1965.*

The cutting sides are inevitably overgrown, but the track formation is clear and occasionally used as a farm track.

From the end of this cutting a few hundred yards away, the formation is carried on a continuous embankment towards Banbury and remains generally well defined, although the banks are lined with young trees. It is virtually intact for several miles, with the exception of two bridges which have been demolished, perhaps by those with with little 'faith' or 'hope' that the link will ever be needed again! The first was the underbridge at

Chacombe Road, adjacent to which there is no trace left of the old platform; the other was under the A361, but this road has recently been diverted and somewhat altered in the immediate area with the advent of the M40 motorway which cuts a ghastly swathe through this magnificent part of the country.

With the forecast that Banbury will transform from a pleasant market town to a thriving industrial centre over the next few years, could this present the Central Railway Group with the opportunity to site a roll-on roll-off terminal here to connect the M40 with the former GC line using the Banbury branch? The chances are remote, as it would be far easier to upgrade the existing BR line from Ashendon Junction, using the grossly under-utilised portion of the ex-GWR main Paddington–Birmingham fast link via Bicester and Aynho Junction, but only time will tell.

Any traces of the junction at Banbury with the 'Gas Works Railway', as GC men derided their rival, north of the town near the convergence of the Oxford Canal and River Cherwell, have to all intents and purposes been obliterated. *Date: 23 October 1989.*

127
Banbury station
151 SP 462406

Having taken over the 10.25 Poole–Bradford train from GWR Hall class 4-6-0, No 6930 *Aldersey Hall*, seen on the right, V2 class 2-6-2 No 60893 waits at Banbury prior to setting off on its journey to the North. It will take a right turn at Banbury Junction, where it will traverse the GC's Banbury branch to Culworth, thence on to Bradford via Woodford, Leicester, Nottingham and Sheffield. An unidentified Hall, with its nameplates removed, waits in the background with its train for another turn of duty. *Photo: Michael Mensing. Date: 6 August 1960.*

Today's version of a cross-country service through Banbury: Class 47 No 47814 gets away from the station with the 'Wessex Scot', one of BR's longest cross-country InterCity services, which plies between Poole–Edinburgh/Glasgow. No longer is the option available that enabled trains either to take this route or over GC metals, they have to go via Birmingham and Crewe.

Although this view does not show much of Banbury station itself, it has only undergone a few cosmetic changes in the ensuing years: the main building remains virtually the same as it did when reconstructed in the late fifties. The station lamp posts have been replaced, but little else is different, save the removal of the track against the platform in the foreground. This was previously the Woodford bay, from which the 'Banbury Motor' plied its trade. The Percy Gilkes' factory in the background has also changed little. *Date: 17 August 1989.*

COMMENT: *The unobstructed view previously had by Michael Mensing was found to be obscured by an 8ft plywood screen around what is now a building site. This necessitated crawling under some wire mesh 100yd away to gain access to the site and then clambering up the unstable earth bank near the A361 road bridge to wedge myself, camera and tripod between the old spike-topped railway fence and the plywood screen in order to take this shot. Very precarious and uncomfortable.*

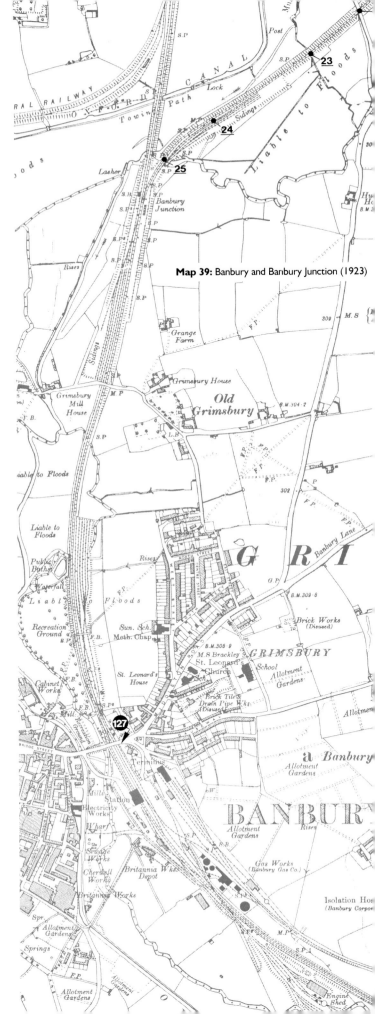

Map 39: Banbury and Banbury Junction (1923)

128
Culworth station
152 SP 564483

There are few photographs better than this to sum up the apparent attitude taken by Sir Edward Watkin and his fellow directors when planning the London Extension: it would be built on a grand scale with space seemingly no object, if this view of Austerity 2-8-0 No 90299 passing the station with an up coal train is anything to go by. With three spans each of 55ft 6in, Bridge 508 in the background was one of the most elegant on the whole length of the line, but only served as a humble occupation bridge, which lends credence to the theory of how no expense was spared to make the line and its structures aesthetically pleasing, or in the quality of materials used.

Culworth, again typical in design for a country station, seemed to have more than adequate space, albeit with limited sidings, for handling any goods traffic that was ever likely to be generated here. The station was actually nearer Morton Pinkney than the village which it purported to serve. Culworth was geographically nearer the Banbury branch. The station closed on 29 September 1958. *Photo: Ivo Peters. Date: 4 June 1963.*

Not such a grand scene now and the only clue regarding the location is given by the fields in the background. The site of the former station is covered by farm buildings, where pigs are intensively reared. The tree in the foreground obscures the view to the bridge, which stands in all its glory, still serving the same purpose and carrying a public footpath between two minor roads.

The line formation north towards Culworth Junction is relatively untouched, as is it south of this point. *Date: 17 August 1989.*

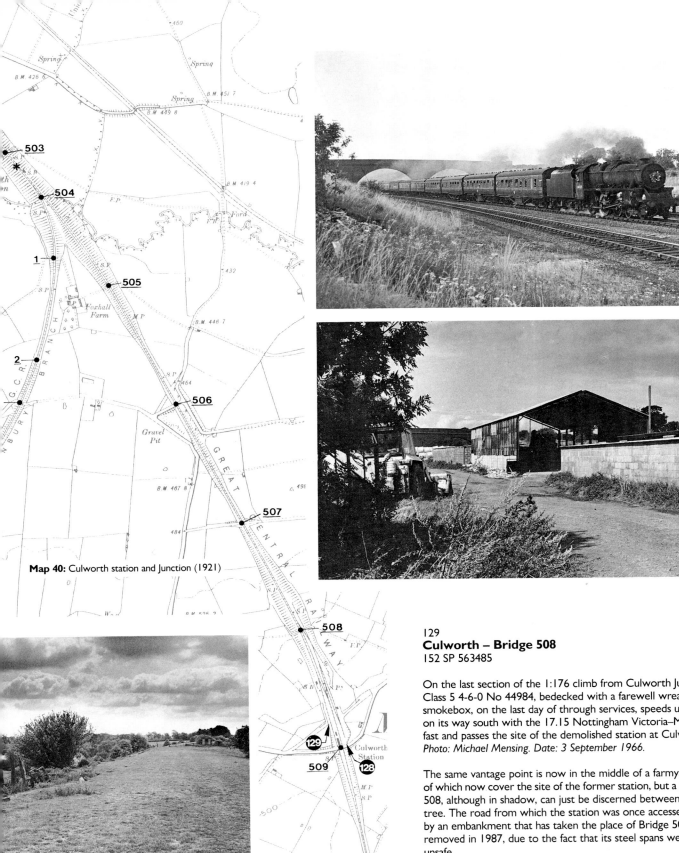

Map 40: Culworth station and Junction (1921)

Culworth Junction today. The charred remains of the signal box are on the left, beyond which the linesmen's hut survives in the fork of the junction. *Date: 25 May 1990.*

129
Culworth – Bridge 508
152 SP 563485

On the last section of the 1:176 climb from Culworth Junction, Stanier Class 5 4-6-0 No 44984, bedecked with a farewell wreath on its smokebox, on the last day of through services, speeds under Bridge 508 on its way south with the 17.15 Nottingham Victoria–Marylebone semi-fast and passes the site of the demolished station at Culworth.
Photo: Michael Mensing. Date: 3 September 1966.

The same vantage point is now in the middle of a farmyard, the buildings of which now cover the site of the former station, but a portion of Bridge 508, although in shadow, can just be discerned between the barn and tree. The road from which the station was once accessed is now carried by an embankment that has taken the place of Bridge 509, which was removed in 1987, due to the fact that its steel spans were deemed to be unsafe.

A certain amount of backfilling has been done either side of Bridge 510 which is 52¼ chains south of this point. A spectacular view of the old GC line passing through the fabulous Northamptonshire countryside can be enjoyed from the minor road between Helmdon and Sulgrave (152 SP 575446), where one can see the formation stretching away into the distance from both sides of the hill. *Date: 17 August 1989.*

130
Helmdon station
152 SP 586430

A scene indicative that all was not well: the buildings are
but untidy heaps of rubble strewn on the platform and
present a sorry sight, as this station was once beautifully
kept by the staff, who lovingly tended their charge.
Ironically, the lineside is in pristine condition, almost as if it
was a matter of pride and an act of defiance in refusing to
accept the imminent closure of the line with the
subsequent loss of jobs it would entail. A way of life would
soon be gone for ever, not to mention a loyalty which, as a
precious but undervalued resource, was to be wantonly
cast aside at a stroke.

The closure of this main line, which had been grossly
under-utilised, was later to be viewed in some quarters as
the settling of an old score by the Great Central's former
rival, the Midland Railway, whose successors had been
entrusted with its running for the previous eight years.

The station closed on 4 March 1964, following the
withdrawal of local services north of Aylesbury. The rot
soon set in and the buildings were demolished early in
1966, a few months before closure of the line, but the
stationmaster's house survived, as did the small goods shed
and store. Goods traffic, mainly consisting of domestic coal,
ceased on 2 November 1964.

In the distance is Helmdon Viaduct, a handsome
structure of nine arches, which spanned both the former
Northampton & Banbury Railway (later to become a
branch of the S&MJ (later LMS), but closed in 1951) and the
River Tove, barely no more than a brook at this point.
Photo: Andrew Muckley/Ian Allan library. Date: March 1966.

The rapid growth of weed-like trees prevents a view from
the platform which, surprisingly, has not been removed,
although many of the edging stones have, as can be seen by
the portion of the up side just visible in the foreground. The
stationmaster's house is occupied by a former railway
employee, who fittingly was once the linesman responsible
for this section.

The small goods yard buildings survive, but are in
generally poor condition. A few pathetic reminders of
bygone days are to be found on the trackbed in the form of
telegraph pole crossbars with their insulators, which lie
where they were felled.

Helmdon Viaduct has not been demolished and is in
generally fine condition. *Date: 22 May 1989.*

Helmdon station
152 SP 586430

A good study of the station buildings taken about five years
before closure shows the layout well, with the
stationmaster's house in the background.
Photo: H. B. Priestley. Date: 13 August 1959.

Helmdon Viaduct
152 SP 583436

The fine viaduct appears to be as good as new. Unusually, not one of the coping stones has yet drawn the attention of the vandals, who so often delight in casting them off the parapets of such structures. The trackbed of the LNWR branch can be seen passing under the fourth arch. *Date: 16 August 1986.*

131
Helmdon – Bridge 519
152 SP 587425

Some 435yd south of Helmdon station the line passed under this splendid bridge, which marked the point at which the line descended for 4½ miles on a ruling down grade of 1:176 to a point between Brackley and Finmere. Bridge 519 carried a busy minor road over the mid point of a deep cutting, which stretched for over half a mile. Each of the three spans, like Bridge 508 at Culworth, is of 55ft 6in.

The scale of the bridge is well judged by B1 class 4-6-0 No 61271 passing underneath with the 12.30 Nottingham Victoria–Marylebone train. *Photo: M. Mitchell. Date: 11 June 1962.*

The cutting north of the bridge has very recently been cleared of undergrowth and shrubs — particularly on the gently sloping embankments — prior to planning permission being sought by a local landfill company to use the area as a tip for building and industrial waste. The south side, from which this photograph was taken, has not as yet been touched and still sports a variety of growth on its banks, although the trackbed is free from such and is well grazed by rabbits.

The line formation towards Brackley is in good shape, much being used as a farm track as all the bridges survive to facilitate this, particularly near milepost 145, which still stands by the side of the trackbed at Radstone. *Date: 24 October 1989.*

COMMENT: Some twenty years ago it was Brackley Viaduct and this particular bridge which fostered my initial interest in the Great Central line. I was immediately struck by the beauty of these structures and awed by the size of them. I thought what stupendous folly it must have been to rip up a main line railway that ran through the heart of England and was built on a scale such as this. My opinions have changed little and current plans for rebuilding part of it would confirm them.

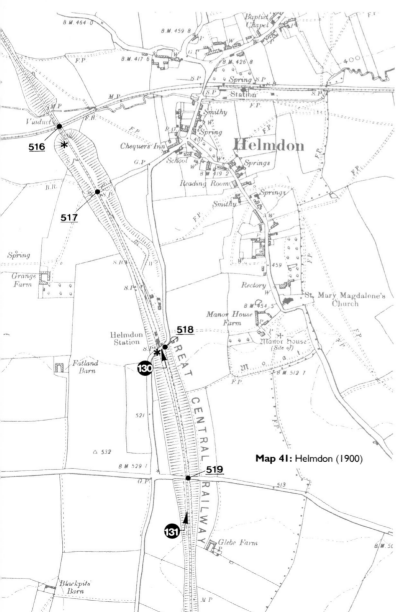

Map 41: Helmdon (1900)

II

BRACKLEY — CALVERT AND GRENDON UNDERWOOD JUNCTION — ASHENDON JUNCTION

132
Brackley Central station (1)
152 SP 590380

Brackley, a small but attractive market town situated near the Oxfordshire/Northamptonshire/Buckinghamshire borders, having a modest population, did not require vast resources to be allocated on building an elaborate station or goods handling facilities, but they were adequate for the purpose and on a par with Rugby. Although spacious, and in common with most stations on the London Extension, the goods yard was humble by way of sidings provided, but it had a fairly substantial shed-cum-warehouse built on the down side.

Plans to link the platform with the station entrance from the bridge over the main Oxford to Northampton road (A43) had to be modified due to concern that it would cause traffic congestion on this busy thoroughfare. A lay-by was built on the west side of the line adjacent to which the booking hall and offices were constructed on an embankment overlooking the line. This involved building a footbridge which spanned the down line enabling access to be gained via a staircase to the slightly truncated platform, a feature which made Brackley unique in this respect.

Drawing into Brackley with the four-coach 14.38 semi-fast Marylebone–Nottingham train is rebuilt Royal Scot 4-6-0 No 46215 *3rd Carabinier*. The up loop is being used temporarily to store some coaches, behind which the rather inelegant water tower, a relatively modern structure, stands out and could be seen from some distance away. Just visible through the haze, is the Brackley to Buckingham road bridge on the other side of Brackley Viaduct, which is obscured by the signal box. *Photo: P. H. Wells. Date: 26 October 1963.*

The modern industrial unit built on the site of the station is owned by a company which manufactures carbon-fibre body shells for racing cars, using the latest materials and technology.

Ironically this unit, together with a few others built during 1990, is the only major development that has been built on the line formation between Claydon Junction and the north side of the West Coast main line at Rugby, apart from the small industrial estate built on the site once occupied by the locomotive depot at Woodford. *Date: 18 August 1989.*

133
Brackley Central station (2)
152 SP 591378

A view looking north taken of the station from beside the goods shed on the Tuesday following closure. The modest size of the platform and layout of the covered footbridge leading from the booking offices to the platform staircase, can be judged well. Bridge 525 carrying the A43 road is visible beyond and the stationmaster's house is seen over the platform sign. The Great Central's intention to build a link to Northampton from here came to nothing, but provision was made for a platform, as seen by the bank on the left under the booking offices and the alignment of the track through the double arch of the bridge, gauged by the smoke stain on its surface.

Following closure, services from this station to London were sorely missed by the line's patrons and the town's people were left with little alternative other than to use Bletchley or Banbury, both of which were some distance away: a situation which still exists today. The other station, Brackley Town, on the LNWR Verney Junction to Banbury Merton Street line, was closed in 1964.

Being endowed with several large schools, Brackley did generate considerable custom for the line in that many children used the station to commute from outlying areas. The beginning and end of terms were always busy periods due to the number of boarding schools in the area. Brackley Central remained open until closure of the line.
Photo: Andrew Muckley/Ian Allan library. Date: 7 September 1966.

Hardly a spectacular contrast, with little to see as reference. The pine tree on the left is the same one as in the previous shot, but has grown considerably. The embankment on the right, previously seen beyond the water column, can be identified. Moulds for various racing car panels and components litter the compound built adjacent to the old goods shed

which survives and is used by the company. The station booking offices are used as an ATS tyre depot. For many years following closure, the station area was a compound for the storage of new cars, an irony since road vehicles were partly to blame for the gradual decline of the Great Central and railway travel in general during the first three decades after the war.

Bridge 525 on the A43 was demolished several years ago when the road was widened, the deep cutting immediately north of which has been filled in for several hundred yards before the formation becomes distinct on the outskirts of the town. *Date: 18 August 1989.*

The goods shed as it was in March 1987, and which remains in much the same condition today.

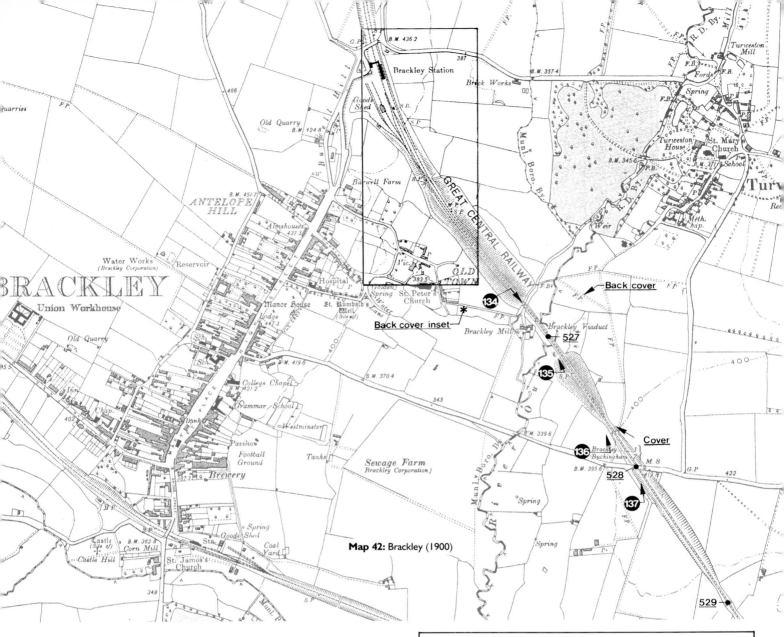

Map 42: Brackley (1900)

Brackley station building in March 1987.

Brackley Viaduct

British Rail was glad to get rid of its responsibility to maintain Brackley Viaduct, as it had been the subject of vandalism. Local children delighted in toppling the coping stones from the parapets into the river below. With the risk of serious injury or death to passers-by or animals in the adjacent fields, demolition was thought to be the best answer, although the main structure was sound. A local businessman bought the viaduct in anticipation of selling the rubble as hardcore for roads that had to be built for major housing developments in the Milton Keynes area.

The viaduct proved a lot more substantial than was first thought: it was believed that the piers were either hollow or filled with rubble, which proved to be false as they were found to be of solid brick. This necessitated special drills being imported from Germany to bore the structure prior to the demolition charges being laid. In the event, the viaduct was reluctant to fall and the first charges set off succeeded in levitating it a bit, then it promptly settled back down again largely intact! Further attempts were made and over the ensuing months huge sections of the arches were toppled, which then had to be broken up with pneumatic drills. The noise and inconvenience to the local residents was considerable, and combined with the large amounts of dust this work created, the contractors were not at all popular. This work went on for many months, and it was at least a year before the site was completely cleared.

134
Brackley Viaduct (1)
152 SP 594373

The need to cross the Great Ouse and the river's flood plain at Brackley necessitated the construction of a 320ft long 22-arch viaduct, which was arguably the most substantial and impressive single piece of architecture built on the line. Large embankments leading to the viaduct were formed using material extracted from the cuttings both to the north and south of the town; an estimated three million cubic yards of spoil were used.

The contractors had difficulty with the viaduct's construction due to moving beds of clay encountered at the southern end. This led to the removal of two arches, which were replaced by two girder spans. A third arch was converted into a buttress to help stabilise the structure and to act as partial support to the last two spans.

Some idea of the scale of the viaduct and the number of craftsmen and labourers — all traditionally attired in waistcoats and flat caps —

employed on its construction can be well gauged in this view taken looking south-east towards Finmere. An impressive aspect of this shot is the massive baulks of timber used as rail bearers, seen being moved into position. The bridge in the background carrying the Brackley–Buckingham road has already been completed. The building in the foreground on the extreme right is Brackley Mill.
Photo: Newton collection/Leicester Museums. Date: c1897/8.

With the viaduct gone, having met its end in 1978, and many of the mature trees lost, possibly the only thing readily identifiable is Brackley Mill. The new A43 Brackley by-pass cuts through the Ouse valley and now hundreds of juggernauts thunder along this busy section of road each hour of the day, shattering the peace and tranquillity previously enjoyed by the residents of the sleepy and picturesque village of Turweston. By way of a contrast trains on the Great Central line were no problem in this regard, as they were carried high over the valley on the viaduct and presented little inconvenience. *Date: 18 August 1989.*

135
Brackley Viaduct (2)
152 SP 596370

A unique photograph taken of the viaduct from the southern end showing it nearing completion in its original form. The last two arches on the right were demolished and the intermediate column converted to support them, whilst the third arch was filled in with brickwork to act as a buttress.

This photograph also shows the scale of the structure when compared to the contractor's rail wagons in the valley below. Brackley Mill is on the left in the background. *Photo: Newton collection/Leicester Museums. Date: c. 1897/8.*

This scene probably represents the country's most potential and all too often environmentally disastrous, but nevertheless vital, modern transport mode in all its congestive horror: lorries and cars thunder along the A43 by-pass, which cuts across the site of the former viaduct. The Great Ouse's course has been altered to accommodate the passage of the road through the valley, and runs under it just beyond the newly constructed wooden footbridge adjacent to the parking sign.

The viaduct's embankment at the northern end can be clearly seen, where a few brick foundations of the buttress remain. This escarpment has provided local youths with an ideal off-road motorcycling area, which has caused much annoyance to nearby householders from time to time. *Date: 18 August 1989.*

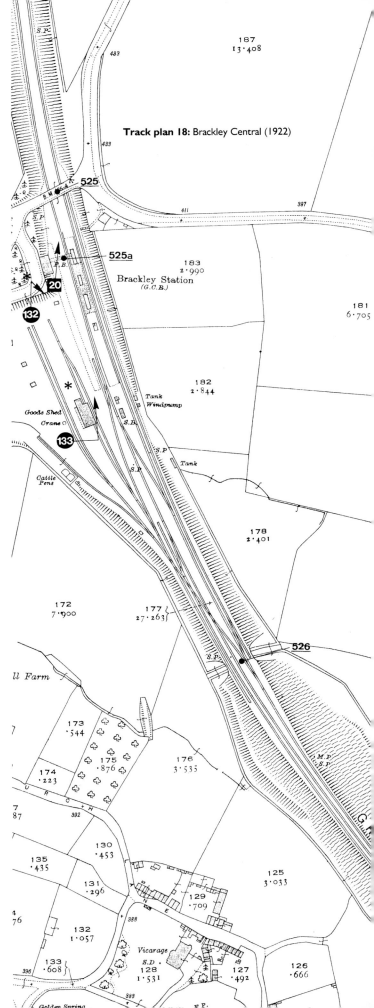

Track plan 18: Brackley Central (1922)

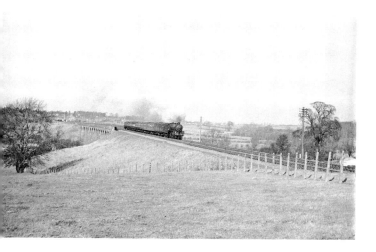

136
Brackley Viaduct (3)
152 SP 597369

A fine study of the viaduct and its surroundings is had in this shot which shows B1 class 4-6-0 No 61078 approaching the A422 Buckingham road bridge with a Sunday morning Woodford–Marylebone train. Brackley Central can be spotted in the distance directly over the viaduct. *Photo: M. Mitchell. Date: 1 March 1959.*

Early morning shadows cast over young growth that has been allowed to grow on the embankment slopes in the foreground, but the north side is highlighted by bright sunlight. A portion of the boundary fence still survives, but many of the concrete posts have broken because of rust eating the steel reinforcing wires.

The trackbed has been used to dump a certain amount of spoil from the recent road improvement schemes, and the short cutting to Bridge 528 has been backfilled. *Date: 24 October 1989.*

137
Brackley – Buckingham Road: Bridge 528
152 SP 599365

Having approached the bridge through a long cutting, BR Standard Class 5 4-6-0 No 73045 passes Brackley's down distant signal and tears under the A422 Buckingham road with the 16.38 Marylebone–Nottingham semi-fast train. The bridge was built on a skew and sloped steeply, carrying the road towards the Great Ouse valley below.

A mile or so south-east of this point the line crossed the Great Ouse again and then immediately over the Banbury to Verney Junction branch of the LNWR on a girder span bridge (No 532). *Photo: Michael Mensing. Date: 9 May 1964.*

The cutting south of the bridge has been subjected to extensive infilling over the past years since planning permission was given to its owners to create a landfill site, which has almost been filled to capacity. The company is now seeking planning permission to extend its activities to Helmdon cutting. At the time this photograph was taken, the company had begun to landscape the surface and was in the process of laying a topsoil covering, a lorry load of which is seen passing on the south parapet of the bridge.

The A422 was re-aligned in conjunction with the construction of a large roundabout on the A43 by-pass and the bridge, on becoming redundant, was backfilled with the road running now adjacent to it on the south side. Before the bridge was all but obscured, thick soot was clearly visible on the underside of the arch — even after all these years.

At the end of the infilled cutting, which extends for twenty-five chains, the next two bridges have been removed, as have Bridges 532 and 533 beyond, at which point pylons carrying main power lines run the length of the formation for some distance before branching away towards Finmere at a point near Bridge 537 just east of Mixbury. The shallow cutting immediately north of the bridge is in the process of being filled in and is being used as a landfill site. *Date: 22 May 1989.*

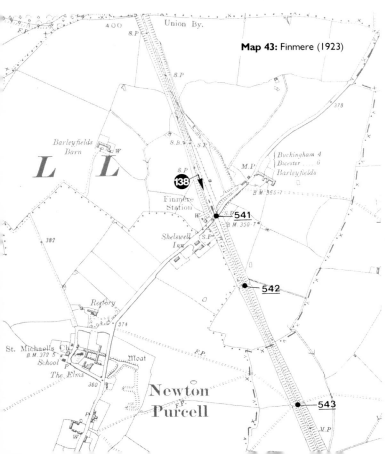

Map 43: Finmere (1923)

138
Finmere station
152/165 SP 629314

Situated close to the Buckinghamshire/Oxfordshire border and set more than a mile south-west of the village on the main Buckingham to Bicester road, Finmere station only enjoyed limited local custom, but due to its proximity to Stowe, the famous public school, was at its busiest at the beginning and end of terms. The war years also proved fruitful due to the number of airfields and camps in the vicinity, which generated passenger traffic. The small goods yard handled normal commodities, mainly cattle and coal traffic.

Apart from normal local trains stopping here, in 1923 a slip-coach service was introduced on certain expresses, probably due to lobbying by distinguished persons living in the area with large country estates; this service continued well into the decade. *Photo: Lens of Sutton. Date: c1963.*

This rather bleak scene depicts the last vestiges of Finmere station, whose island platform survives under the brambles and grasses that now cover its surface. Bridge 541, whose parapet can be seen in the background over the A421 road, is still extant and in reasonable shape, despite needing a lick of paint. Note the sole surviving telegraph pole on the extreme right beyond the bridge. At the entrance to the old goods yard the small checker's hut still stands, but minus its windows.

The long cutting between Bridge 538 over the B4031 north of here and the station has been partly infilled, but the formation is still quite distinct and the two intermediate bridges survive. *Date: March 1987.*

139
Claydon LNE Junction – Bridge 561
165 SP 681256

It was not until 1940 that a spur linked the GC with the Oxford–Bletchley line (often called the Oxford–Cambridge line) brought about by the needs of war, which also enabled a connection to be made with the London Brick Company's sidings at Calvert, situated a short distance away. The junction was made just a little east of the GC main line and adjacent to Shepherd's Furse Farm.

A diesel multiple unit from Bletchley to Oxford has just passed under Bridge 561 carrying the GC main line and approaches a minor road bridge over the ex-LNW line. The signals and box at Claydon Junction can just be discerned beyond the GC bridge, whilst in the far distance a steam train disappears towards Bletchley. *Photo: Dr G. C. Farnell.*
Date: c. 1962.

Caught just in time: the Oxford–Bletchley line was in the process of being singled and gangs were on the west side of the bridge, removing one track. The GC bridge was removed a few years after the line's closure and today no trace remains — even the abutments have been demolished and just a grassy bank marks their position.

Claydon Junction now provides access for a once-daily rubbish container train sent from the Bristol/Avonmouth area, that comes via Oxford on its way to the old clay pits at Calvert, and periodically for the Chiltern Line's DMUs utilising the Bletchley maintenance depot's heavier repair facilities.

At the time of writing there were unconfirmed reports that BR was to re-introduce a passenger service on the line between Oxford and Cambridge, which would take a somewhat circuitous route via Bletchley, Bedford, Kettering, Manton, Ely and Peterborough. Regular services were withdrawn a number of years ago. However, special shopping trains are put on at Christmas between Aylesbury and Milton Keynes via Claydon Junction. From Calvert the trains then traverse the only remaining section of the London Extension north of Quainton Road (where it originally joined with the Metropolitan Railway) over which BR operates any kind of passenger service; a chance for the enthusiast to savour, although not often, and unfortunately not steam hauled.

The formation of the GC line back towards Finmere is largely untouched and only Bridges 547, 550 and 559 have been removed. This is the last section of the dismantled part of the main line, with the exception of a portion of the link with GWR Paddington to Birmingham line from Grendon Underwood Junction, between Akeman Street and Ashendon Junction. *Date: 18 August 1989.*

140
Calvert
165 SP 688247

An aspect looking north from Bridge 563 adjacent to Calvert station showing the main line rising at 1:176 towards Finmere. Just beyond the signals is the spur to Claydon Junction.

In anticipation of the main line's closure two months hence, gangers are out in force modifying the track layout and are about to install pointwork on the up road for access to Calvert's down road, which will be truncated and be no more than a siding north of the crossover.
Photo: Andrew Muckley/Ian Allan library. Date: July 1966.

The end of the old Great Central main line is beyond where it curves right towards Claydon Junction and marks the point north of which it ceases to exist. Mother Nature is gradually staking her claim to the territory, unless the Central Railway Group's plans will deny her that!

The modified layout to handle the rubbish container trains at Calvert is seen in its present form, with the crossover installed and the truncated down line converted into a headshunt or siding, but this is seldom used. The occupants of the former stationmaster's house on the north-west side of the bridge rarely get an undisturbed night's sleep, due to the Northolt train which arrives in the early hours of the morning, and then proceeds to indulge in some shunting.
Date: 18 August 1989.

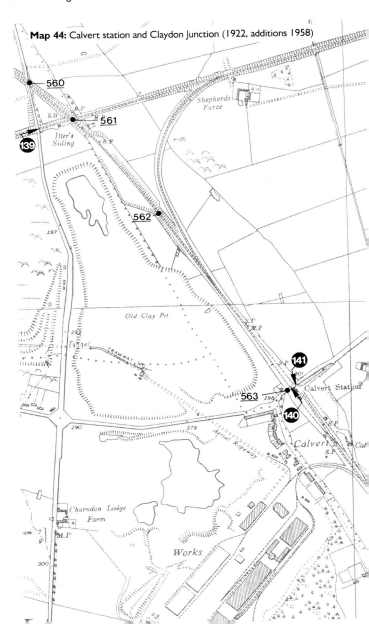

Map 44: Calvert station and Claydon Junction (1922, additions 1958)

141
Calvert station
165 SP 688247

Calvert station was the southern-most of the island platform design to be built by the Great Central on the London Extension before it joined the Metropolitan Railway at Quainton Road. The small goods yard which accompanied it handled the usual commodities such as coal, timber, cattle and dairy produce, besides bricks from the adjacent works.

This photograph shows the station in rather a forlorn state prior to demolition of the buildings, which were of the standard pattern for the line. Rather poignantly, a closure notice remains pasted on the wall of the booking office, succeeding in adding to the scene of dereliction. The track, however, has been recently re-laid and awaits ballasting.

A local landowner, Sir Harry Verney named the station after his family name, Calvert, in memory of his mother. It was only after he inherited the family estate he assumed the name of Verney (the nearby junction where the LNWR and Metropolitan lines met had already been named in honour of this family). The station initially served a small community, primarily from nearby Charndon, since there was no village of Calvert, although a large brick industry evolved in the immediate vicinity over the years and a small cluster of housing was built adjacent to the works for some of its employees. *Photo: Andrew Muckley/Ian Allan library. Date: 9 June 1966.*

Calvert station as it is today; only the platform survives, but is covered with weeds. The former down line is used to hold containerised rubbish trains, two of which are handled here every twenty-four hours. The gantry crane in the background removes the containers and then the contents are taken to be tipped into disused clay pits nearby. One train arrives from Northolt via Aylesbury. The other comes from the Avon area via Claydon Junction, having picked up containers at Bath, Bristol, Avonmouth and Westerleigh on the former Midland line near Yate. *Date: 18 August 1989.*

142 (Opposite)
Grendon Underwood Junction
165 SP 709220

A connection with the Great Western Railway's Paddington–Birmingham main line was brought about by the need to avoid congestion on the Metropolitan route south of Aylesbury, which could have led to the delay of express workings. This would give the Great Central the option of running via Neasden South Junction through High Wycombe and Princes Risborough, with the potential to run services into Paddington. Despite the Metropolitan Railway objecting to the possible loss of revenue, a bill was passed in 1898 for the Great Central to construct a short link between Grendon Underwood and Ashendon, which opened for goods traffic in November 1905 and for passenger traffic the following April.

Some two miles south of Calvert station, Grendon Underwood Junction was set in beautiful countryside, but was remote from any centre of population or road, so was a fairly lonely outpost for signalmen, one of whom seems pleased to see the photographer in this view taken at the turn of the century. The route to Ashendon is the line seen branching to the right with the gate across its path, which signifies that it was not yet open to traffic and was still to be completed, as can be judged by the corrugated-iron hut set at the end of the down line's catchpoints; although painted in railway colours, it was probably being used as a temporary store by the contractors.
Photo: Newton collection/Leicester Museums. Date: c1905.

The former main line was singled in the late sixties and now only regains double track at Aylesbury, whilst the link route towards Ashendon Junction is just a spur which extends for a little over two miles to an agricultural fertiliser depot near Akeman Street.

At Grendon Underwood the signal box has long since been replaced with a ground frame, which is electrically released. Despite this, there are a few things that remain to which one can refer, such as the bridge (No 568) in the background; also two of the trees previously seen on the horizon between the signal box and the cabin still survive and can be readily identified. *Date: 8 August 1990.*

(Above left)
Grendon Underwood Junction today looking north towards Calvert, where smoke from the brick kilns can be seen rising into the air beyond Bridge 567 in the background. *Date: 6 November 1989.*

Map 45: Grendon Underwood Junction (1923)

143
Akeman Street
165 SP 705180

Two small halts were constructed on the Ashendon–Grendon Underwood link. One was at Wotton (opening in November 1905 and closed on 7 December 1953) and the other here at Akeman Street near the main A41 trunk road of that name, although it is not pictured in this view looking south towards Ashendon; in fact the halt was on the other side of the road.

Class 5 4-6-0 No 44691 approaches Akeman Street box with the 18.18 Marylebone–Sheffield train, which the year before had been the 'Master Cutler'. By this date, although leaving at the same time — and still with restaurant car facilities — the train no longer carried the name of the line's premier express, following its transfer to the King's Cross–Sheffield Victoria via Retford route as a Pullman service. Despite this, the 18.18 from Marylebone continued to run as an express until eventual withdrawal of all such workings in January 1960, from when trains would only be operating as semi-fast services. *Photo: M. Mitchell.*
Date: June 1959.

There is not much to see at Akeman Street today except the wide formation that is carried on an embankment to the immediate south of the main A41 road where the bridge has been removed, leaving only the abutments on the north side. Just beyond this point, the truncated link from Grendon Underwood Junction ends and the line remains to serve the UKF fertiliser depot of Fermin Coates Ltd via a siding accessed by trailing points spurred from it. British Rail makes a once-weekly delivery, usually on a Saturday.

It is strange to think that the original Roman dirt road has lasted a lot longer than the GC's iron road! *Date: 23 October 1989.*

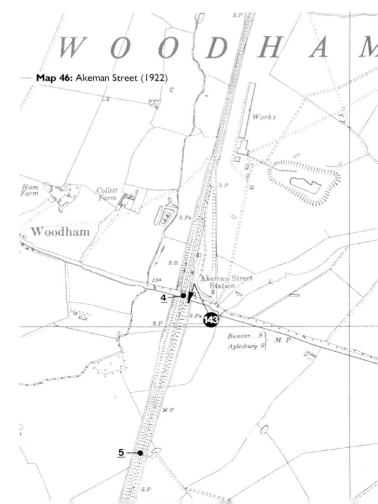

Map 46: Akeman Street (1922)

144 (Overleaf)
Ashendon Junction
165 SP 692136

When the final section of the GWR's direct route from Paddington to Birmingham between Ashendon to Aynho, known as the Bicester cut-off, commenced construction in 1905, a flying junction was created here to facilitate the convergence of the joint GW/GC lines. Like Grendon Underwood, Ashendon was located in the heart of the countryside and was over a half-mile from the nearest road or track. The 4¾ mile section between these two junctions, having a general speed limit of 90mph (only dropping to 75mph, then down to 60mph as Grendon Underwood was approached), enabled some fast running by GC expresses to be achieved. The Bicester cut-off was opened for GW goods traffic on 4 April 1910 and for passenger trains on 1 July the same year.

At Ashendon the GW lines parted, with the up line carried on an embankment with a girder bridge to pass over the GC, which joined from a north-easterly direction. This was different to that at Grendon, which was a conventional flat type, and the junction at Northolt (at the southern extremity of the joint GW/GC line), which was of the burrowing variety, where the down GC line passed under that of the GWR.

A summer cross-country working: Class B1 4-6-0 No 61225, with a Hastings–Sheffield train, passes under the GWR up line and takes the GC route towards Grendon Underwood; in the process it will travel at speed through some splendid countryside in the Vale of Aylesbury.
Photo: Stanley Creer. Date: 27 August 1955.

The ex-GWR Paddington–Birmingham main line was singled from Princes Risborough to Aynho Junction, a few miles south of Banbury, in the late sixties and the up line was then lifted. The girder bridge was subsequently removed and scrapped, with only the abutments remaining today. One survivor is the lineside ballast bunker which still lies beside the GC's formation.

At the time of writing the only passenger train other than the normal DMU workings between Marylebone and Banbury to use the old GWR main line, is the weekday 18.12 Paddington–Banbury service, usually hauled by a Class 50 diesel-electric locomotive. The up service leaves Banbury at 06.54 and arrives in the capital at 08.26. Perhaps this situation will change in the future if electric trains heading north to Rugby via the revitalised junctions of Ashendon and Grendon Underwood are to run over the route. *Date: 6 November 1989.*

COMMENT: *Two trips to the former junction were made: the first involved a trudge across several fields of heavy clay soil for over a mile. I was utterly exhausted upon my return. Fortunately, thanks to the courtesy of a local farmer, the second was made by car, which had to be driven across several steeply sloping fields, much to the curiosity of the occupants!*

The former booking office and waiting rooms of Wotton Station have been converted into a house, now called 'The Old Station'. Surprise, surprise! The underbridge (No 9) was removed in 1970.
Date: 8 August 1990.

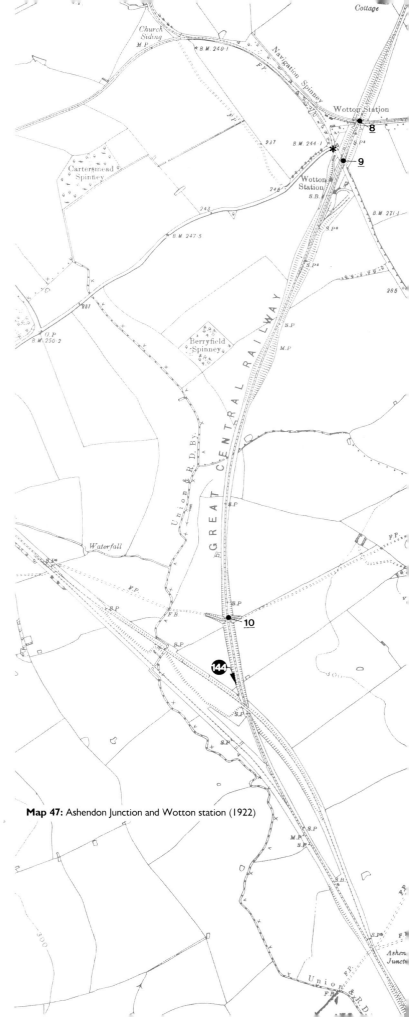

Map 47: Ashendon Junction and Wotton station (1922)

QUAINTON ROAD — MARYLEBONE AND PRINCES RISBOROUGH

The Chiltern Line

This chapter covers the portion of the former GC/Metropolitan Railway route from Quainton Road to Marylebone and the GC/GWR joint line that ran from Neasden South Junction through to Ashendon Junction via High Wycombe and Princes Risborough, from where a single track branch connected with the GC/Metropolitan line at Aylesbury. All these routes survive in much the same form apart from the section between Princes Risborough and Aynho Junction, which has been singled (save for a passing loop at Bicester), but from the point where GC trains took a right turn at Ashendon Junction, it was solely GWR territory on from there.

Because the 'Chiltern Line', as it is now called, is very much the same as it was in 1966 when through services on the GC routes were discontinued, only lip service is paid to this section and its stations. There is no point in taking 'then and now' photographs that show little or no change in the past twenty or thirty years, apart from a few cosmetic ones, so the purpose of the few sample photographs included in this section are to highlight the fact.

Both routes of the Chiltern Line are the province of ancient diesel multiple units sets working out of Marylebone, which had been threatened with closure.

A £76 million investment programme is under way to upgrade the line, with continuous welded rail replacing much of the old, while new signalling is being installed; the last of the semaphore types will have been removed by the time this book is published. The new Class 165 Networker Turbo diesel units are to replace the old DMU sets over the next few years. Various stations have been modernised and platforms re-surfaced, even extended in some cases; barrel vaulted shelters have replaced many of the buildings, as well.

Quainton Road station seen from the down platform.
Date: 22 October 1989.

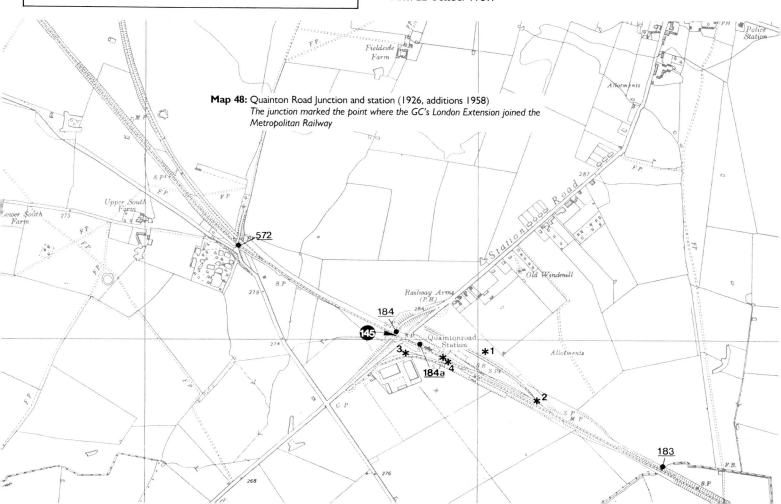

Map 48: Quainton Road Junction and station (1926, additions 1958)
The junction marked the point where the GC's London Extension joined the Metropolitan Railway

145
Quainton Road station
165 SP 737190

Quainton Road station is situated in the heart of the Vale of Aylesbury and was the former meeting place of three railways: the Metropolitan (formerly the Aylesbury & Buckingham) Railway that ran to Verney Junction from Aylesbury; the Brill Tramway (opened in 1871 and closed in 1935), and last but not least, the Great Central's London Extension which arrived in 1899.

The station was first opened in 1868 by the A&BR and built to a conventional layout of two platforms on the main line with a third subsequently constructed on the west side for the Brill Tramway. The station lost its passenger service in 1963, when it closed.

This photograph taken from the road bridge on the north side of the station shows the conventional layout of the platforms, together with that of the ex-Brill Tramway, which is visible on the right. The up sidings still appear to be busy in this view, and two engines, one of which appears to be a B1 class 4-6-0, can be seen in the yard at the far end over the footbridge. *Photo: M. Mitchell. Date: 25 May 1959.*

Under the auspices of the Buckinghamshire Railway Centre, the station survives in very good condition and has received extensive refurbishment over the years. There is much to see at the Centre which has the usual facilities, including a buffet, bookshop, exhibition hall, small relics museum and miniature track railway.

From this facsimile there appears to be little that has changed its character which has been preserved, although the track has been singled through the station, and the new buildings, including the restoration sheds, one of which is seen in the up yard beyond the station, have blended in reasonably well.

As in many of the previous photographs, it is sad to see how many mature trees have been lost over the years; this area is no exception. *Date: 22 October 1989.*

The Buckinghamshire Railway Centre

Chosen for its historic importance as the meeting place for three railways, in 1968 a group called the London Railway Preservation Society selected Quainton Road station as a centre for their activities, with the intention of preserving a broad spectrum of railway equipment, which would not be confined just to engines and rolling stock. Over the years a great number of other artefacts have found a home in the 'Quainton Collection'. In 1969 the LRPS became the Quainton Railway Society Ltd, a registered charity, whose members now own and operate the Buckinghamshire Railway Centre.

The Centre is not blessed with the ability to run over the track through the station, as the points connecting the yards and sidings have been removed, due to the fact that BR uses the old main line for containerised rubbish trains plying once-daily between Calvert and London. Despite this aggravation, which has divided the Centre into two separate parts, it makes good use of the other facilities available to it, and has exploited the use of the former up and down yards to full advantage; new restoration sheds have been built in both. Trains run to and from a new platform created in the up yard, whilst the former Brill Tramway's platform is used on the down side for passengers enjoying rides on that side of the former main line.

Over the years various locomotives, both steam and diesel, have been or are in the process of being restored to working condition. An immaculate example is the former Metropolitan 0-4-4 tank No 1, painted in appropriate maroon and yellow livery. Other resident locomotives include GWR 2-8-2T No 7200, a heavy tank engine; Peckett 0-4-0 No 2087; Ivatt Class 2MT 2-6-2T Nos 41298 and 41313, also 2-6-0 No 46477. In addition, there are a variety of diesel shunters and locomotives kept here, including Class 25 No 25057.

The most significant restoration project, which came to fruition in the spring of 1989, was the completion of the sixteen-year programme by the 6024 Preservation Society, an associated group, to rebuild to main line running condition GWR King class 4-6-0 No 6024 *King Edward I*. This was a truly magnificent effort considering the daunting task which initially faced the volunteers, and of which they can be justifiably proud now that their ambitions have been fully realised. The King's main-line certificate has been issued by BR following a successful trial with a 12-coach 391-ton train hauled from Derby to Banbury on 1 February 1990.

Apart from the variety of locomotives to be seen at Quainton Road, there are some splendid examples of coaches and rolling stock, including LNWR 1st class Dining Car No 77 built in 1901, which in its latter years before withdrawal in December 1966 was allocated as a secondary vehicle attached to the Royal Train for railway support staff.

2: This aspect looking south towards Waddesdon from the end of Quainton Road's up yard gives a good impresson of the undulating nature of the line. *Date: March 1987.*

3: A view inside the down yard's restoration shed showing an industrial saddle tank locomotive and a beautifully preserved London, Chatham and Dover Railway first class carriage in residence. *Date: 22 October 1989.*

4: A variety of preserved locomotives are seen in the down yard with the restoration shed beyond. A portion of the former platform of the Brill Tramway is visible in the foreground. *Date: 22 October 1989.*

1: The immaculately preserved Metropolitan 0-4-4T No 1 standing at the new station platform built in the up yard. *Date: 22 October 1989.*

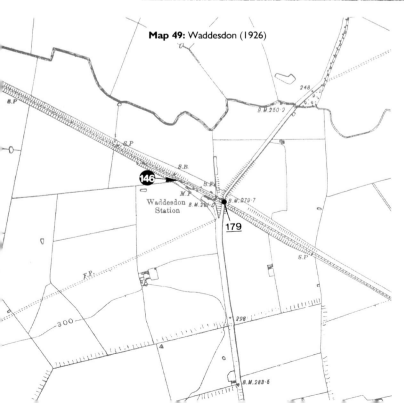

Map 49: Waddesdon (1926)

146
Waddesdon
165 SP 756181

A small two-platform halt was built by the A&BR ostensibly to serve the village of Waddesdon, about a mile to the south-west; limited facilities for passenger comforts were provided. Being only a short distance from Quainton Road it saw limited use, and trains ceased to call here from an early date.

In this rare view of Waddesdon, B1 class 4-6-0 No 61116 passes the disused platforms with the 18.06 Marylebone–Woodford 'ord' and heads north towards Quainton Road station a mile distant, where it will hope to find some custom. *Photo: M. Mitchell. Date: 4 July 1959.*

The platform on the down side of the line survives more or less intact, but that on the up side has not been so lucky and just a pile of rubble remains. Careful study will reveal the gravel bunker still in situ off the end of the platform, although it is partly obscured by long grass and has been moved from its original position slightly. Bridge 179 (to recognise its original Metropolitan Railway number) in the background carries the minor road between Pitchcott and Waddesdon.

The line and formation between here and Aylesbury, although singled, has changed little and just the former up side is used by the containerised rubbish trains heading to Calvert. *Date: 23 October 1989.*

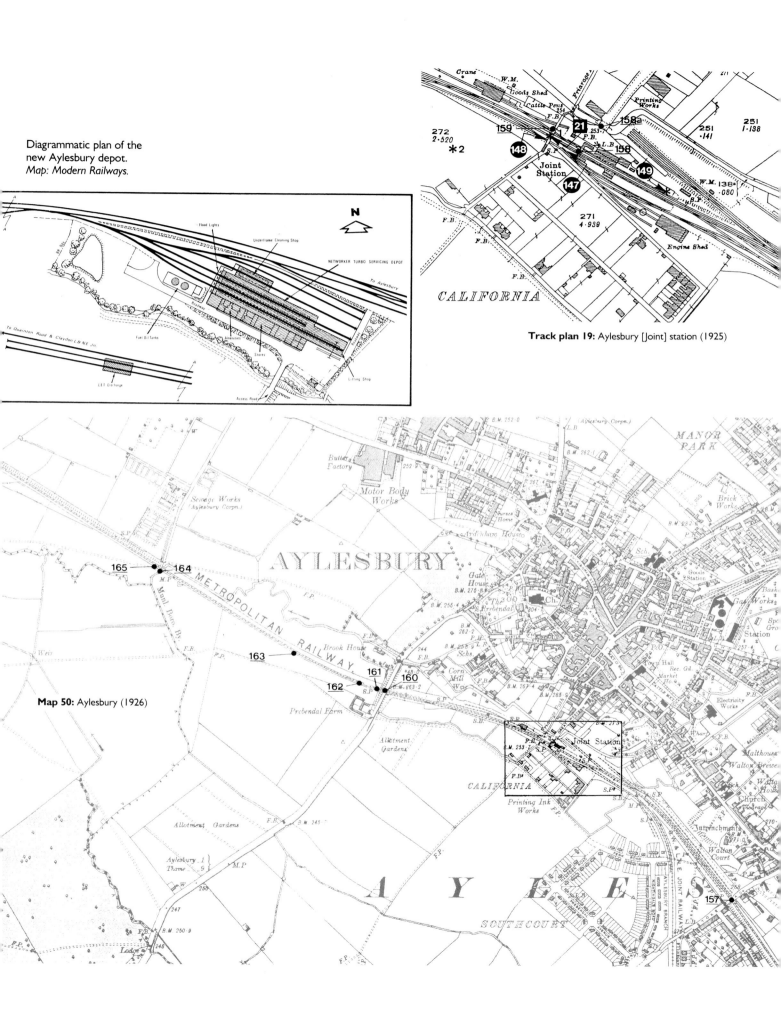

Diagrammatic plan of the
new Aylesbury depot.
Map: Modern Railways.

Track plan 19: Aylesbury [Joint] station (1925)

Map 50: Aylesbury (1926)

147
Aylesbury Town station (1)
165 SP 817134

Aylesbury, the first town with a sizeable population south of Rugby, had expanded rapidly in the latter half of the nineteenth century with the advent of the Metropolitan Railway, which encouraged people to move from the inner city areas of London into the countryside north of the capital, with many suburban developments burgeoning from previously rural areas and villages along or near the line. The town to all intents and purposes marked the northernmost limit of this development.

The Great Central shared much of the Metropolitan's route from Quainton Road to Baker Street, which was not electrified until it reached a point south of Amersham, where the Chesham branch joined the main line near Chalfont & Latimer (originally the electrification had only extended to Rickmansworth).

From Neasden South Junction, near to the site of the locomotive depot there, it then ran parallel to the electrified Metropolitan line on its own tracks for some miles before swinging away at Canfield Place in South Hampstead to enter the Hampstead, St John's Wood and Lord's tunnels before finally reaching its newly built terminus at Marylebone.

A single-line branch was also constructed from Aylesbury Town through Little Kimble and Monks Risborough & Whiteleaf to join the GWR at Princes Risborough, being on the alternative route from

Grendon Underwood, which ran through to Neasden Junction via High Wycombe and Northolt Junction where the GC and GWR lines diverged.

At the northern end of the station, a water column is being well and truly used by the driver of an ex-GWR 0-6-0 pannier tank No 6429, which having previously arrived at the station with the Princes Risborough auto-train, is having its water supply replenished to the absolute brim. Note the rather forbidding sign on the column relating to an anti-pollution measure adopted by the railway authorities — perhaps rather more in hope than earnest! *Photo: Dr G. C. Farnell. Date: August 1960.*

This now marks the point which is effectively 'the end of the line' as regards passenger services over the former GC/Metropolitan route. A DMU, having arrived from Princes Risborough on the equivalent service previously operated by the pannier tank, has run beyond the station to cross the points to set back into the old down platform, but will not require watering! Note the patch on the platform surface where the column once stood. The gradient post, although having lost its indicators, still remains by the lineside on the extreme left.

In July 1989 the building of a new £4 million Networker Turbo depot to be sited to the north of the station on the west side of the line had yet to commence, but by the summer of 1990 work was well advanced, and during the spring of 1991, it was completed. *Date: 28 July 1989.*

1: The Networker Turbo depot under construction. *Date: 8 August 1990.*

2: A view inside the completed servicing depot shows the second of the new 75mph Class 165 Networker Turbos, No 165002, in residence; the prototype, No 165001, was still undergoing further trials at Derby. An initial order of 77 vehicles for the Chiltern Line at a cost of £43.5 million was placed, with a further 12 to cater for traffic growth authorised subsequently; these will be made up into 11×3-car and 28×2-car sets. *Date: 11 June 1991.*

148
Aylesbury Town (2)
165 SP 817134

A view of the station taken from the pedestrian bridge at the north end shows the layout well. Thompson B1 class 4-6-0 No 61201 stands at Aylesbury Town before leaving with the 13.40 Marylebone–Woodford train on a dank and dismal day. The booking hall and main buildings hide the bay platform, which can just be seen under the covered footbridge. Aylesbury South signal box controlling the junction to Princes Risborough is also just visible over the island platform's canopy.

The small shed on the right in the background had two roads, where an Ivatt Class 2MT 2-6-2 tank waits outside for another turn of duty.
Photo: M. Mitchell. Date: 22 November 1958.

This shot taken on a hazy day from the same spot but on a replacement footbridge goes to prove that little has changed here. The buildings and layout are almost the same, with the exception that the shed has been demolished and much of the area has been sold off to industrial development. The station is, however, in much better overall condition: its buildings and canopies have been renovated and the replacement lamp standards have been recently painted bright red, giving it an infinitely less gloomy and run-down appearance.

The chronically old drop-side wagons seen passing through the station make up an engineers' train, which having deposited ballast for the track improvements north of the station, is on its way back to Marylebone via the Princes Risborough route, hauled by Class 47 diesel No 47341.
Date: 13 September 1989.

149
Aylesbury South Junction
165 SP 818134

South box controls this junction just off the end of Aylesbury Town station and marked the point where the branch to Princes Risborough left the main line, which can be seen swinging away to the right.
Photo: H. B. Priestley. Date: 30 May 1971.

With a matter of months to go before they are demolished, the semaphore signals are still performing a valuable function some nineteen years later. The signal box will also be made redundant when the line is upgraded and new signalling equipment installed.

Class 47 No 47341 gets the right of way to the Princes Risborough branch and starts from Aylesbury station with its tatty train of engineers' wagons. *Date: 13 September 1989.*

COMMENT: *The hazy conditions with thunder rolling in the gathering clouds did not help to make this photograph as crisp as the former shot, but I felt it was important to record the semaphores, as a final salute, before they disappear from this line for ever.*

Some months later the new electronic signalling system was in the process of being installed at the southern end of Aylesbury station and soon to replace the semaphore types beyond. *Date: 8 August 1990.*

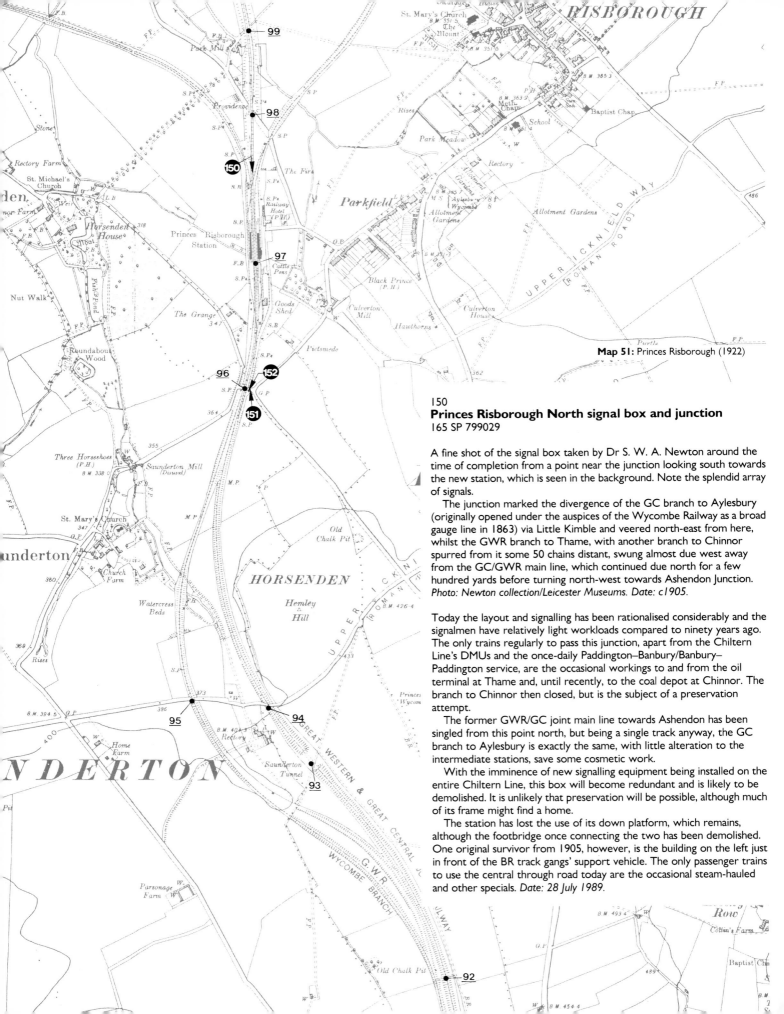

Map 51: Princes Risborough (1922)

150
Princes Risborough North signal box and junction
165 SP 799029

A fine shot of the signal box taken by Dr S. W. A. Newton around the time of completion from a point near the junction looking south towards the new station, which is seen in the background. Note the splendid array of signals.

The junction marked the divergence of the GC branch to Aylesbury (originally opened under the auspices of the Wycombe Railway as a broad gauge line in 1863) via Little Kimble and veered north-east from here, whilst the GWR branch to Thame, with another branch to Chinnor spurred from it some 50 chains distant, swung almost due west away from the GC/GWR main line, which continued due north for a few hundred yards before turning north-west towards Ashendon Junction. *Photo: Newton collection/Leicester Museums. Date: c1905.*

Today the layout and signalling has been rationalised considerably and the signalmen have relatively light workloads compared to ninety years ago. The only trains regularly to pass this junction, apart from the Chiltern Line's DMUs and the once-daily Paddington–Banbury/Banbury–Paddington service, are the occasional workings to and from the oil terminal at Thame and, until recently, to the coal depot at Chinnor. The branch to Chinnor then closed, but is the subject of a preservation attempt.

The former GWR/GC joint main line towards Ashendon has been singled from this point north, but being a single track anyway, the GC branch to Aylesbury is exactly the same, with little alteration to the intermediate stations, save some cosmetic work.

With the imminence of new signalling equipment being installed on the entire Chiltern Line, this box will become redundant and is likely to be demolished. It is unlikely that preservation will be possible, although much of its frame might find a home.

The station has lost the use of its down platform, which remains, although the footbridge once connecting the two has been demolished. One original survivor from 1905, however, is the building on the left just in front of the BR track gangs' support vehicle. The only passenger trains to use the central through road today are the occasional steam-hauled and other specials. *Date: 28 July 1989.*

151 (Opposite)
Princes Risborough – Bridge 96
165 SP 799023

Just south of the station a minor road bridge provided a fabulous vantage point to photograph trains on the main GWR/GC joint line plying between London, the North and Midlands. Enthusiasts could satiate themselves on a feast of locomotives representing most regions: Kings, Castles, Halls, Granges, Directors, Jubilees, Royal Scots, Class 5s, A3s, V2s, B1s, K3s, L1s, Austerities, and Standard classes of all descriptions, let alone the bustling GWR pannier tank engines going about their business on local trains, retrieving slip-coaches or shunting in the yard. The list was almost endless, such was the diversity of motive power and traffic on this line in its heyday, particularly after nationalisation.

Seen here is a typical GC line special working either to Wembley or Marylebone from the North via Ashendon Junction, as B1 class 4-6-0 No 61177 tears round the bend having passed Princes Risborough station in the background, whilst the driver keeps a lookout for the next set of signals. *Photo: Dr G. C. Farnell. Date: July 1957.*

Not much diversity of traffic is to be seen from here these days: only the ubiquitous DMUs plying between Banbury and Marylebone, or those to Aylesbury via Little Kimble. Perhaps the occasional oil train working can also be seen by the more patient observer, but the line is totally under-used and only a shadow of its former self.

Although the units are usually driven with spirit in true 'GC' style, this DMU takes the bend at much more sedate pace as it rounds the same curve with the 13.44 Aylesbury–Marylebone service. It is interesting to see how few buildings survive from the previous shot, although the cottage on the left is still the same. Many new industrial units and housing have been built in the area. *Date: 28 July 1989.*

152 (Above)
Princes Risborough – Saunderton bank
165 SP 799023

To enable trains to have an easier climb through the Chilterns, the up and down lines parted between milepost 33¼ at Saunderton, before meeting again at milepost 35¾ on the south side of the road bridge near Princes Risborough. The summit of the down line was reached at milepost 34¼, then descended for 1½ miles at 1:100 and 1:88.

Coming down the final gradient at 1:88 towards the road bridge at Princes Risborough is B1 class 4-6-0 No 61334 with the 12.15 service to Manchester. The speed down Saunderton bank was usually very high and express trains quite often achieved the line limit of 90mph. *Photo: Dr G. C. Farnell. Date: July 1957.*

(Right)
A diesel multiple unit with the 11.15 Marylebone–Aylesbury service crosses over the points installed near the bridge to take the former up line, the only one at the station used by regular passenger trains today, to enter Princes Risborough station half a mile away. Note how the up sidings have been removed during the track rationalisation that has taken place over the years. *Date: 28 July 1989.*

COMMENT: *A rapid sprint was made from the station to the bridge and arriving just in the nick of time to catch this train, otherwise a lengthy wait would have been necessary had it been missed. One camera lens did not survive the jolting and was severely damaged in the process . . . ah well, such is one's dedication to duty!*

153
Rickmansworth
166/176 TQ 059946

Class A3 Pacific No 60104 *Solario* rounds the sharp curve on the approach to Rickmansworth station with the 15.20 Marylebone–Manchester express, whilst LPTB No 4 *Lord Byron* waits in the up platform with 15.36 Saturdays-only train to Baker Street.

Having a severe speed restriction on the approach to the station, and being on the electrified portion of the Metropolitan line where both GC trains and those running on the suburban services shared track, Rickmansworth provides a good example of how express trains could be held up on this section and a number of them, such as the 'Master Cutler' and the 12.15 service to Manchester, took the alternative route through the Chilterns via Neasden South Junction, High Wycombe and Princes Risborough.
Photo: R. M. Newland/Ian Allan library.
Date: 10 September 1955.

A slight difference in motive power otherwise nothing much has changed here, although the crossover and one track has been removed. The signal box is demolished and replaced by a more modern structure on the platform. Although the trees on the right obscure part of the station, another train was waiting in the up platform where No 4 *Lord Byron* stood — and at about the same time!

One of the Metropolitan electric locomotives has been preserved and is kept at Neasden. No 12 *Sarah Siddons*, now beautifully restored, occasionally works special trains on the line. *Date: 28 July 1989.*

COMMENT: *The dark patch on the photograph could not be avoided because the footbridge is now protected with a fine pressed steel mesh cladding and this meant that the camera had to be positioned very critically to minimise shadow and not to obscure the central view.*

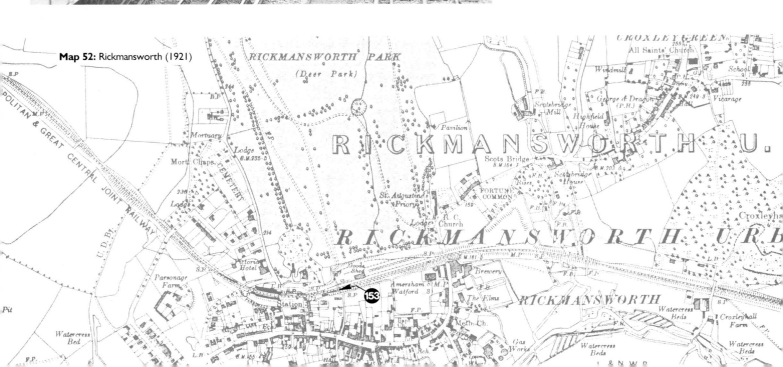

Map 52: Rickmansworth (1921)

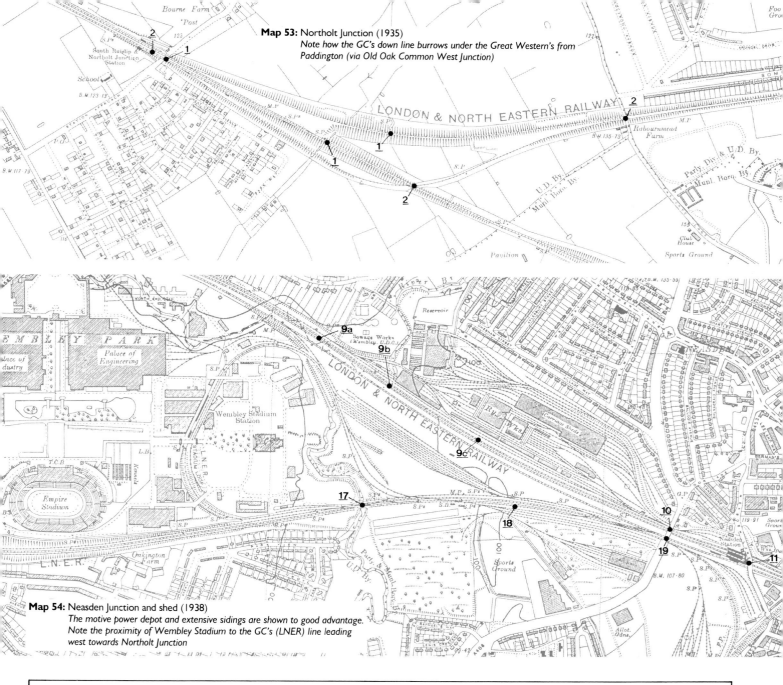

Map 53: Northolt Junction (1935)
Note how the GC's down line burrows under the Great Western's from Paddington (via Old Oak Common West Junction)

Map 54: Neasden Junction and shed (1938)
The motive power depot and extensive sidings are shown to good advantage. Note the proximity of Wembley Stadium to the GC's (LNER) line leading west towards Northolt Junction

Marylebone station

With funds running low and not helped by the enormous added cost of three tunnels which had to be dug, forced on the company by strong opposition to the route through St John's Wood and past Lord's cricket ground, Watkin's grand scheme to drive on to the South Coast ended in a whimper with a modest terminus being built, designed by the railway's engineering department, and fronting Marylebone Road.

Opening officially on 9 March 1899, the station was initially planned on a much larger scale. In the event it was reduced by as much as 50 per cent in area, but nevertheless the whole site still took 70 acres of land, which included a goods yard and enormous warehouse built on the north-west side, with the carriage sidings and shed being constructed on the up side at the north-east corner of the complex. A turntable was sited adjacent to the Rossmore Road bridge at the end of the station on the down side. Locomotives were based at Neasden, where sheds were constructed to house them.

The station itself had three clerestory roofs, which were designed to cover two island platforms each of 1,000ft long, but although it was intended to have seven lines run into it, only five were laid. The available

space filled in between the platforms on the east side enabled a more than generous carriage and cab rank to be sited there, which in effect, took up at least 40 per cent of the station's covered area.

Sandwiched between the booking hall and platforms, an adequate glass-roofed concourse had the usual facilities provided on it for a main line terminus, including a rather charming 'finger'-type destination board, restaurant, buffet, waiting rooms, newsagent's shop, and lavatories.

In recent years Marylebone was under the threat of closure and a scheme was devised to convert it into a coach station. The plan was abandoned, partly due to the fact that the tunnels under St John's Wood and Lord's cricket ground would have prevented coaches operating safely through them. It was found that they were too narrow for the safe passage of such large vehicles en route to and from the M1. Traffic lights and one-way working would have been required, thus creating bottlenecks.

British Rail subsequently had a change of plan, and the station has recently undergone an extensive refurbishment and alteration. The long term future is less certain, as the proposed cross-London line from Liverpool Street to Amersham may eventually render Marylebone redundant.

154
Marylebone station (1)
176 TQ 275822

A general view of the station taken from a position near the Rossmore Road bridge shows its modest construction. A diesel multiple unit service for Nottingham via Princes Risborough waits in platform 5. By this date the station had a neglected appearance and gave the impression of forlorn quietude between trains. The modern office block on the right is Melbury House. *Photo: Andrew Muckley/Ian Allan library. Date: July 1965.*

Snap! Nothing has changed in twenty-four years, not even the motive power. The 11.10 service to Aylesbury gets away several minutes late from Marylebone, leaving a failed portion in the station, whose interior is filled with oil and diesel smoke from this rather tired unit.

The station itself has adopted a much more modern and less neglected appearance and now faces a reasonably secure future in the medium term, having being threatened with closure in recent years; considerable sums of money are currently being spent on its fabric. The reversal of the decision to close the terminus was brought about by the fact that Paddington would have been unable to cope with the rise in commuter traffic that has been generated on the line in the last few years.

The former carriage sheds survive as a depot to carry out first-line examinations, running repairs, fuelling and cleaning work on the DMUs; it is treated as a sub-shed of Bletchley Depot, which undertakes any higher maintenance work. The Marylebone depot will close when the purpose-built depot at Aylesbury to service the new Networker Turbo DMUs is commissioned, but a new carriage cleaning plant is to be built at Marylebone, so this duty will still be able to be carried out here. *Date: 13 September 1989.*

COMMENT: *Since September 1989, work has proceeded apace in the £1 million refurbishment and reconstruction of Marylebone. A major development is that a further two platform lines have been laid on the former cab rank, as was originally intended. All the new platform surfaces have been laid with the attractive standard Network terrazzo-style slabs, replacing the concrete paving stones and tarmac that did not help to lessen the station's run-down look. By April 1991, the bay (platform 6) on the right, from which many steam-hauled specials have run in the last few years, had been demolished along with its neighbour and the apex roof section covering them. New carriage lines were in the process of being laid, albeit in truncated form, as part of the area they once occupied is to be sold off for commercial development, as is Melbury House, the latter day offices of the British Waterways Board and Railfreight Construction, which is soon to be demolished.*

1: Redevelopment work in progress at Marylebone. Note the new GEC-Alsthom colour light signals, now in operation near the Rossmore Road bridge in the distance. *Date: 5 April 1991.*

2: A general view of the station which shows the platforms have nearly been finished; however, only two complete roof sections, plus the cantilever canopy salvaged from over the former platform 6, are now needed to cover them. Note how the latter has been grafted onto the westerly uprights of the former centre span. *Date: 5 April 1991.*

155
Marylebone station (2)
176 TQ 276821

The classic scene: the line's premier express standing at its terminus in the capital. Having arrived from Sheffield with the up 'Master Cutler', V2 2-6-2 No 60854 takes a well-earned breather, whilst the train's passengers make their way along the platform towards the concourse.

The tall signal box at the end of the covered area, although disused by this date, was demolished in the late fifties, but was used by platform staff as a rest room for many years previously. *Photo: C. P. Boocock.*
Date: 28 September 1957.

Far from a classic scene: an uninspiring Class 115 DMU arrives at Marylebone with the 09.48 service from West Ruislip some two minutes late. DMUs are the only trains to operate out of the station today, apart from the occasional steam-hauled specials that have started from here in the last few years – and hopefully will continue to do so. The turntable survives on the other side of the Rossmore Road bridge, and has occasionally been used by visiting steam locomotives.

By this date work was already well under way on the modernisation of the station and workmen were busy digging up the cab rank on the right in preparation for the laying of two new tracks and platforms.
Date: 28 July 1989.

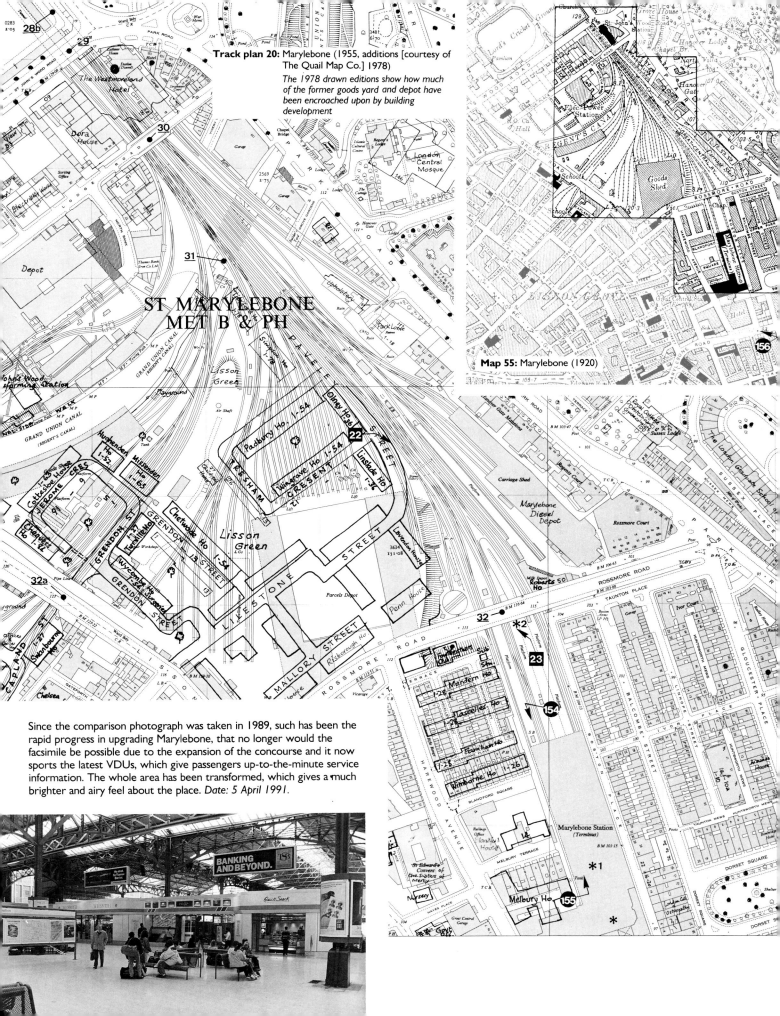

Track plan 20: Marylebone (1955, additions [courtesy of The Quail Map Co.] 1978)

The 1978 drawn editions show how much of the former goods yard and depot have been encroached upon by building development

Map 55: Marylebone (1920)

Since the comparison photograph was taken in 1989, such has been the rapid progress in upgrading Marylebone, that no longer would the facsimile be possible due to the expansion of the concourse and it now sports the latest VDUs, which give passengers up-to-the-minute service information. The whole area has been transformed, which gives a much brighter and airy feel about the place. *Date: 5 April 1991.*

156
Great Central Hotel – 222 Marylebone Road
176 TQ 276819

If the station was modest, the hotel was not. It was built in true grandiose style of the period, like those buildings fronting most other London termini, seemingly as if the Great Central Railway needed to have its own status symbol to advertise its apparent potency and arrival in the capital. Perhaps this was seen by the more cynical observer as if it were in a valiant attempt to hide behind its decorative mantle the humble terminus immediately behind, an arm from which joins the hotel's rear in the form of a glazed covered way stretching over the cab rank, like a rather shy and plain child clutching at the skirt of a *grande dame*. However, all is not what it seems: the railway company board, with funds exhausted, could not afford to build the hotel itself and was forced to sell the site, but with an undertaking that one would be built. It was fortunate that Sir John Blundell Maple, the successful furniture magnate, wanted control of a prestigious London hotel to guarantee a lucrative furnishing contract which would then act as a showcase and shop window for his wares. Although Sir Edward Watkin's dream of forging a fast link from Manchester to the Continent via a channel tunnel never became a reality, and the line which he built to London never prospered, Maple got the furniture showcase he wanted.

Designed by R. W. Edis, the hotel was a masterpiece of Victorian craftsmanship with many of the public rooms being decked out in marble and carved stone. It could also boast one of the largest dining rooms in Europe. In this view the hotel is still under construction and encased in scaffolding. The sign written in the period salesman's true hyperbolic style proudly proclaims it as the 'Hotel Grand Central', which is being equipped 'with all the latest Sanitary improvements' . . . in other words all the mod cons!

The hotel was requisitioned by the army in World War I, after which, with its market gone, it went into gradual decline. In 1939 the last guests left and it was taken over as railway offices, then eventually became the headquarters for the British Railways Board . . . and thereafter was affectionately known as 'The Kremlin' by BR employees!
Photo: Newton collection/Leicester Museums. Date: c1900.

With the British Railways Board headquarters' move to another location, the building became vacant and was purchased by an Arab syndicate for £6 million, who then sold it a year later for approximately £20 million to a Japanese property company. Renovation works commenced in 1989 to convert it back to a luxury hotel. *Date: 13 September 1989.*

COMMENT: *Since this facsimile was taken, the Hazama Corporation (UK) Ltd purchased the Grade II listed building from the previous developers in September 1991 and over 3½ years it had in excess of £75 million (about £240,000 per room) spent on its painstaking refurbishment. Restored to its former glory and finished in lavish style, the hotel, now called The Regent, London and operated by Regent International Hotels, opened its doors for business on 20 February 1993, rivalling the finest in standards of luxury and cuisine.*

ACKNOWLEDGEMENTS

One of the privileges of being able to prepare such a volume as this is to experience the kindness and help from so many people, most of whom were previously strangers to me, but in many cases have since become firm friends; this book has been no exception.

It is always difficult to single out individuals for special mention, but I feel that this must be done in the case of Robert Robotham who, as an author himself, has produced two books on the line: *The Last Years of the Great Central Main Line* and *The Great Central from the Footplate*, the latter of which he did in conjunction with Frank Stratford, an ex-GC engineman. Robert has given me invaluable help in contacting many of the leading exponents of the Great Central; in addition, he has unflinchingly imparted his own extensive knowledge of the line and allowed me to delve into his fascinating photographic albums for subject material. He also had the kindness to read through my manuscript, which was of great help — at least any errors of fact can be put down to him!

I would particularly like to thank the following who have kindly helped with information, or allowed me to reproduce material from their photographic collections, often going to a lot of trouble in printing them specially for me. They include: Tom Boustead, Mike Mensing, Dick Riley, Les Nixon, Horace Gamble, Mike Mitchell, G. C. Farnell, P. H. Wells, Barry Hilton, Frank Stratford, Dave Wellington, Brian Morrison, William P. Power, J. F. Henton, H. C. Casserley, R. M. Casserley, Roy Hobbs, Colin Boocock, Hugh Nicoll, H. B. Priestley, Roger Kaye, Gordon Buck, Bob Tebb, B. N. Collins, J. S. Hancock, Rex Partridge, Andrew Muckley, D. Holmes, Leicester Museums, Colour-Rail, National Railway Museum, Lens of Sutton, Ian Allan Ltd, the Central Railway Group, Great Central Railway (1976) PLC, and finally my good friend, Ivo Peters, who sadly died during the preparation of this book.

I am also especially grateful to those companies and people encountered during my travels along the line who allowed me to photograph from their properties. They include: Private Patients' Plan, Coltman Brothers, The Stag Furniture Company, Havenplan Ltd, The Victoria Shopping Centre, The Gimson Timber Group, T. J. Keeves & Sons, Mr J. Antony, Mr & Mrs Wright, Mr & Mrs A. Laughton, Mr & Mrs R. Hague, Mr & Mrs G. Tweedy, Mr & Mrs K. Lea, Mr Peter Jackson, Mr & Mrs P. Rowe, Mrs Carol Nesterow, Mr A. S. Khattab, Mr & Mrs J. Snowden, Mr & Mrs D. Gisborne, and many others besides.

In addition, I would like to express my gratitude to John and Elizabeth Holman of Turweston, also to the management and staff of the Westminster Hotel in Nottingham, where I took refuge during my trips to the Midlands and the North. My thanks go also to the County Record Offices of South Yorkshire, Leicestershire, Nottinghamshire, Derbyshire, Northamptonshire, Warwickshire, Oxfordshire and Buckinghamshire whose staff were of enormous help in obtaining old maps; to British Rail who kindly allowed me to see the Great Central Railway's route plans and bridge data, and to the city councils of Leicester and Nottingham for their generous assistance.

Finally I am grateful to my wife Jenny, whose support is my strength; as always, she has acted as my much treasured chief critic, proof reader and sometime safari companion.

SELECTED INDEX

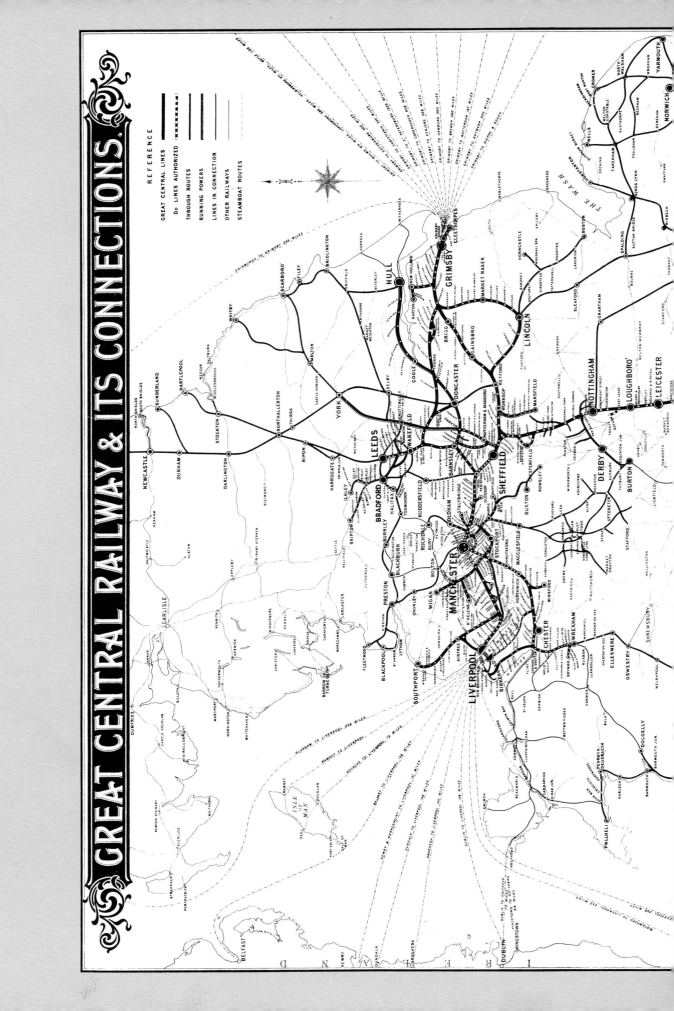

GREAT CENTRAL RAILWAY & ITS CONNECTIONS.